Meditations on Business isn't just another business book. It is a unique and insightful view of the future—challenging, stimulating and a little disturbing. I enjoyed it immensely.

Bruce Peer
President, European Division,
Labatt Breweries of Europe

In an era of the "Management Book of the Month" John Dalla Costa's essays on North American business are thought-provoking and controversial. He challenges business to address the 1990s issues of environmental protection, human enrichment and feminism head-on.

Robert Serenbetz
Vice President,
Warner Lambert Company
President,
American Chicle

MEDITATIONS ON BUSINESS

0 57812 72520 1

MEDITATIONS ON BUSINESS

Why *Business As Usual* Won't Work Anymore.

John Dalla Costa

Prentice–Hall Canada Inc., Scarborough, Ontario

Canadian Cataloguing in Publication Data

Dalla Costa, John
  Meditations on business

ISBN 0-13-572520-8

1. Business. I. Title.

HF5011.D35 1991   650   C91-094468-7

Prentice-Hall Inc., *Englewood Cliffs, New Jersey*
Prentice-Hall International, Inc., *London*
Prentice-Hall of Australia, Pty., *Sydney*
Prentice-Hall of India Pvt. Ltd., *New Delhi*
Prentice-Hall of Japan, Inc., *Tokyo*
Prentice-Hall of Southeast Asia (Pte.) Ltd., *Singapore*
Editora Prentice-Hall do Brasil Ltda., *Rio de Janeiro*
Prentice-Hall Hispanoamericana, S.A., *Mexico*

Editor: William Booth
Cover & Design: Suzanne Boehler
Composition: Hermia Chung
Manufacturing Buyer: Lisa Kreuch

ISBN: 0-13-572520-8

Printed and bound in the U.S.A. by Arcata
Graphics Book Group

1 2 3 4 5 AG 95 94 93 92 91

This book is printed on acid-free paper

DEDICATION

There is a proverb among Native Americans that says that we do not inherit this earth from our parents, but rather borrow it from our children.

This book is dedicated to children. Both those children who will grow and live in the society we leave for them, and those children that we carry inside each of us who keep us open to change, renewal, and awe.

A modest donation from the sale of this book will be made to the Children's Aid Society of Metropolitan Toronto Foundation, an organization dedicated to helping prevent the abuse and neglect of children.

TABLE OF CONTENTS

ACKNOWLEDGEMENTS

How This Book Came To Be

The process of writing this book has been very rewarding. I was able to explore issues that are very important to me, but that I would likely not have studied in such depth without the impetus of doing a book. I also learned a lot about myself, about the values I profess, the convictions I feel, and the contradictions I live with. Experiencing, firsthand, the process of writing has also given me new insights and new appreciation for the still not very well understood dynamics of creativity.

This achievement, and the learning that it afforded me, would not have been possible without the support of many people.

Throughout this project, Louise Blouin and Gordeen Donovan provided friendship and caring wisdom. Their affection and support helped me through the alternating currents of cockiness and insecurity, of over-confidence and self-doubt, that characterized this act of creation.

Marty Myers and Laima Cers spent hours reviewing the manuscript. They applied their penchant for words and their understanding of business to catch the logic loops and thinking irregularities that my "too-close-to-it perspective blinded me to.

Deborah Pappis dedicated a good part of her summer vacation from graduate school to do the research for my, at that time, still nebulous topics. The materials she collected made it so much easier for me to synthesize and write.

My family—parents, sisters, and soul-brother, Dom— were with me in spirit all the way.

This project would not have been possible without the support and vision of the people at Prentice-Hall Canada. Tanya Long had the inspiration for the concept of this book. And Bill Booth provided encouragement, and his very valuable editorial input helped smooth some of material's rough edges.

All of these people deserve thanks, and share in the accomplishment that this book represents.

INTRODUCTION

There are many factions in our democratic society. Some are very strongly pro-business. Others, and these are growing, are pro-environment. Still others, and these are generally struggling, are pro-people.

With such markedly different, and often conflicting, agendas, it is not unusual for these various factions to fight one another. Environmentalists are often anti-business. Business is often antisocial, preferring the dynamics of the market to the interference of government in solving problems. And many people, dulled by their jobs, or excluded from the wealth created by commerce, are broadly suspicious of the motives and behaviour of business.

Somewhat obscured within the conflict between these factions is their growing interconnection. The issues of commerce, of the environment, and of humanity profoundly affect one another. These can no longer be segregated, no longer be dealt with as separate problems requiring dedicated solutions.

Business is an essential fact of life in our modern world, and our competitiveness as a nation will determine both the quality of our lives, and our flexibility in evolving and changing those standards of life in the future. But business, while commercial in its focus, cannot remain vital within our society without re-weighing its priorities to include environmental and human factors. Business cannot be sustained without developing a much less exploitive, more harmonious, relationship with nature. Nor can it meet the challenges of global competitiveness without engaging the full creativity and broad commitment of the people who work in its companies, buy its products and services, and live in its communities.

Irrefutable Interdependence

While this book is primarily about business, its principle theme is of *interdependence*. Business can no longer take its natural or human resources for granted. This acknowledgement of interdependence is essential for the health of our planet, and the fulfilment of our greater human potential. The companies that operate with this spirit of interdependence, integrating concern for the environment and people within their business goals and philosophy, will achieve the improvements in efficiency, productivity, and human development that will enhance their long-term business performances.

I realize that the challenges of interdependence are many. While it's tough enough to make a profit, it will be considerably harder to balance this need for financial achievement with the broader goals of social responsibility. But, no matter how difficult it may be, we who work in business, manage its activities, and lead its companies, must accept the wider obligations that go to an institution that so deeply affects the planet we live on, and the society within which we function.

The reality of interdependence requires that we rethink the operating philosophy of business. A new paradigm is needed, one that melds the positive drive, initiative and creativity of business with concern for our natural environment, and respect for the full humanity of the people who make up our society.

The Model of Reciprocity

For both pragmatic and idealistic reasons, the guiding principle of this new business paradigm must be based upon *reciprocity*—giving back to nature, to our people, and to our society, as much as we in business extract from them. This is not a "nice-to-do," but a "need-to-do" issue. Business, with its economic influence, is the most dominant, most pervasive of our human institutions, and there is little choice but for it to take the initiative in establishing this reciprocity, in creating the values, systems and structures that accommodate mutual, rather than exclusive, interests.

Importantly, a more socially responsible business will also be more competitive. North Americans are losing many of the battles being fought in the global economy. Our culture will not allow for the regimentation and heightened work ethic of economies like Singapore's and Korea's, against which we are increasingly competing. To improve our productivity, to unleash the creativity and ingenuity of our work-force, North American managers must achieve the fullest possible participation of our society. Reciprocity is a means for earning the heightened commitment that business so needs, to meet the challenge of heightened competition.

In exploring interdependence, I've necessarily crossed the comfortable boundaries that have been created by tradition to segregate economic and business preoccupations from those of nature and humanity. Whether we acknowledge it or not, business has operated with an apartheid-like attitude of exclusivity. Its focus on profit, governed by rigid principles of accounting and economic measurement, has advanced only its interests. To factor into the business equation a sense of the sacredness of nature, or of the broader, human needs of people, is unfathomable and uncomfortable for most business people.

To break this exclusivity, this form of business apartheid, we need to infuse new values into our commercial institutions. Since these values are expansive, extending beyond self-interest to embrace the broader needs of nature and humanity, I've called them spiritual.

Historically, spirituality is to business what communism is to capitalism; a source of conflict, best managed by keeping them as far apart as possible. But the spirituality I envision within business is not based on any traditional religion, but rather on the heightened respect and dedication to reciprocity that flows from accepting interdependence. Fostering such a spiritual sensibility within business does not soften the competitiveness of our companies. Rather, in allowing people to explore and express their full humanity, a spiritually attuned company has the potential to tap new levels of commitment and creativity, thereby developing an indispensable asset for the future.

To make my case, I've borrowed concepts and notions from economics, political theory, history, psychology, theology, anthropology and sociology. However, my expertise and experience are derived as a business practitioner, so I don't presume to have mastered any of these disciplines, nor do I pretend to be an expert in any of these fields.

I am also not an academic. The ideas I've formulated have come from working in business, and the supporting research I've provided is derived from the many books and articles I've read and the seminars and courses that I've attended. And, while I've attempted to interweave appropriate substantiation, this book is clearly more an expression of my passion than of any scholarship.

My basic view is that business can be a very positive, very liberating influence. In channeling its immense resources, both financial and human, business can serve as an agent of change, helping humanity deal with its many problems, while building value for shareholders and generating profits. To realize such an expansive potential involves changing more than our expectations of business. We must acknowledge its inadequacies and set about making the corrections to how we view and value a business enterprise.

Looking at business through the filter of my own humanity and my personal concern for the environment has helped define some of the inadequacies and shortcomings that its companies and corporations must overcome. I've also tried to suggest new concepts and ideas, which may help business evolve its attitudes and systems to better meet its expanded responsibilities. Some of these recommendations are immediately workable, and represent progressions on directions and steps that business is already taking. Some are more radical, requiring the experimentation and input of managers and specialists who have more expertise than I do. And some of the suggestions are half-formed, because the scale of the problem and the complexity of the reform are beyond my capacity to solve.

As I've confronted these issues and have sought to define a realizable and progressive potential for business, I've discovered that there are no easy answers. The pressures of the competitive marketplace are such that it is very difficult for anyone who is leading a company or managing a project to look beyond the scope of the business priority at hand. Yet, because what we do in business touches so many aspects of our society, we who are in business have a responsibility to ask the most difficult and demanding questions about our performance.

Asking the questions, and living with the ambivalence of some of the answers, are part of how we can use our work, our commitment to business, to develop and express our own humanity. The German poet, Rainer Maria Rilke, in *Letters to a Young Poet*, wrote about questions. "Be patient towards all that is unsolved in your heart. Try to love the questions themselves. Do not now seek answers which cannot be given because you would not be able to live them. And the point is to live everything. Live the questions now. Perhaps you will then gradually, without noticing it, live along some distant day into the answers."

The questions about business and its role in our society are too important to not confront, even if we don't have all the answers. With the challenges to North American competitiveness, with the degradation of our environment, with the widespread dislocation of many people who work within, and are affected by, business, we have no choice but to "live those questions now." With the goodwill, commitment and creativity of the people responsible for the performance and behaviour of business, I am confident that we will find and fulfil the dynamic answers.

FOREWARNED

Who I Am, and Why I Wrote What I Wrote

The unconventional topics I've written about are, in many ways, the result of my unconventional background.

I am a businessman. I love what I do, and I've had the good fortune to be successful at something that stimulates and intrigues me, something that rewards me emotionally as well as financially.

I am what people call a "whiz kid" and a "fast-tracker." I was a vice-president of a major Canadian advertising agency at twenty-six. I joined a start-up at twenty-eight, became a partner at twenty-nine, president and CEO at thirty-two. My three partners and I built our company from scratch, with all the angst and accomplishment that that entails. Today, our enterprise employs forty-five people, serves fourteen clients, and generates gross billings of over $35 million. The eight years I've spent managing this company have been a process of on-the-job training, and I've paid dearly for my precociousness with some very hard-learned lessons.

I am not a traditional business person with a traditional MBA. In fact, before getting my first job in advertising, I had spent seven years in a Roman Catholic seminary, studying for the priesthood. That I made the instantaneous transition from theological studies to advertising has amused many of my colleagues. That I have thrived and succeeded in this, what is often called "cutthroat" business, after spending my high school and university years in the isolation of divinity school, has also perplexed them.

It isn't so surprising, when you consider that advertising and religion actually share many fundamentals. Both involve preaching. Both are designed to convert people to a point of view. Advertising works best when it has a compelling message, a story that has resonance with the people it is targeted to. Religious leaders knew this long before advertising types started plying their trade. Advertising, like religion, works on a basis of reach and frequency. Getting to as many people as possible and repeating the message until it becomes ingrained in their psyches was the strategy used by missionaries for the Church, long before advertising people became the missionaries for commerce.

From Scriptures to Scripts

With hindsight, I can acknowledge that many of the skills I learned in the seminary have had application in my career. The Church is very hierarchical, and the very competitive spirit that pervaded the seminary I took with me into business. Academic studies were the primary vehicle for advancement, and the discipline and intensity I absorbed in the seminary study hall contributed to the drive and determination that have fuelled my business achievements.

I also inherited my work ethic from the seminary. Priests work weekends as well as weekdays, and the training of seminarians was geared to that. We got up early every day, performed household cleaning tasks before breakfast, prayed and studied throughout the day, played basketball or soccer for an hour, and then prayed and studied some more, until evening prayer. We accepted such discipline for a vocation that was facing a labour shortage, so you can imagine how easy it was to be driven and disciplined when I found myself in a highly competitive job market.

The functional skills I've needed to do well in business also had their roots in my seminary training. At a very early age, we were taught to stand at a podium in front of hundreds of parishoners, and read and preach to them. Mastering an overhead projector was a fairly easy transition from that. We seminarians were also expected to write clearly, since we would one day have to write our own sermons to both instruct and inspire. That ability to communicate is obviously indispensable in a business that hinges on communication between departments, between client and agency, and between agency and the end customer for the products and services we are trying to sell.

One of the most defining experiences I had in the seminary was the "volunteer" work that we were forced to do for six hours a week. Throughout my four years in high school, I spent Friday afternoons working with severely handicapped children at Willowbrook State School for the Mentally Retarded, on Staten Island, New York. In university, my volunteer work included a year of visiting several "special friends" at a nursing home, and visiting juvenile delinquents at the Cook County Detention Center in Chicago.

These experiences, sometimes overpowering, instilled what business teachers call "people skills." The memories are haunting, and still serve to defeat the self-importance that is so easy for people in advertising to develop, when we see our work flashed on TV, spilling across the pages of newspapers and magazines, and peering down from the outdoor boards.

That I've applied my seminarian training to advertising may be a personal peculiarity, but it also says a lot about the changing roles of religion and business in our society. I was in the seminary during the late sixties and early seventies. Great changes were then transforming society. The civil-rights and anti-war movements were creating a new level of public expression. Rock music, the women's movement, drugs—illegal ones like LSD and legal ones like the Pill—were wreaking havoc on society. The Church recoiled from what was happening in what we called "the real world," retreating ever deeper into its dogma and traditions, which had provided the Church with its stability and power for so long.

While we seminarians were only allowed one hour of TV a week (to watch *Star Trek*), it was impossible to shield us from the values-change that was rewiring our society. We could see that the change occurring on the streets was deep and dislocating. And, over time, as we seminarians were affected by the frenetic pace of change besetting our generation, it became obvious that the Church's conservatism was hindering its ability both to respond, and to minister effectively, to the society that it was dedicated to serve. The growing gap between the needs of people and the effectiveness of the Church led to the sobering realization that the institution we were dedicating our lives to was losing its relevance in society.

Of an original class of twenty-five seminarians, I was the last one to make the difficult decision to leave what I had believed was a calling to serve God. My faith, although not gone, was fractured, and I was deeply disillusioned by the failure of the Church to keep pace with the changing world. During the long year of my deciding to leave, I came to see the Church as but one of the institutions created by men, which carried with it all the flaws and failings of humans. I could devote myself to business because it was another man-made institution, also flawed, which was at least more direct, because it was very clear about its temporal motives.

In a strange way, business today is going through many of the changes and difficult challenges that I watched the Church stumble through. Just as vocations for the priesthood dried up, business today is facing a new labour shortage; a shortage of engineers, designers and professional managers to lead its enterprises in the future. Like the Church, business in North America is in a period of losing its primacy. The mistakes of North American business, the successes of our global competitors, have shown the fallibility of our system. People who work for companies, and society in general, have become somewhat alienated from business, particularly now as we collectively deal with the abuses that are the legacy of the 1980s.

In these pages, I explore themes that come out of my experience as both a seminarian and a business person. The perspective may be atypical, but the issues I've identified and tried to work through are ones that I believe are very important for business, and for our broader social and environmental community.

In any event, I can't escape the man I am. As a business person, I want to find pragmatic solutions to the problems that affect my company, those of my clients, and, if possible, those of companies across North America. As a human being, I also want to find the connections between what I do for a living and the other dimensions of my life, and of our broader community.

Business Lessons and Life Lessons

This book has been a labour of love. The issues I've investigated are all of personal interest and importance to me. I've learned a lot, both in the research for this book, and from the actual process of conceiving its ideas and crafting its wording. However, I'm not a researcher, not a business journalist, nor a business academic. I am a business practitioner who spends most of his day trying to do the best job possible for his clients. It is this practical experience that I hope ties together the ideas and concepts formulated here.

My experience is, happily, quite rich. That I work in an advertising agency has afforded me the special opportunity of looking through the windows of the nearly fifty companies that have, at one time or another, been clients I've worked with; multinational companies, such as Proctor & Gamble, Sony and Subaru, and Canadian companies, such as Telecom Canada, Speedy Muffler King and Imax Systems Corporation. The thousands of experiences viewed through these windows have contributed to my notions.

I've not only viewed the operations and styles of numerous client companies, but also had the opportunity to participate with my partners in creating our own company. As we've grown from start-up, through the phase of being a creative boutique, then a small agency, and now a mid-sized company, we've essentially been through quite different management experiences within the same company.

Through our entrepreneurial period, my partners and I devoted our drive and creativity to breathing life into our enterprise. The sleepless nights, some filled with worry, some filled with the excitement of dreams being realized, are indelible experiences, which I bring to this book. Later, as our company grew, my partners and I had to learn new skills to provide the organizational structure and management discipline that a larger company requires.

With resilience and humour, my partners and I have been through business wins and business losses. We've created new companies, and watched some of them fail or break away. We've been courted by companies that wanted to buy us. We tried unsuccessfully to make our own acquisitions. And we ultimately negotiated an alliance with an international partner.

For me, as CEO, this was really on-the-job training. There were many successes, many failures, and important new lessons, which inflicted their wisdom on me every day. The problems and pains, the rewards and satisfactions of this journey are part of every page I've written.

What I wasn't learning at work, I tried to learn from the many business books and articles that I so enjoy reading. These, and the seminars and courses I enrolled in to refresh my managerial self, are all part of the material included in my essays.

That I've written a book also means that I've had to learn to write one. This has not been easy, particularly while also trying to manage a company during a recession, and both serve clients and go after new business in the currently very intense Canadian agency market. I persisted because I learned so much through this process.

When I worried that I was only just learning, and not yet applying, some of the measures I advocate in my book, a particularly wise friend of mine counselled me that "you learn what you teach." This book draws many conclusions and makes many recommendations, but its lessons are those that, frankly, I'm still learning and absorbing.

Confronting the dilemmas that face today's business leaders has provided lessons for me, which are personal as well as professional. We seem to have so little time to distance ourselves from our daily activities and view our lives from a broader perspective. Author and psychologist John Bradshaw complains that our society's preoccupation with activity has changed us from human beings into "human doings." After so many years of measuring myself as a "doing," writing this book has allowed me to reflect, to slow the whirlwind of my business activity, to consider the wonder of being.

This process of reflection led me to the title, *Meditations on Business*. Even planning has become such a frenetic activity that business people, particularly in North America, have lost the capacity to see the whole, to be in awe of the interconnections between business and life. Through reflection, we can learn to see this broader reality and come to involve all aspects of our humanity in the activities of business. And among the aspects to be involved should be our human yearning for spiritual fulfilment.

This expansion of the role of business, to involve and accommodate the fullest human potential, is controversial. To mix the objectives of business with those of the human heart and soul goes against the grain of our traditions. But the spirituality I am advocating is not based on any traditional religious construct. I have no dogma to preach. Instead, the spirituality I envision for business is one that simply grows out of the undeniable interdependence between business, the natural environment of our planet, and the people who make up our human family.

It is my deeply held belief that such a spiritual orientation can provide the impetus to renew business, to increase its value and productivity, while also contributing to the well-being of our broader, natural society.

■

PERSPECTIVE: WHY *BUSINESS AS USUAL* CAN'T BE, ANYMORE

Business represents both what is great and what is dangerous about human beings. It has created wealth and a more comfortable lifestyle for hundreds of millions of people. Yet it has abused the planet from which it draws its livelihood, to the point of destroying hundreds of thousands of species and risking our very existence. Business often liberates the individual to create, to innovate, to achieve. Yet it also suppresses many, alienating and demeaning those who do not contribute to its interests.

All of this is to be expected. As a human institution, it's only natural that business would embody the good and the bad, the hope and the despair, the success and the failure, that are intrinsic to our species. However, today the power of business is such that any imbalance in this paradoxical behaviour is bound to have serious repercussions throughout our society.

There is no doubt that business is becoming the dominant institution on our planet. The democracy movements that we've seen in Asia and in Eastern Europe are not only about freedom, but also about business. People want the lifestyle, the ability to compete, to get ahead, to consume, that the "free enterprise" commercial system of the West has created.

It is not without irony that the Soviet KGB, after several generations of trying to undermine all things Western and capitalistic, has recently announced that it is setting up an information-gathering unit, to provide market research for companies looking to develop new consumer franchises in the Soviet Union. While the outcome of economic reforms in that country is still very much uncertain, this move to market the services of the stealthy secret police suggests how far the world has come in adopting the principles of free, or relatively free, enterprise.

While people have generally become more fundamental in their religious beliefs and more tribal in their nationalism, business seems to be the great unifier. For three summers, beginning in 1988, I had the opportunity to take a three-week advanced management programme at the Harvard Business School, which was specifically geared to "Owner-Presidents." My fellow students numbered over one hundred, and came from India, Australia, France, Turkey, Kuwait, New Zealand, Pakistan, Taiwan, Colombia, Canada and the United States.

During our nine weeks together, we worked intensively, dissecting cases, debating in class, and working through our solutions and points of view in formal study groups. This experience underscored how much business unites us. The language of the spreadsheet is universal. And, although we came from different cultures, and ran companies of widely varying sizes in very diverse industries, we found that we shared many similar problems, passions and dreams.

As was evident in my Harvard class, the principles of business have been embraced with equal fervour by Christian Europeans, Hindu Indians, Muslim Pakistanis, Shinto Japanese and Buddhist Chinese. The language of the bottom line has transcended long-established, often antagonistic cultural differences. In this sense, business has become the great equalizer, rewarding enterprise and paying-out initiative, regardless of race or nationality or creed.

As the influence of business spreads, it is logical that it assume ever-greater responsibility for the people, countries, cultures and planet that it affects. This is a contentious belief. Many business people see business single-mindedly, as a means to deliver profit to shareholders. Any extensions of business into areas of social responsibility have, for the most part, been regarded as misplaced altruism.

But business is no longer a segregated institution, accountable only to its own rules, objectives and devices. Business permeates our culture. Business drives our society. Business touches each and every one of us. Extending so pervasive an influence demands that we expect more from business than simply profit and market share.

Such expectations of business are relatively new. For much of our history, business was a sideshow, while politics and religion held centre-stage. People and communities defined themselves and competed through their political allegiance and by their religious beliefs. English versus French. Protestant versus Catholic versus Jew.

The dominant institutions of politics and religion were often in conflict until, over time, the uneasy truce separating Church from state was established. This same separation of institutions has also applied to business.

Governments occasionally have nurtured business, or restrained it, depending on the needs and attitudes of constituents. And religious forces occasionally have intervened to prick the conscience of business. But, by and large, these institutions have operated with autonomy, recognizing the different pressures and logic processes unique to each.

With the world embracing business as its greatest hope for development and peace, political and religious institutions are finding themselves usurped. To paraphrase General Motors' view of itself within the U.S. economy, "The business of the world increasingly is business." In this context, segregating business from the other institutions within our society is not only no longer viable, it is no longer desirable.

If business is surpassing politics and religion as the defining influence of our era, then it is important that we challenge its traditions, its structures and its operating principles from this new perspective. If business is to remain vital and realize its full potential as a tool for human development, then it must be reconstituted to a new paradigm.

As a businessman, I live within this institution every day. I've played by its rules. I've been enriched by its rewards. And, while I'm excited about its potential, I am concerned that business is unprepared for the broader role that history is thrusting upon it.

The management models for business that operated within the confines of a province or a country are too unsophisticated to deal with a business that is run globally. The system of accountability that has been developed to satisfy shareholders and the stock-market is hopelessly inadequate in owning up to the vast ecological damage that business is directly responsible for. And the financial formulas for return on investment are far too simplistic to accurately measure the human and social costs that business incurs in meeting its goals.

So, while business is clearly emerging as the best hope for humankind, it must undergo a significant transformation. It must redefine itself, both to live up to its expanded obligations as the dominant institution on our planet, and to correct the excesses that, if left unchecked, will lead to its inevitable demise. "Business as usual" is no longer possible. In fact, "business as usual" is dangerous to both people and business, because we are already precariously close to the point of exhaustion of resources and expiration of life.

WHY
MEDITATIONS?

Searching for the Spiritual
Possibilities Within Business

Business has borrowed most of its structural
ideas from the military, and most of its method
from science. Recently, as its influence has
grown, and as it struggles to motivate a new
generation of workers, business has turned to
religion for "inspiration."

A myriad of business books and seminars
have been devoted to helping business managers
define their "visions" for their enterprises.
Many corporations now proudly display "mission statements" in their lobbies, to provide
higher "guidance" for the behaviour of the organizations and all their employees. The traditional management theory, based on control,
is slowly being replaced by that of "empowerment," acknowledging the "trustworthiness" of
the individual to help the company achieve its
targets.

Such fundamental change in the operating
style of business was brought about, in most
instances, by necessity.

For generations, business has been focused on mass production. The more units produced, the greater the efficiency, the lower the cost per unit. The management imperative, in an organization dedicated to mass production, is based on measurement and control; measurement of tolerances, measurement of conformity to specifications, measurement of costs and energy expended per unit made.

Mass production emphasizes standardization, so it is only natural that business evolved comprehensive systems of control. Control is best achieved by breaking down tasks into smaller components, and scrupulously supervising each task.

We forget, because our experience with business is so pervasive, that the theory and practice of management are relatively new arts. Early corporations were often tyrannical, run by the iron hands of visionary founders such as Henry Ford, John D. Rockefeller and Bud McDougall. The Second World War stretched business to new limits, and it made sense to borrow the military model of management to produce the incredible quantities of armaments needed for the war effort, and to expedite the incredible logistics of procurement, which were critical to victory.

With very little refinement, business continued to use this model for decades after the war. And, while many companies have adopted enlightened mission statements, they persist in using a management structure that is essentially unchanged since being formalized by the military of the Roman Empire.

Several factors have rendered this structure almost obsolete.

Competition has become far more intense. In striving for advantage in meeting the needs of the marketplace, business people have devoted themselves to ever greater customization of the products and services they provide. The focus on "economies of scale" is inadequate to meet the competitive demands for goods of higher quality, unique features, and distinct imagery. It is no longer enough to manage for standardization. Success demands that we also manage for innovation.

The cliché that says that the military is always ready to fight its previous war speaks to the difficulty that bureaucratic organizations have in stimulating and nurturing innovation.

A rational culture is almost always antithetical to creativity. Even nature, with all its wizardry, could only accommodate the human capacity for the rational and the creative by segregating the two functions in two distinct lobes of the brain.

The rational management structures of control inhibit the very creativity that business needs today, to remain current with its customers. Companies like Xerox and IBM, which compete in the innovation-intensive information marketplace, have organized the groups responsible for new products outside the mainstream of their respective corporations. Xerox's product-development facility, in Palo Alto, California, actually pioneered the "user-friendly" mouse and desk iconography that Apple used to revolutionize computers. Its bureaucracy prevented Xerox from applying its own innovation to its own competitive advantage.

Current corporate behaviour essentially contradicts one of our dearest-held myths about North American enterprise. We have long viewed ourselves as the world's greatest commercial innovators, yet the evidence suggests that our management structures and systems are largely inept in delivering innovation.

Unlike North American companies, which swing away for the innovation home run, many European and Japanese enterprises have integrated innovation throughout their operations. They innovate in increments, trying to improve each step, every component, to achieve a holistic result. This commitment to integrating constant improvement, not tacking it on as an afterthought, is why the quality standards for so many products are being set elsewhere.

Toyota and Honda constantly outscore North American autos in quality measures, and in surveys for defects and workmanship. The Buick division of General Motors has actually built an advertising campaign around the fact that it was the only North American car to break into the top five in the J.D. Power customer-satisfaction survey. Bragging about breaking into the top five is a testament both to how far North American cars have come, and to how far they still have to go.

Companies like Sony actually define their business as creativity. This spirit of innovation is not restricted to the R&D labs, but rather permeates all the disciplines within the company. The constant questioning and searching, which leads to the impressive stream of new products, new uses, new categories for which Sony is famous, is only possible in a management environment that doesn't pretend to have all the answers.

Rigid hierarchies stifle innovation. They also frustrate and undermine the very people upon whom the modern corporation is dependent for ideas and success.

Peter Drucker calls these people "knowledge workers." He believes that "the centre of gravity in employment is moving fast from manual and clerical workers to knowledge workers, who resist the command and control model which business took from the military."[1]

"Knowledge workers" are the primary assets of businesses competing through innovation, yet in many cases they are managed with the same tools and disciplines that business pioneered to control the mechanical, repetitive, thoughtless processes on an assembly line. Again, while many companies have acknowledged the differences, and have even sought to "empower" their employees, the hierarchy in place in most companies ultimately frustrates and dissipates innovators.

A new managerial approach to replace the military model is desperately required. In *The Frontiers of Management*, Peter Drucker provides an analogy for management. "Because the 'players' in an information-based organization are specialists, they cannot be told how to do their work. There are probably few orchestra conductors who could coax even one note out of a French horn, let alone show the horn player how to do it. But the conductor knows how to focus the horn player's skill and knowledge on the orchestra's joint performance. This focus is the model for the leader of an information-based organization."[2]

The example of the symphony is a very rich one for business.

Music, like business, has a very rational component. Notes provide the intellectual foundation for music, much as a business plan does for a company. But the music only happens when the full range of human experience is engaged in its expression. Performers infuse the logical, mathematically precise string of notes with emotion, to bring music to life. Some music goes even beyond the emotional plane. It sometimes touches our spirits, moving us in a dimension that can only be equated with the religious.

Managing As If People Had Souls

The practice of management essentially involves leading and motivating people, so management excellence will increasingly demand that we, too, engage the full spectrum of human experience. As we continue to shift the priorities of management from simply production quantity to genuine concern for the customer, and for the employees who produce the goods and services for that customer, it is sensible that we de-mechanize management and instill it with the diversity and depth of our own humanity.

The emphasis on the rational has deprived many corporations of the creativity and ingenuity that springs from the intuitive side of our being. General Motors did the rational in the last decade, by spending over $40 billion to modernize its plants. Logically, GM invested in the most sophisticated technology and software available. Yet it continues to lose market-share in North America.

The rational investment was not matched by an infusion of the intuitive, with the result that GM's cars have largely failed to capture the emotions, the imagination, of the public it serves.

GM has also spent $3 billion to create its new Saturn marque. As important as the product produced by this new division, is the management approach GM is using to design and build its cars. Traditional organizational structures and systems have been scrapped. Management doesn't even wear ties. Teamwork is promoted by involving as many people as possible in the decisions that affect them. Using experiences like Outward Bound to build a basis of common goals and a sense of interdependence, Saturn has adopted for North America many of the cooperative management practices used so effectively in Japan. Each employee understands his or her stake in what Saturn is doing, so that their commitment goes beyond the rational.

Developments at Saturn are promising. While it's too early to tell whether this venture will be a success, the process itself is interesting. Through Saturn, GM can be seen to be searching for its soul. This concept of soul, applied to business, is not hyperbolic. Theologian Otto Rank defines soul in part as the "power of rebirth," which is exactly what Saturn represents to GM.

As at many other North American corporations, the leadership at General Motors has come to realize that the motivations for its employees will need to go beyond pay and benefits, and provide for emotional connection and fulfilment. Similarly, its products must perform beyond functional expectations and deliver a jolt, and an ethereal, yet visceral, degree of satisfaction.

The Japanese are well along in developing this next stage of quality. Having mastered the fit and details that are the sensory expressions of quality, design and engineering efforts are now being focused on dimensions that are intuitive, creative, reflective. The *kansei* concept, described in Mazda's advertising, attempts to express this feeling, which transcends the five senses and provides a holistic experience between driver and machine.

While not religious, such concepts finally begin to acknowledge the spiritual component of modern management. Companies will be far more innovative, and far more successful in meeting the needs of customers, if they succeed in making the corporate experience, at every level, one that respects and nurtures the human spirit.

In Drucker's conductor analogy, music is not created simply by coordinating the professional skills of the performers. Music has soul, and the conductor must inspire the artistry, the creativity, the spirit of the musicians in the ensemble.

Operating with this spiritual sensibility does not make a business soft. Rather, it affords an opportunity for heightened performance, unleashing the creativity and commitment that people provide only when they derive a broader meaning from their activities.

For knowledge workers, this opportunity for meaningful self-definition is particularly important. Their job is working with information, analyzing data, formulating conclusions, and creating new connections to solve problems and capitalize on opportunities. Using both their intellectual capacity and their creativity means that their individuality is more fully engaged by the company. Understandably, they are unwilling to settle for the traditional "pay-for-labour" contract, which still guides most corporations.

Drucker writes, "For knowledge workers, the institution they work for is not primary; their knowledge, their craft is. Business is thus only the place where one works."[3] To earn the commitment of these highly prized workers, management must create an environment of reciprocal fulfilment.

Fulfilment comes from meeting shared objectives, satisfying goals for both the corporation and the individual contributing to that company. Fulfilment also comes from a sense of greater purpose, of using one's capacities and capabilities not only to earn a living, but also to make a difference.

Now, not everyone will want the same degree of involvement in their work. Nor will everyone seek the same degree of fulfilment. This, too, is OK. The point is to respect people, and allow them to make the fullest contribution they can. Max Depree, the recently retired chairman of the Herman Miller office furniture company, suggests that business leaders must first understand the diversity of gifts that different people bring to their jobs. "Understanding the diversity of these gifts enables us to begin taking the crucial step of trusting each other. It enables us to begin to think in a new way about the strengths of others. Everyone has certain gifts, but not the same gifts. True participation and enlightened leadership allow these gifts to be expressed in different ways and at different times."[4]

Reconstructing companies, to reflect the need for heightened spiritual fulfilment, is among the most important challenges we face in preparing North American business for the next millennium. This is not alarmist hyperbole. Rather, it is a pragmatic assessment of what our companies need to do to survive. Without this spiritual sensibility, the quality of our products will continue to suffer. Without the opportunity for spiritual fulfilment in our enterprises, the people on whom companies rely for innovation will grow more dissatisfied and more disillusioned. Without a sense of spiritual responsibility, the planet that sustains business will shortly be ecologically bankrupt.

The Art of Meditation Applied to the Art of Management

Changing the values of business on this scale requires a whole new tool-chest for management. Already, the accepted disciplines of planning, training, promotion, service, selling, and accounting are proving inadequate in sharpening the competitive skills, vision, and spiritual awareness of North American business.

In an article on management in *Fortune* magazine, C.K. Prahalad, professor of corporate strategy and international business at the University of Michigan, worries that the traditions of North American business are failing it. He says, "In most American companies, the urgent has driven out the important." Managers, and the motivational system within which they operate, focus on "critical present-day tasks of boosting sales, increasing market-share, and enhancing profits." The long-term suffers.

Fortune asks, "Why did American companies pull out of the colour TV business? Because traditional strategic analysis said it was a 'mature' industry." Traditional strategic analysis is a tool for the rational organization. As the Asian take-over of the "mature" TV industry suggests, such purely rational strategic analysis has become dangerously obsolete.[5]

Jack Welch, the visionary CEO of General Electric, is "trying to create what he calls a boundaryless organization in which technology, information, managers, and management practices flow freely from one division to another." Such an organization will use all its rational disciplines, but it will only work if these disciplines are complemented and enhanced with the emotive, creative, and risk-taking attributes of the people within the company.

The precepts of an organization without boundaries are still being written, but, if we imagine them, they are essentially spiritual. Individual and widely held self-worth and self-confidence are prerequisites for successfully managing the autonomy that such a structure suggests. Both of these flow from spiritual consciousness. Without boundaries, and without the rigid protocol that such boundaries provide, people will only be able to interact successfully if their relationships are based on total and mutual respect—another fundamentally spiritual attribute. The accountability for results within a boundaryless company cannot be imposed from the top, but must emerge within each individual. Such responsibility is ultimately spiritually fulfilling for the individuals involved.

In *The Power Pyramid*, Diane Tracy writes, "Most people contribute only a small fraction of their full capabilities, simply because they don't feel a sense of personal power. They are bound by a bureaucratic management system that does little to encourage initiative and high performance. Almost all power within the organization rests with those at the very top. Powerless in their ability to achieve results, most people eventually lose interest and settle for mediocrity."[6]

Spiritually involved individuals are less likely to settle for mediocrity. Engaged and rewarded in their fullest human sense, people will bring boundless pride and commitment to the enterprises that employ them. As Diane Tracy notes, "The satisfaction of your people and the satisfaction or success of the company are not mutually exclusive. Each is dependent on the other."[7]

Arriving at the management insights that will provide spiritual context and renewal is a relatively new, still largely unformed process. Fortunately, history shows that humans have a natural propensity for spiritual exploration. We've shown ourselves to be restless, trying to derive meaning and formulate insights about the deeper value of our lives. Business people, therefore, need not look beyond the common sense of our own hearts to find the guidance for building and managing spiritually aware business organizations.

What we desperately need in business is reflection. Not more planning. Not more strategizing. More reflection. Theodore Levitt, a professor at the Harvard Business School and, until recently, the editor of the *Harvard Business Review*, believes that the structure and style of the modern corporation work against such reflective thinking. "As with any other skill or art, disuse produces disability. Those who, by virtue of their position, rely increasingly on their staffs to do their analyses and thinking for them are increasingly incapacitated to do precisely what is so vital at increasingly higher ranks."[8]

Meditation takes thinking even further, because it allows for the wisdom of the heart to interweave with the knowledge of the head.

In an article in *Business Week*, entitled "Zen and the Art of Middle Management," Neil Gross describes the meditation training received by a group of fifty-six mid-level managers from Fujitsu Ltd., Japan's largest computer company. Zen, taught by a senior priest, is part of an intense training programme, which includes seminars on economics, management theory, and business strategy. Dozens of other companies incorporate such programmes in their executive-development programmes.

Chisho Misawa, the senior priest guiding the Fujitsu managers through their training, explains that "meditation prompts the brain to produce alpha waves. Such brain wave patterns signal profound relaxation, but also indicate alertness." This state is very similar to that point of consciousness between being awake and being asleep, a time when many find themselves most creative in their ability to find new solutions, new ideas.

The zen training is not easy, nor is it intended to provide instant solutions. Rather, it is a tool that these executives are encouraged to incorporate in their day-to-day business practices. Misawa reinforces to these managers that "zen need not be related to a specific religion;" it is a discipline for self-enrichment.

One of the managers at the particular programme that Gross attended works as an integrated-circuit designer at Fujitsu. He explains the benefits of meditation in pragmatic, productive terms. "In the design process, you need to work quickly, but you mustn't hurry. If you could just relax, you might get a broader vision or see the problem from a different angle."[9]

After having had the discipline of meditation imposed upon me during my seven years of religious training, it was one of the many aspects of that experience that I let lapse as I took on the lifestyle of an advertising executive. Things monastic just seemed ill-suited to the hustle and bustle of business. Only as I assumed greater management responsibility, and confronted my sense of inadequacy and immaturity in leading people, did I again resort to meditation. This discipline of reflection helped me to know myself as a business person, so that my decisions, and the guidance I provided the people who worked with me, were anchored in my deepest convictions.

Energy Is No Substitute for Reflection

I was a young president. My fears in facing up to the responsibilities of the job often led me to impose decisions, rather than work them through with the individuals who reported to me. These decisions were reactionary, coming in reflex to issues and circumstances that surprised me. Although we had made plans, I lacked the maturity and sense of distance that only come from thoughtfulness and reflection.

My company suffered from the inconsistency that was the result of my immaturity as a CEO. As I've learned some of the lessons of the job and have begun to bring more reflection to the role, it is now benefiting from the greater stability and clarity that meditation has helped me realize. Through meditation, I've learned to visualize, to project ahead to find new solutions to nagging problems. I've also learned to concentrate, to focus on the issue to better see its relationship with our overall plan and goals. This has helped me to grow as a manager, and to better anticipate the exigencies that are intrinsic to a service business.

Through the mirror of meditation, I've also gotten to know my own heart better. Business is primarily a mental exercise, preoccupying our minds. But, while mental experience gives us intellectual reference points for decisions, true wisdom is achieved only when that intelligence is filtered through the values and emotional understanding of the heart. Meditation helps me align thoughts with feelings, decisions with values.

My system of meditation is not foolproof. When I let the pressures of projects distract me from frequent meditation, I quickly loose the perspective, the objectivity, and the potential for insight that only flow from reflection.

While such reflection has become invaluable to me, I realize that time is already in short supply in most companies, and that encouraging more reflection seems to defeat the productivity gains most of us in management have devoted ourselves, for the last decade, to attaining. The last few decades have shown us that one of the weaknesses of North American companies is our short-term perspective. The frenetic, accelerating pace of work will only exacerbate this problem. Meditation is a tool for breaking the cycle of the short-term. Only reflection, the calm, centred consciousness that is derived from the meditative state, can free managers and leaders to find the more imaginative solutions to problems that the competitive business environment demands.

Tom Peters and Nancy Austin suggest such a meditative approach in their book, *A Passion for Excellence*. "Goethe said that in order to understand the world it's necessary to select an *eckchen*, a small corner of it for contemplation. We sorely need, in managing our enterprises, to get beyond our total dependence on committees, staff, reports, and rules. We need desperately to select an *eckchen*, to begin to get back in touch. We need to depend on people, the power of commitment, ownership, verve, zest, enthusiasm, celebration and love."[10]

Verve, zest, celebration, and *love* are not words found in many business plans, which underscores the shortcomings of traditional strategic planning. The full range of human contribution is simply not accessed in such a strictly rational process.

Planning is deductive, building its case in an obvious, methodical, measurable manner. Meditation is inductive, allowing for thoughts, assumptions, fears and hopes to randomly interconnect and weave an original view. Planning is a tool managers use to control the application of resources and the results of their enterprise. Meditation is a tool for creating vision and formulating direction.

The products of meditation are, therefore, the attributes of leadership. Leadership sees what can be. It leaps the obvious. It defines potential. If leadership were rational, leadership would be common. But leadership is essentially irrational, or, more precisely, supra-rational. While facts and data can be known and understood by many people, the leader is the person who can construct a new, compelling reality out of that commonly held information.

Meditation provides the context, the opportunity, for these data to be reconfigured. It does not preclude doing the homework of analysis, but rather uses the raw materials of rational thought to intuit and create an original conclusion.

Meditation involves the whole person, allowing the head, the heart and the soul to exchange thoughts, feelings, aspirations. While business has generally been uncomfortable with a concept that is so ethereal, so difficult to quantify, it desperately needs the leadership that meditation produces.

The connection between meditation and leadership is centuries old. John Heider, in *The Tao of Leadership*, uses the concepts of Lao Tzu, who provided counsel to Chinese rulers in the fifth century, B.C. "Tao" is basically an understanding of "how things work." This is the first principle of leadership. Lao

Tzu writes, "Tao cannot be defined, but Tao can be known. The method [for knowing] is meditation, or being aware of what is happening. To become aware of what is happening I must pay attention with an open mind. I must set aside my personal prejudices. Prejudiced people see only what fits those prejudices."[11]

The process of bringing meditation into the workplace begins with the commitment of the individual. Companies can provide the environment and even supply the training. But the discipline of setting aside time every day to relax and immerse oneself inside his or her own being is one that must be embraced by the individual.

To show their support for heightened reflection, companies can allocate space specifically designated for meditation. Some companies have special rooms for thinking, for creativity or for play. A meditation room would acknowledge the importance of thoughtful, contemplative time to employees. There is a cost to space, so it may, in fact, require some creativity to make a place available. My own experience is that most boardrooms live up to their names, and since boards rarely sit, they make ideal rooms for people who wish to escape the distractions of their own offices, to immerse themselves in quiet meditation.

Applied Meditation

The actual training for mediation can take various forms. There are many "generic" systems of meditation, those that have no religious affiliation or bias. These can be explored through innumerable books and audio tapes.

Classic meditation training can involve study with a zen master or even a guru. Because of my general suspicion of organized religion, I've avoided exposing myself to anyone for whom my desire for meditation training may represent an opportunity for proselytization. Most companies that have formalized some type of meditation within their organizations share, if not that suspicion, at least the desire for an objective, not a religious, source for their training.

Consultants such as Stephen R. Convey incorporate techniques for visualization and meditation in their management-development programmes and seminars. Convey is not a fringe player, having worked extensively with companies like Procter & Gamble. His work is based on helping managers achieve a fullness and harmony as individuals. With spiritual centredness, people are more conscious of their capabilities and motives, and better able to apply those fuller aspects of their individuality to the problems and issues they face at work.

In his book, *The Seven Habits of Highly Effective People*, Convey writes, "The spiritual dimension is your core, your centre, your commitment to your value system." Meditation enters that core. It "draws upon the sources that inspire and uplift you, and tie you to the timeless truths of all humanity."

Different people use different devices to inspire meditation. Convey adds, "Immersion in great literature or great music can provide a renewal of the spirit for some. There are others who find it in the way they communicate with nature. Nature bequeaths its own blessing on those who immerse themselves in it."[12]

All of these possibilities for meditation are widely available to us. The key is to suspend our inbred business desire to do, in order to allow the meaning and context of what we do to emerge through reflection. Perhaps surprisingly, our first case at Harvard, taught by Professor Marty Marshall, was designed to make exactly this same point. The case was called "Study the Fish."

The case was very short, its lesson very memorable. A graduate student in natural science sought to fulfil a dream and study with a world-renowned biology professor. He desperately wanted to prove himself to his professor, who finally gave him a challenge. The professor took a small fish out of a jar of formaldehyde and asked the student to "study the fish."

The student was very excited. He set about making observations and taking notes about the size, shape, weight and colour of the fish. After several hours of intense study, the student approached the professor to share what he learned. Without reviewing what the student had learned, the professor told him to go back and "study the fish."

Reluctantly, for more hours, the student examined the fish. He counted the teeth and noted how the angle of their placement made it easier for them to tear flesh from their prey. He also began to better understand how the colours of the scales helped the fish camouflage itself, increasing its stealth as a hunter and making it harder to find, for those fish that would prey on it. At the end of the day, with a great many more lessons and observations, the student again approached the professor to review his progress and ask for his next assignment. The professor rather brusquely told him to "study the fish."

For several weeks, this pattern continued. Although the student thought he had all the answers, each time the professor sent him back to "study the fish," he learned important new information, made ever more significant observations, and gained ever deeper insight into the nature and complexity of the fish.

There are no shortcuts to understanding. The discipline to think, to reflect, to meditate, demands an investment of time and a deep personal commitment. Although it's hard work and it seemingly detracts from the time we have to put into the "doing," meditation ultimately helps managers create a broader context for their decisions. Meditation is a tool for "studying the fish," for mining the lessons of experience, for distilling wisdom. Importantly, meditation also helps connect individuals, in a fuller way, to what they do for a living. The creativity and convictions of heart, mind and soul are synthesized through meditation, helping the work experience become more fruitful for the company and more fulfilling to the individual.

BUSINESS AND THE QUEST FOR MEANING

Business is rightly judged very harshly for its lack of humanity, and for its absence of greater purpose. It does not make the excesses of business easier to accept, to realize that our political and religious institutions have also let us down. Politics and religion, although flawed, have resonance with the noble side of the human spirit. Business, on the other hand, has always been a secular activity, one rooted in the material, focused on the temporal.

This failure to integrate spiritual consciousness within the practice of business has been very costly. Without a conscience to regulate it, business has horribly abused nature. Without any spiritual sensibility, business has also misused its human resources. The net result is a looming crisis, which threatens not only the viability and profitability of business, but the very survival of our natural environment, of our societies, and of our species.

Environmental awareness has grown during the last few years, and businesses, along with governments, have begun to respond. But the scale of the problem is such that even enlightened environmental policies by our most prominent companies are not enough.

A National Forum, convened by the U.S. National Academy of Sciences and the Smithsonian Institution in October 1986, warned that we are experiencing a wave of mass extinction, "one that would approach the magnitude of that which wiped out the dinosaurs and half of all other extant species some 65 million years ago. Whereas the earlier cataclysm was of natural origin, the one now unfolding is of human origin."[1]

The immorality of such destruction has not weighed as fully as it should on the shoulders of business, because morality has never been as important as profit in its practices and operations. But now it is becoming obvious that even the singular pursuit of profit is in jeopardy if business does not undergo the significant transformation of accepting a fuller responsibility.

The business logic for such change is compelling. As the Worldwatch Institute wrote, in their 1986 issue of *State of the World*, "While the global economy has expanded continuously, the natural systems that support it unfortunately have not." Worldwatch quotes economist Herman Daly, who suggests that, "as the economy grows beyond its present physical scale, it may increase costs faster than benefits and initiate an era of uneconomic growth which impoverishes rather than enriches."[2]

The goal of business for profit, to the exclusion of all other considerations, cannot sustain itself. Therefore, for its own survival, business has no choice but to integrate environmental considerations into its behaviour. This cannot be achieved by simply adopting "green policies" as part of a corporate mission statement. Instead, it requires an essence shift, an acknowledgement that protection of the planet is a legitimate pursuit of business.

This is a radical proposition. However, only by formalizing environmental goals with the same discipline, planning and follow-through that companies use for financial ones will we be able to take the first step in developing the desperately needed spirituality within business.

Joseph Campbell, the scholar, author and teacher who rekindled awareness of mythology for millions, emphasized the relationship between nature and spirituality in many of his books. He paraphrased a saying in one of the Upanishads: "When before the beauty of a sunset or of a mountain you pause and exclaim 'Ah,' you are participating in divinity." Campbell explains. "Such a moment of participation involves a realization of the wonder and sheer beauty of existence. People living in the world of nature experience such moments every day. They live in the recognition of something there that is much greater than the human dimension."[3]

Enrich the Person to Enrich the Business

By acknowledging that business is dependent on nature and not its master, we develop the potential for such spiritual recognition. This is a deeply satisfying prospect for those of us who devote so much of our lives to business. In opening our managerial minds to awe and respect for nature, we can come to *feel* a passionate connection to it. From this sense of connection springs our spiritual awareness and responsibility.

An intimate connection with nature is very difficult for most of us to achieve. Businesses are usually headquartered in cities, and the people who make decisions are usually ensconced in hermetically sealed buildings, which even recirculate their own used, de-oxygenated air. From the vantage point of a controlled environment, separated from nature by glass, steel, concrete, it's no wonder that the environmental policies of so many companies lack urgency and fail to realistically acknowledge the damage that business has wrought. With used ideas recirculating like stale air, it's not surprising that most companies have failed to expand their definition of success to include their broader impact on the ecology of our planet.

Although it requires a fundamental change in perspective, even city people can make connections with nature. Once we've sensitized ourselves to its splendour and fragility, we confront the wonderful possibility that working within a business can also provide new dimensions of personal fulfilment. Work, career and business achievement are no longer exclusively secular. In addition to livelihood and advancement, time spent in activities of business can, in the context of spiritual awareness, also provide the inner nourishment, the fulfilment and sense of meaning that humans crave.

There has been a lot of resistance from business leaders, economists and academics against trying to imbue business with responsibility for more than for profit. Henry Mintzberg, professor of the business school at McGill, and one of Canada's most respected consultants to business, says that "only a conceptual ostrich, with his head deeply buried in the abstractions of economic theory, could possibly use the distinction between economic and social goals to dismiss social responsibility."[4]

Managing with a heightened sense of social responsibility means that the planet and its people are as important as profit, to those engaged in business. This is not a repudiation of profit. Profit, in so many ways, represents the potential for renewal and rebirth. It provides both rewards to the deserving, and investment for the future benefit of the company and its constituents. So the imperative is not to displace profit within the spiritually aware corporation, but rather to use the skills of management and leadership to artfully balance its priorities with those of people and the planet.

Achieving momentum for such broad-scale reconfiguration of business will require that we redefine the operating beliefs of many of the institutions that support our system. Economics, education, banking and the law will need to go through a similar metamorphosis.

Progressive scholars, such as Herman Daly of the University of Louisiana, are already using the models and logic of economics to jump-start the restructuring. He writes, "All economic systems are subsystems within the big biophysical system of ecological interdependence. The ecosystem provides a set of physical constraints to which all economic systems must conform."[5]

E.F. Schumacher, in his seminal book, *Small Is Beautiful*, introduces a notion of meta-economics. This enhanced economics would "derive its aims and objectives from a study of man, and...derive at least a large part of its methodology from the study of nature."[6]

The new methodology would include a more realistic evaluation of the true cost of creating a product or providing a service. The true cost of depleting limited natural resources. The true cost of not only production, but also after-use clean-up. The true cost of labour, not as simply a unit of productivity, but as the human component of manufacture, which deserves dignity, security, variety and safety.

Recently, executives at Coca Cola suggested to their industry peers and suppliers that packaging costs be increased, to more accurately reflect the price of using a depleting resource and of recycling. Neville Kirchmann, president and chief executive, suggested that a "levy at the point of production, which would be passed on to customers, and eventually consumers, would bring market forces into play and compel companies to cut costs by using recycled materials."[7] Other industries, including agriculture and energy, are already beginning to redefine "cost of goods" to include ecological, as well as commercial, values.

From the new economics, it will be possible to evaluate business performance in a new way. Instead of the myopic focus on quarterly profits, investors and managers will judge the health and attractiveness of a company by how well it performs across the spectrum of meta-economic measures.

Just as government ministries that regulate securities require that publicly traded companies provide audited financial statements, environmental ministries should require statements of ecological performance. These, too, would be included in a company's annual report, providing a more complete picture of performance and results. The ecological audit would review energy consumption, raw-material depletion, and initiatives of renewal undertaken by the company to restore the environment and clean up waste.

Reworking Rewards

The reward structure and the system for managerial promotion will also have a new basis for evaluation. The orientation to the multiple bottom lines of profit, people and planet is especially exciting because it will serve to revitalize the profession of management. The numbers mentality, which has so stupefied North American business, will give way to a far more creative, visionary style of management.

Again, this revitalization of management is necessary, not as altruism, but for the survival of business itself. Professor

Mintzberg, in his book, *Mintzberg on Management*, writes, "Professional management, by putting systems ahead of the people, has had the effect of bleeding out of organizations, slowly and gradually, their capacity to do mental work as it must be done—with energy, vigour and imagination. 'Scientific management' has exacted its toll not only on the workers who don't care about the products of their labour, but also on the managers and analysts who have been equally dehumanized by the whole effort."[8]

Adopting the principles of meta-economics is basically good business. Its alternative, which Mintzberg calls "the cult of rationality," has "served to destroy the deep-rooted effectiveness of our large [business] organizations by squeezing out their very humanness."

With the infusion of spiritual values into North American business, we stand the best chance of recapturing some of the lost competitiveness that is so worrying to our political leaders. Spiritually aware companies provide far more fulfilment for the people who work in them. This works to attract the best and the brightest. It also helps foster the initiative and commitment that cannot be imposed, but must be self-developed.

Akio Morita, the co-founder and principal voice of Sony, believes that his main responsibility was not the development of new technology, but the development of people. Sony is one of the premier high-technology companies in the world. Its brand name is the third most recognized on the globe. His goal has been to advance his company by advancing his people.

Morita suggests that the "post of manager could perhaps better be called the post of 'encourager.'" This encouragement is focused on "developing a fate-sharing attitude to work," in which the individual contributes to the group by achieving his or her own personal potential. Morita believes that "you encourage them best, not by offering more money, but by offering more meaning. Providing meaning and a sense of purpose in life: for me, this must be the central element of the corporate philosophy which management must create."[9]

The notion of providing meaning as a motivator for workers is not widely practised nor discussed in North America. The approach to compensation and motivation has evolved considerably during the last two decades. The traditional compensation contract of payment-per-task has been largely replaced by more sophisticated incentive programmes. Bonus and pay-for-performance systems are being adopted by more and more companies.

Progressive organizations have introduced still more participatory practices, to allow workers to share a degree of ownership in their respective ventures. This ownership can be literal, in the form of employee stock-option plans, or it can be attitudinal, emphasizing the "empowerment" of the individual within the corporation to make the decisions and take the actions that best serve the objectives of the company.

These more sophisticated programmes for motivation are essentially temporal, what Michael Maccoby calls "partial man" theories. Maccoby is the director of the Project on Technology, Work and Character, in Washington, D.C. He has written several books about management organizations, leadership, and personnel motivation. Using quantitative surveys, interviews, and a major participant study, involving AT&T, an insurance company and several U.S. government agencies, Maccoby researched the values and behaviour of people in the modern work force.

In his book, *Why Work?*, published in 1988, Maccoby writes, "The academic theories [of motivation at work] see man as *economic man, sociological man, political man*, and *psychological man*. They are partial theories about partial man who is motivated by money, power, status, or a hierarchy of needs. Each of these theories is partially true; none is fully true. They are designed for partial people in narrow, routinized jobs."[10]

A "fully human" theory of motivation is the antidote for much of the listlessness that people throughout North American corporations are experiencing. *Fully human* acknowledges that the men and women who work in business have overriding values and beliefs, which influence their performance, their happiness, their pride, and their fundamental conception of self-worth. These values are intrinsic and universal. They are what make us all spiritual, not in a religious sense, but in the way in which we strive to give purpose to life.

Victor Frankl, the psychoanalyst who survived a Nazi concentration camp, has written extensively about this human drive for purpose. In *The Will To Meaning*, Frankl writes that "man's heart is restless unless he has found, and fulfilled, meaning and purpose in life."[11] What meaning is derived is unique to the individual, and to the circumstances in which that person's values are being expressed. But what unites us as humans is this search for meaning.

Success, the traditional measure of achievement for people in business, is not necessarily enough to bestow meaning on one's life. Frankl reports on a study conducted among a Harvard University class, twenty years after graduation. The findings show "a huge percentage of people who complained of crisis. They felt that their lives were pointless and meaningless—and this they did although they had been very successful in their professional lives."[12]

Today's managers are facing a work force that is increasingly demotivated by the "pointlessness" of their professional activities. The popular press has documented the change in work behaviour among baby boomers. After a decade and more of sacrificing all to career and job, this group is shifting priorities. They are "returning" to more traditional family activities. The home, and its role as a "cocoon," have kept marketers busy creating new products for this expanding group of ex-corporate-ladder-climbers.

The broad shift to a more centred lifestyle is, in part, to be expected after the obsessive pursuit of career and material possessions that characterized the 1980s. But it also speaks to the failure of the work environment to provide sufficient stimulation and renewal to keep these people interested. It shows that work does not yet provide the meaning that people need, to feel fulfilment in their lives.

In his book *Modern Madness: The Emotional Fallout of Success*, psychologist Douglas LaBier reports on his seven-year study of the emotional lives of young executives. Many people, even some who seem to be well-adjusted and thriving within corporate life, are, in fact, experiencing severe stress and dislocation from their jobs. This stress is not only derived from the pressures of competing and succeeding, but is often the result of a conflict of values. LaBier concludes that "contemporary work within large organizations and institutions can generate crises and conflicts as the person adapts to values or conditions within the organization that are good for advancement but impoverishing to the spirit and sense of identity."[13]

It's obvious that the emotional dislocation of working in companies whose values do not align with our personal ones will hinder both personal fulfilment and, ultimately, productivity and efficiency. However, very few companies acknowledge, let alone respond to, the needs for spiritual fulfilment among their people.

How Meaning Builds Business

Herman Miller Inc. is an exception. Herman Miller is among the most successful office-furniture manufacturing companies in North America. Its business achievements are extraordinary, exceeding its competitors on profitability and productivity measures, year after year. Herman Miller is also among the most progressive companies in terms of its designs, creating functional furniture of high quality, which also contributes to the aesthetics and joy of a work environment.

As proud as he is of these results, Herman Miller chairman Max Depree believes that business is about more than reaching goals. He writes, "As individuals and as a group, we need to reach our potential. Nothing else is good enough." This is not to diminish the importance of goals, but rather to acknowledge that the goals of business can best be met and stretched by people who are fully involved, and enriched on a spectrum of human dimensions. Depree adds, "The condition of our hearts, the openness of our attitudes, the quality of our competence, the fidelity of our experience—these give vitality to the work experience and meaning to life."[14]

Companies that fail to provide the culture and values to allow such meaning to be derived are hurting their own performances. The most important assets of a business are its people, and many of the most creative, questioning and innovative among them are withdrawing from corporate North America. A recent cover story in Fortune documented the exodus of many bright executives from large companies. Often, people left because the values of the corporation were out of sync with their own. Others left to better combine their professional interests with their personal ones. Some left for what Victor Frankl calls "despair despite success."

The price of these departures, to the companies involved, was very high. Not only was the investment in training and development of these people largely wasted, but these companies also lost some of the very people that they needed to be more competitive.

Progressive business leaders are responding to the changes and are realizing significant benefits, both financial and organizational. Levi Strauss & Company, led by CEO Robert Haas, has evolved a highly effective corporate culture, based on the broader values of its people.

Haas and his people created an "Aspirations Statement," to shape the company for the 1990s and beyond. Unlike most mission statements, the Levi's aspirations reflect the full spectrum of human needs and capacities. Pride. Learning. Growth. Respect. Balance. Friendship. Fun. These are among the aspirations that are defined in the statement. Sharing and reinforcing these aspirations have evoked greater dedication and satisfaction not only from Levi's employees, but also from its suppliers and customers.

Drawing from the total humanity of its people, Levi's has achieved remarkable business success. Creativity and commitment were channeled into new products, including the Dockers line of clothing, one of the fastest-growing new products in apparel-industry history. Sales from 1985 to 1989 increased thirty-one percent. Profits quintupled.

Because of its Aspirations Statement, Levi's success is not simply contained on its balance sheet. Its human-resource policy has been among the most progressive in helping people overcome the frustrations, fears and humiliation of adjusting to new technology. A task force is looking at how the company can help its people achieve a better balance between work and family commitments. And, reflecting Levi's deeply felt responsibility for social issues, Haas himself has assumed leadership within the business community in dealing with the AIDS crisis.

The process of defining such lofty and motivating aspirations proved to be surprisingly simple, because they flowed from the hearts of Levi's people. Haas explains. "Most people want to make a contribution and be proud of what they do. But organizations typically teach us bad habits—to cut corners, protect our own turf, be political. We've discovered that when people talk about what they want for themselves and for their company, it's very idealistic and deeply emotional.

This company tells people that idealism is OK. And the power that releases is just unbelievable."[15]

As shown by Levi's, companies can gear themselves to bestow more meaning on the lives of the people they employ, the suppliers they use, and the customers they finally serve with their products. Business operates against goals, so the first step is to broaden the goals of a company to include the aspirational. And, to genuinely fulfil people, it's only logical that they should be included in the process of constructing those goals.

Every company will have a different culture to sharpen, and a different character of employees to satisfy. Involving the people who work in companies to help set the "goals for meaning" is a way of ensuring that the vision is, in fact, meaningful and possible. Commitment flows from involvement. The more involved people feel in the goals, the more personal their contribution and ultimate satisfaction.

Meaning is, in large part, derived from how what one does affects others. The goals that provide meaning are those that bring an added dimension of caring and teamwork to the work environment, or that affect the broader community in some positive way. The task for managers is to create the conditions within a company in which people feel that they can make a difference to their fellow workers and to their society.

Just as profit and cost-control goals are formalized within a company, the objectives for infusing greater meaning must be specified. While more noble, meaning will not occur happenstance, no matter how well-intentioned people are. Constructing a value system within a company, which evokes greater personal meaning, requires the same discipline and dedication to strategy as do the other, more conventional, goals of business.

While a corporate mission statement may ultimately reflect a company's quest for meaning, its source remains the hearts of the people involved. Business leaders and managers need look no farther than their own sensibilities for what's right, their own values for what's important to them as human beings, to set goals of meaning and fulfilment. The adage that "no one, on their death bed, ever says they wished they worked harder" provides a sobering acid test for what we do in business.

Are we creating real, lasting, meaningful value? Are we contributing to ourselves, our families, our communities, in ways that transcend the economic impact of what we've achieved?

In the past, we've drawn a line between what's right in life and what's right in business. This arbitrary distinction has proven dangerous. Ultimately, the good judgement we have as human beings provides the best judgement for what we need in business.

BUSINESS AND
THE SIN AGAINST
THE PLANET

There is no way to bring a spiritual sensibility to business without first reconciling its hostile relationship with nature. The recycling programmes and other "green" initiatives undertaken by business during the last few years, while admirable, are largely cosmetic, often pursued under pressure. While there has been progress, most business leaders and their managers regard the environment dispassionately. They view it through the filter of traditional business thinking, so that the relationships between their companies and nature remain exclusively economic.

Thinking about what constitutes the "bottom line" has not been expanded sufficiently to incorporate the true value of the environment to business. Why else would the seven automobile manufacturers around the world, who have developed, built and tested cars that can achieve more than sixty-seven miles to the gallon, have yet to launch a single such fuel-efficient model anywhere?[1]

Without a change in values, there is the very real risk that the environmental concerns of corporations and businesses will remain in the sphere of public relations. How companies are perceived on the issues of the environment will continue to be more important than their actual behaviour.

Many of the giant logging companies of North America have, for a long time, made it a policy to cut down trees only beyond the sight lines visible to motorists on public roads. A tiny strip of trees provides the illusion to passing drivers that the area is untouched by loggers. Concealed behind this strip are the horrifying after-effects of logging. Only from the air can the true devastation of the forest be seen, but because few people see it from this vantage point, the public perception is not as critical as it should be.

Real integration between business and nature cannot be achieved in reaction to public-relations pressure. The attitudes, assumptions, beliefs, systems and structures that underlay our system of enterprise must be reconsidered, and evolve to reflect the urgent need to reconnect with nature.

The tradition of regarding nature as subservient to humans is deeply ingrained in our Western culture.

The mythology and thought structure that the West inherited from the ancient Greeks divided the the world of nature from that of the spirit. Not only was the division arbitrary, but nature and the world of the material were seen as flawed. The spirit, on the other hand, was pure and transcendent. In the classical context, rational thought was a spiritual instrument, because it created order, while nature was mired in dark chaos.

The bias against nature was reinforced by the Judeo-Christian belief structure that pervades Western history.

In Genesis, the world that is the natural home of human beings is, in fact, the distorted place we inherited after "the Fall." From this perspective, the natural world is without the approval of the divine, and in need of redemption, just as humans were after their "original" sin.

In the hierarchy of existence established in the Bible, humans are lower on the scale of development than angels, who are ethereal, but higher than all the other creatures of nature, who are material. Furthermore, the Bible confers mastery over nature to humans, by giving us the power to name the animals and plants within creation and use them for our advancement.

Such a mythological and spiritual context inevitably led our culture to debase nature. With the sacred aloft in another dimension, nature was, by implication, profane.

In *Conquest of Paradise*, Kirkpatrick Sale looks at the arrival in the Americas of Columbus, and the Europeans who followed him, from the new point of view of the ecological disaster and cultural turmoil they wrought on the indigenous environment and people. He believes that the cultural bias against nature made it easy for the explorers and settlers who came after them to fail to see the wonder of the New World. "From these elemental patterns in Europe's tapestry of nature—ignorance and fear, separation and hostility, dominance and exploitation—a discernable image emerges: of a world more mechanistic than organic, more artificial than intrinsic, more corporeal than numinous, from which intimacy, sacredness and reverence have all but vanished..."[2]

It would be a mistake to assume that the abuse of nature followed industrialization. Even when the economy of the Mediterranean region was primarily agrarian, humans were relentless in their destruction of the natural habitat. At ancient sites, such as Ephasis, archaeologists are uncovering evidence that the decline of once-great cities and states was, in great part, the result of environmental abuse.

Ephasis was an ancient centre for trade and commerce. Its architectural and artistic achievements were such that the city's amphitheatre seated over fifty thousand people—only a few thousand fewer than Toronto's SkyDome. On the surface, the decline of Ephasis seems to have been political or economic; just another casualty of military competition or commercial decline. In reality, the decline was largely environmental.

The rich forests around Ephasis were completely cut down, to accommodate the cultivation of crops. This deforestation was huge, on a scale that we assume only people with chainsaws and lumber-trucks to be capable of. Farming methods were very efficient, but, as with modern agriculture, the tilling and planting were relentless. Soil erosion decreased the productivity of the land, requiring still more forests to be cut down. The combination of loss of trees and soil erosion resulted in the desertification of the region. Not only did the land become incapable of sustaining agriculture, but the eroding soil also washed away, filling in the natural harbour that had made Ephasis such an attractive centre for trade.

The failure to operate within nature led to the decline of this city, its culture, and its enterprises. Now, on a much broader and more catastrophic scale, we are repeating this failure. The machines and methods of modern business are so powerful that we face nothing less than the *ephasisication* of the whole planet. But again it would be a mistake to assign responsibility for the destruction of nature solely to these machines and methods. Business does not operate in isolation from the beliefs and attitudes that pervade our whole society. It is these beliefs and their source values that must be reconnected to nature.

The Clumsy Touch of "The Invisible Hand"

Adam Smith is widely credited for providing Western society with the theoretical basis for its economic system. Much of the "free enterprise" rhetoric of the Reagan-Thatcher-Mulroney era was derived from Smith's work. However, it is important to remember that Adam Smith was not an economist, but a moral philosopher. His thinking stretched the moral and scientific construct of Western thinking to include the changes that rapid mechanization and industrialization were creating.

Smith was a Christian, so his view of the natural world was utilitarian. Smith was also an academic, teaching at the University of Glasgow, so he valued the rational above all. Ultimately, Smith was a Renaissance man, so he believed passionately in the progress of science and industry as a means of elevating all mankind.

The importance of Smith's thinking comes from providing a logical process for economic activity, which fit society's moral view of itself. The liberal concepts of the Enlightenment stressed the value of the individual. Smith built on this moral premise. He saw the value of the individual, particularly the love of self that all individuals are worthy of, to be the guiding mechanism for economic and social order.

Smith based his economic theory on the very simple premise of human self-interest. He wrote the often-quoted explanation that it is "not from the benevolence of the butcher, the brewer or the baker, that we expect our dinner, but from their regard to their own self-interest." In economic activity, self-interest is healthy because it creates the competitive motivation for constantly improving the goods and services available to the market. Competition also provides the checks and balances for preventing abusive business practices because, in Smith's logic, it will be in someone else's self-interest to correct, and therefore capitalize on, that abuse.

Smith believed that the *reasonable* counterweight of competitive self-interest would guide economic activity "as if by an invisible hand."[3] Letting the market thus follow and correct its own course would provide the greatest economic benefit and gains for society.

In providing a *reasonable* argument for self-interest, Smith continued the long tradition of Greek and biblical thinking, which placed man high in the hierarchy of creation.

Thomas Berry, an American monk, has written passionately about spirituality and the environment. "The industrial-commercial mode of consciousness within our society has co-existed with traditional spiritual coding in the pattern of Western classical spirituality. These two patterns cause little trouble to each other because neither the modern scientific mode of consciousness nor our spiritual consciousness is concerned with the integral functioning of the earth community. Indeed, both modes of consciousness experience the human as Olympian ruler of the planet, the planet as naturalistic functioning, and Earth's resources as objects for unlimited human exploitation."[4]

Smith's economic vision reflected the human-centred morality of his time. As industrialization exploded and the staggering developments in mechanization and technology took hold, Western society genuinely believed that the attendant progress was an improvement on the natural order. Nature remained outside the loop of human consideration. There was no "natural interest" to influence the movements and counter-responses of the market's "invisible hand."

Today, although we may not yet see it fully, the self-interest of humans finally coincides with that of nature. This affords great hope, because the market dynamics that Smith envisioned have been wonderfully adept at responding to market pressures out of self-interest. That nature's needs are now in sync with the self-interest of humans means that the considerable drive and creativity of self-interested people and self-interested companies will finally be put at the service of nature, helping to solve the daunting, inescapable, very serious problems of the environment.

The voice of nature, though still being filtered through the transparent needs and self-interest of humans, is, at least, finally being heard. Progressive marketing companies have adopted the environment as yet another expression of their orientation to satisfy consumer needs.

Procter & Gamble has introduced refillable packaging for many of its liquid cleaning products. McDonald's has bowed to public pressure and finally scrapped much of its styrofoam packaging. GE has introduced a new bulb that lasts significantly longer and consumes far less energy than conventional incandescents. Borden has cleaned up its waste-discharge system, and actually increases the efficiency of its plant and saves money. Black & Decker has announced a line of solar-powered lawn-mowers.

All of these moves are part of the ping-pong process of improvements that has characterized the competitive marketplace. Companies, looking for an edge to improve efficiency or better differentiate their products, implement initiatives that reduce trash, increase recycling, or benefit the environment in yet another way. Competitors must play the ball back, looking for improvements on improvements, efficiency on efficiency, innovation on innovation.

This high-stakes ping-pong game is, in fact, a demonstration of Smith's "invisible hand" at work. At last, the needs of nature are high enough on the priorities of human self-interest to be in the game. Now that nature has made this breakthrough and represents a business opportunity, we will likely see a lot of progress on reversing the abuse of the environment in the next decade.

The considerable creativity and power of invention within business is already being directed at solving environmental problems. Huge business opportunities await those who master less ecologically damaging new technology. The costs of cleaning up the air, the water, and the land are enormous, representing opportunities of equal scale to the entrepreneurs and corporations that build expertise in this burgeoning field.

The Market May Be Too Slow

The problems contributing to our current environmental crisis were built up over time, and with time, the millions of incremental changes that will be implemented by business will go a long way towards alleviating the pressure on nature. The sad reality is that this process is too slow.

While General Motors boasts of winning "1991 Car of The Year" honours for its anachronistically boat-like Chevrolet Caprice, the planet chokes, trying to absorb five billion tons of carbon released into the atmosphere every year. While Archer, Daniel, Midlands brags in its advertising about the ecological benefits potentially to be obtained by converting cars to corn-derived methanol, the earth loses twenty-four billion tons of topsoil to erosion every year. So, on a very personal measure, the oil and gas we consume, and the food we produce, costs the equivalent of one ton of airborne carbon and one half-ton of topsoil erosion *every year, per human being*.[5]

Incremental improvements in energy use from cars that get higher mileage are laudable. Incremental reductions in waste going into landfill by, as P&G has suggested, recycling diapers into plastic lumber, are marketing steps in the right direction. But the progress of the "invisible hand" is too little, too late.

The "natural interest" must be given equal weighting to the "self-interest" of humans, to achieve a workable economic model. In their 1987 *State of the World report*, the Worldwatch Institute suggests restructuring the established measurement of Gross National Product to reflect the environmental interdependency that all industrial nations can no longer escape.

The measures of GNP were formalized only a half-century ago, to help countries quantify changes in industrial output over time. "GNP measurement includes depreciation of plant and equipment, but it does not take into account the depreciation of natural capital, including non-renewable resources such as oil, and renewable resources such as forests."[6] In our current environmental context, GNP fails to measure the true assets and liabilities of industrial development, because it assigns no value to the dwindling natural resources upon which business is so dependent.

Until we acknowledge that ecological assets have a legitimate place on the balance sheet, business remains more of a problem than a solution to the environmental debacle. Until sufficient economic liability is assigned to the abuse of natural resources, business will persist in exercising its short-term self-interest over the long-term, common, planetary good.

The economic costs of natural degradation are finally evident in developed countries, such as Germany, where the acid-rain damage to its Black Forest now affects an area the size of Austria, and costs industry about a billion dollars a year in lost revenue. The high costs of natural degradation also played an important role in the crash of communist industry. Poland, Romania, East Germany and Russia now face catastrophes in air and water pollution of unimaginable proportions. The cost of clean-up is so far beyond their economic capability that communism itself has ceased being viable.

In a world of environmental degradation, the poor only get poorer. Deforestation of Latin America and the Amazon basin continues unabated, despite the evidence that farming cannot be sustained for very long on jungle soil. It is another expression of the inadequacy of modern economic measurement that the countries with many of the most valuable resources for sustaining the health and vitality of our planet are labelled undeveloped. The under-appreciation of these assets has accelerated the devastation of the few remaining virgin forests. While these jungles serve as "the lungs of the earth," our inaccurate appraisal of their value has led to a situation in Central and South America in which only one tree is planted for every ten harvested. In more fragile North Africa, the ratio is one for every twenty-nine.[7]

As we've seen with oil spills, acid rain, and nuclear leaks, environmental damage cannot be contained. Like a spreading cancer, ecological pain spreads across the artificial boundaries of state, economic system and economic development created by humans, and attacks the entire planetary organism. While frightening, the very fact that environmental degradation cannot be contained carries within it the possibility and hope of galvanizing humans to realize, once and for all, that the self-interest of nature is inexorably interconnected with that of all people, in all countries.

The United Nations has already begun to study the changes required in international law and commerce, to begin to attend to the needs of the earth and secure a workable, vital environment for future generations. The World Commission on Environment and Development, headed by Gro Harlem Bruntland, the former Prime Minister of Norway, published its analysis and recommendations in 1987, in a book entitled *Our Common Future.*

The report represents four years of study, incorporating information from scientists, economists, politicians and citizens from around the world. The data supporting the dangerous exhaustion of nature is incontrovertible. The recommendations for corrective action are pragmatic, and worthy of serious study and implementation. One aspect of the report that is particularly inspiring is the implication from many contributors that the one-sided exploitation of the environment can only be addressed through a new spirituality.

The need for such eco-spirituality was embraced by people of competing political and economic systems. I.T. Frolov, editor-in-chief of Moscow-based *Communist Magazine* suggested, "To successfully advance in solving global problems, we need to develop new methods of thinking, to elaborate new moral and value criteria, and, no doubt, new patterns of behaviour." A speaker from the floor at the WCED hearing in Jakarta said, "We in Asia want to have equilibrium between the spiritual and material...Is it not exactly the mistake in the West of developing technology without ethics, without religion? If that is the case, and we have a chance to develop a new direction, should we not...pursue a different kind of technology, which has as its base not only the rationality, but also the spiritual aspect?"[8]

While the leaders of business and industry were conspicuously absent from the hearings that contributed to the WECD report, it is obvious that the values-change and need for spiritual sensibility apply to them, as well as to the consumers of the products they produce. Such spirituality comes from the acknowledgement that all human activity, including the actions of commercial enterprises, are interlinked, interrelated and interdependent. No one person or institution is complete unto itself. Nor are any of us free from an intimate dependence on nature. By realizing this inherent interconnection, we have no choice but to assume the full responsibility and accountability for how our human activities have trespassed against nature.

If we acknowledge the sacredness of nature, then we must accept culpability for the sins committed against it by business. So great is our technological prowess that, in only a few generations, we've destroyed natural resources that took millions of years to nurture and evolve. Such desecration cannot be rationalized by any economic formula.

All of us who participate in business, either as managers, employees, or consumers of its products, must accept our share of the responsibility. Only if business admits its complicity in this crime, and accepts accountability, can it hope to reform its systems and structures sufficiently to operate viably into the future.

Business that operates with such spiritual sensibility and accountability can become a potent source of change. The technological advances of business are already doing a lot to clean up the environmental damage of our global lifestyle. The creativity of its people can be fruitfully applied to the business opportunities in the areas of environmental protection and management. The Bruntland report provides evidence that environmentally enlightened business practices have significant economic benefit. "A 1984 survey by the Organization for Economic Cooperation and Development...concluded that expenditures on environmental measures over the past two decades had a positive short-term effect on growth and employment. The benefits, including health, property, ecosystem damages avoided, have been significant. More important, these benefits have generally exceeded costs."[9]

With spiritual sensibility, by acknowledging past sins, and by accepting accountability for future actions, business can begin to apply its energies, assets and resources to creating commercial enterprises that yield profit, not from the exploitation of nature, but from its nurturing. The scale of change, while daunting, is manageable. It, too, begins with the human heart.

MicroChange

Business executives generally acknowledge that the people who work in factories and offices need the refreshment of vacation.

They also believe that, as companies grow and evolve, new blood must be brought into the enterprise, to renew and restore it. Finally, smart executives understand the principles of capital investment—the need to add new equipment to replace the worn-out and the old, and to expand capacity and improve productivity. When we open our hearts to nature, these rational principles of renewal and refreshment have equal validity and application to our environment.

The instincts of the heart help create a basis for reciprocity between business and nature. What we've historically taken from nature has been justified by the rational economic construct that has governed business. Adding the emotive guidance of the heart means that the health of the partnership takes precedence over the self-interest of either individual party. And this is exactly the equilibrium we so desperately need, to reconcile the needs of business with those of the small planet that sustains it.

Opening our hearts as business people sounds naïve. But, unless we allow ourselves to be awed, we will never have the humility to accept nature as a partner of business, rather than its tool.

Thomas Berry writes, "Without a fascination with the grandeur of the North American continent, the energy needed for its preservation will never be developed."[10] Berry is suggesting that we can't change our behaviour towards nature without opening ourselves to the possibility of holding it in awe. The quantitative measures of business and science, and the glamour of our own technology, have demystified nature. Only from the heart can the evocation of mystique be reactivated.

This small, personal commitment to open our hearts, within the affairs and judgements of business, will lead to the much larger initiatives upon which the commercial-environmental equilibrium ultimately rests. Many longstanding business traditions, such as depreciation and balance-sheet accounting, will need to be revised to reflect emotive concern for the environment. Investment priorities will need to be realigned. Tax laws will need to be redirected, and international business practices standardized to a new accountability for nature. Big challenges require big changes, none of which can come about if our hearts aren't in it.

Unlike the rational mind, which is constrained by the pragmatic and the possible, the heart is motivated by conviction.

Such convictions, the stuff of dreamers and poets, is the untapped raw material that is indispensable if business is to meet the staggering challenges that it—that we—face.

With our hearts in it, those of us who lead small companies will make small contributions to the needed equilibrium, and those in bigger corporations will make bigger contributions. The net effect of these collective efforts will be substantial, and will build the momentum necessary to counter the destruction to date.

More and more leaders of business are turning their energies and the vast resources of their companies to the issues of the environment. The November 5, 1990, issue of *Maclean's* magazine reported on the conversion of Sir James Goldsmith to the cause of ecology. Goldsmith has a well-deserved reputation as a shark. He built a substantial fortune as a corporate raider, and is widely known for his predatory business practices and ruthless negotiation skills. Yet even Sir James had a change of heart, retiring from business to devote himself to the environment.

Maclean's reported that "business communities on both sides of the Atlantic were getting used to the idea of a new, gentler Goldsmith—a protector of nature rather than a ruthless hunter of vulnerable companies." Goldsmith expressed his goal as not "anti-industrial," but "to persuade business people of the importance of the environmental crisis facing the world."[11] Lobbying on this level is critically important, for it is those who have the greatest power who also have the greatest responsibility.

Heartfelt change, reflecting awe for nature, is necessary throughout our society. It must occur among customers and consumers, for their choice in products and services can do the most to influence business leaders to adopt ever more progressive green practices. It must occur among employees, for their ideas and attitudes can help improve manufacturing efficiency and waste reduction. It must occur among our political leaders, whose regulations and taxation policies do so much to direct the investment decisions of business.

The millions of small steps, taken by millions of people who have opened their hearts to the awe of nature, will make a profound difference in the relationship we have with nature. These steps will also help build momentum for some of the larger initiatives that are necessary to move back from the precipice of ecological disaster.

For business managers to build an intimate connection to nature will not be easy. The opening of hearts and the development of a spiritual respect for the environment are not subjects taught in business school, nor skills fostered in corporate training programmes. Pressures from competitors will continue unabated, making the transition to eco-responsibility sometimes risky. Huge investments will be required. New technology must be designed and engineered. New corporate skills must be learned. New accounting practices must be evolved. Such massive undertakings will only be viable if we take some very bold, large-scale initiatives.

Peter Drucker has suggested that corporate business investments in new plant and technology are justified only by a tenfold increase in cost-effectiveness. Dollars expended, which do not yield such improvements, can be viewed as surrendering competitive advantage. Making the massive investments required to adapt business to its new environmental responsibility may not yield the dramatic gains in traditional productivity that have warranted such expenditures. To promote this level of investment, while maintaining competitive balance, is the "Catch-22" baffling even the most genuine of environmentally attuned business leaders.

This conundrum is one that my classmates and I explored at Harvard, while working on a case entitled "The Tragedy of the Commons," by Garrett Hardin. The commons is a piece of public land, a pasture available to all the herdsmen in a town. Each herdsman, being a rational being, "seeks to maximize his gain," and, over time, each adds additional cattle to the pasture. In exercising their right to share the common, reasonable men follow the pattern of reasonable men and add more and more cattle to the commons, until it is overgrazed and spent. As Hardin notes, "freedom in the commons brings ruin to all." This overgrazing of the commons is analogous to both our relentless exploitation of nature to provide raw materials for industry, and our relentless dumping of pollutants into the air, water and soil of our planet. We've struggled with the problem and have reached an impasse, because to act or limit the actions of either exploiters or polluters would violate their rights and impede their competitiveness. It should be

obvious that we have, in fact, defined rights incorrectly, or at
least from too limited a perspective. Hardin states that "morality is system-sensitive," a reality that ethicists from previous
centuries could ignore, because of the seemingly unlimited
abundance of nature. Now that we know its limitations, its
fragility, we must develop a moral sensibility based on interdependence.

My classmates and I could not resolve the paradox of the
"tragedy of the commons." As I've thought more about it, it
seems that, until we develop this new morality, we should at
least implement steps to extend the viability of the broader
commons that all commercial institutions and people share
with other species.

MacroChange

One such unorthodox step would be for business and governments around the world to declare a "Year of The Environment."
During this year, the efforts of business and governments would
be singularly devoted to restoring the environment. Taxation
policies would be reworked to strongly encourage business to
invest in the plant, equipment and training that will most directly benefit the ecology. Companies would dedicate their
profits for this year to environmental initiatives, buying or developing new technology to increase the energy-efficiency of
their plants and to reduce the waste they create.

The moratorium on the degradation of nature would involve all segments of society. Shareholders would forsake their
dividends for this one year, to allow companies maximum
reinvestment in nature. Employees would get involved, contributing their portion of profit-sharing and their own volunteer
time to specific environmental programmes in their workplaces and communities.

Designing and implementing such a year is a formidable
task, but only brave initiatives will generate the needed scale
of results. The war against Iraq showed how the UN can be
galvanized around a cause. Applying the same pressure on an
issue that is even more far-reaching, that touches all of humanity, should be a priority.

By making it an international event, no single country or company surrenders any competitive advantage. An important benefit is that the co-operation that such a year of activity would entail would provide a forum for sharing technology and practices that benefit the environment, between the industrial powers and the developing countries of Eastern Europe, Asia, Africa and South America.

It may seem idealistic to assume that shareholders would forsake their dividends for the year of the environment. In reality, such renewal of nature and such investment in more environmentally benign plant and technology, only serves to increase the value and long-term viability of industry. This year will, therefore, only increase shareholder value, even if it means delaying the clipping of coupons and the collection of dividends.

In an article in *The New York Times* business section, accounting professor Marc J. Epstein reported on quantitative research he conducted among a random sampling of shareholders with ownership of at least one hundred shares of a stock listed on either the New York or American exchange. Epstein found that the shareholders' "responses made one thing very clear: they want corporations to direct more money toward two areas—cleaning up plants and stopping environmental pollution, and making safer products. And they want to put their money where their mouths are. They say they want companies to invest in these areas rather than allocate the money for higher dividends. Higher dividends ranked number 3 in a list of 10 spending items."[12]

In research, we often find that intent is easier to elicit than actual commitment. Nevertheless, the evidence suggests that shareholders and the other stakeholders of companies within society are more open to concepts of environmental management and investment than ever before. What we now need are visionary political and business leaders, who will provide the ideas and concrete direction for actualizing these good intentions.

This year dedicated to the environment should not be a one-time event, but should recur perhaps every seven years, or every decade, so that the investment in the environment will become an accepted part of the business cycle. Farmers have long practised the necessary tradition of allowing the land to lie fallow, to recuperate its powers of growth and nourishment. Our industrialized society must learn the same lesson, and come to accept the broader need of our natural environment for widespread and serious renewal. If nature is our greatest factory, then we must apply the same discipline in replenishing nature that we use in business to maintain equipment, to restore capacity, to rebuild and restock our factories.

The environment touches everyone, and everyone can contribute to the success of such a year. Lawyers can dedicate themselves to creating new codes of responsibility and liability for environmental damage created by oil spills, or the very destructive and expensive release of zebra mussels into the aquasystem of the Great Lakes. Accounting companies can organize new auditing procedures, which reflect not only financial value, but also environmental cost and energy-efficiency. Industry associations, often toothless organizations, can earn their dues by providing companies with standards and environmental solutions that apply to their specific fields.

Focusing the considerable investments of business and government on the environment for one year will start, in earnest, the process of developing a new relationship of respect with nature. Think of the possibilities. New technology will be commissioned, designed, engineered and put in place to clean up the practice of business. Resources will be studied and protected, so that their richness can be used without the depletion and exhaustion that robs future generations of their birthright. R&D efforts will give nature the priority it deserves, so that future advances in technology and science are based on reciprocity instead of exploitation.

The incredible problems of waste will be attacked, so that the business process emulates more closely the patterns of nature, which recycles its own by-products to provide nutrients for future growth. After several centuries of taking from nature, such a year would commit the potent energy and innovation ability of business to giving back, to creating business practices that acknowledge the true value and indispensability of our environment.

With the leadership of business, all the other institutions in society can be focused, for this year, to enhance our collective respect and appreciation for nature. The media, with their great capacity for programming and editorializing, can be marshalled to provide the information base to help our society create a new, more enlightened relationship with our environment. The arts, with their ability to evoke passion and stimulate the imagination, can help us develop a spiritual sense of the majesty and beauty of nature.

Our academic institutions will have the opportunity to teach all segments of society, helping kids and adults see our history and culture, as well as our future, through the new perspective of eco-responsibility. Interdisciplinary task forces, made up of economists, ecologists, business people and poets, can use the year to create the needed theories and measurement tools for establishing the new GNP of "gross *natural* product." Profoundly difficult questions wait to be tackled, and such group efforts throughout society will finally begin to crack the complex issues that have business at an impasse with nature.

Everyone in our society is touched by business and, through its efforts, society as a whole can participate in the renewal of our partnership with nature. This is where we can begin to develop the new morality.

Forging an Eco-Industrial Strategy

For Canada, nature and the cause of the environment may provide a source of political and economic cohesion that we are sorely lacking. Free trade has changed the flow of our national energy from east-west to north-south, contributing to the fragmentation of our national psyche. The early evidence from trading in the larger North American market suggests that Canadian business is not competitive. Plant closings have already displaced hundreds of thousands of people. Now, while we face the difficult challenges associated with the expansion of the free trade area to include Mexico, and with the growing intensity of international competition, we find ourselves questioning the very viability of our confederation.

Canada has long relied on its natural resources to cushion its position in the world economy. The abundance of natural endowments, sprinkled over a vast land and available to a disproportionately small population, has had a reverse effect on both our environmental and economic performances.

In a study that measured emissions of tonnes of carbon and other greenhouse gases, *The Economist* reported that Canada is second only to East Germany in per-capita emissions. Over four and one-half tons of such airborne pollutants are released for every single person who lives in our country.[13] We are profligate users of energy, even in comparison to industrialized countries like Sweden, which shares the cold climate we use to justify our high consumption of fossil fuels. Canadians, while outraged about their dying lakes, have been responsible for more than half of the emissions that contributed to the acid-rain damage of our own forests.[14]

While our consciences are eased by the expanding use of blue boxes, we remain, along with the U.S., the heaviest users of packaging in the world. Despite having the second-largest land mass of any country in the world, we're running out of room for our garbage. Despite having the most fresh water available to any country in the world, many of our rivers are polluted, and many of our lakes are dead. The few remaining ancient forests are being systematically denuded. The very fact that we have so much, as a country, seems to have made us complacent about managing this incredible inheritance.

Beyond the environmental loss, our reliance on, and abuse of, our natural resources also represents an economic loss. Propping up our exports through sales of timber, natural gas, minerals and coal has anaesthetized us, as a country, against the true intensity of international development and competition. While we perceive Canada to be a developed country, our reliance on resource exploitation makes our economy much like those of more primitive, developing countries. We have what Kenichi Ohmae, the Tokyo-based McKinsey consultant, calls "a provider's mentality."

In his 1990 book, *The Borderless World*, Ohmae writes, "Even such advanced countries as Australia and Canada often fall into this dilemma. They think that because they are resource rich they can live on their own resources, dipping leisurely into their pot of gold at need. But it doesn't work that way. Unless they are the sole source of some absolutely critical material, the resources on which they count can be easily arbitraged. They have become commodities. When no value is added, none can be collected."[15]

Canada's trees and minerals are valuable, but, because these are also the resources that developing countries are using to fuel their economies, we find ourselves in Ohmae's commodity spiral. Logging, mining, and energy industries in Canada have been through very painful cycles of commodity pricing, so that, while we are depleting these non-renewable resources, we are doing so in an economic environment that does not fully value them. It is very telling about Canada's eroding place in the world economy that, while we are the largest provider of coal to Japan, Malaysia has become Japan's largest source for microchips.

Adopting a "Year of The Environment" in Canada affords an opportunity to kick-start a new economic plan, one based on the protection, rather than depletion, of natural resources. Following the model for industrial strategy used by Japan, Canada's politicians, business leaders and educators must co-operate to develop an *environmental strategy*. This strategy would dedicate Canada to becoming the world's expert in resource management, pollution control, and waste clean-up.

Government taxation and grants policies would focus on encouraging business to develop new technology and new expertise in environmental management, much like the Ministry of Industry and Trade focused Japanese companies on high-value-added exports, such as cars, electronics and computers. Canada's universities would engage in far more environmentally related research, developing global credentials for this expertise. Supported by government, and with access to the research flowing from universities, entrepreneurs and business leaders would be able to develop new technology and new services, to implement at home and export abroad.

The world is going to desperately require environmental-management technology and expertise. Adopting this as our national niche allows us to focus our limited human resources on a market of considerable opportunity. It may also have the tonic effect of bonding us as a country. The resources we share, and the expertise we would develop as a country, would provide a reason for bonding, for cooperating, for standing proudly as a nation contributing to the planet.

In addition, an eco-based industrial strategy would allow for full participation and contribution from Canada's indigenous peoples. The spirituality of our Native people is nature-based. Who, then, is better placed to teach us in business how to respect nature, how to see its sacredness, how to connect to it with much-needed awe?

Louis Bruyere, president of the Native Council of Canada, spoke to the World Commission on Economic Development in 1986. "Indigenous people are the base of what I guess could be called the environmental security system. We are the gate-keepers of success or failure to husband our resources. For many of us, however, the last few centuries have meant a major loss of control over our lands and waters. We are still first to know about changes in the environment, but we are now the last to be asked or consulted.

"We are the first to detect when the forests are being threatened, as they are under the slash-and-grab economics of this country. And we are the last to be asked about the future of our forests. We are the first to feel the pollution of our waters, as the Ojibway peoples of my own homelands in Northern Ontario will attest. And, of course, we are the last to be consulted about how, when, and where developments should take place, in order to assure continuing harmony for the seventh generation.

"The most we have learned to expect is to be compensated, always too little, too late. We are seldom asked to help to avoid the need for compensation by lending our expertise and our consent to development."[16]

An *environmental strategy* for Canada will provide an economic framework for helping us remain competitive in the global marketplace. It will also give us the spiritual basis for nationhood that we've lacked for most of our history. And it will integrate the Native people, who have been so abused by our resource technocracy.

The naysayers, who maintain that the purity of free enterprise would be compromised by an industrial strategy, have failed to learn the lessons of the most progressive and economically successful developing countries. Those who resist factoring in a new value for the impact of business on nature are ignoring the competitive benefits such appreciation can realize.

The Japanese, short of resources of their own, have become world leaders in efficient energy use. An article in *Newsweek*, about the consequences of the Gulf War in Japan, notes that, since 1973 and the first Arab oil embargo, Japan has "relentlessly implemented conservation policies." That country now produces 81% more real output, with the same energy that it consumed in 1973. "It also uses about 30% less energy, relatively, to fuel its homes, cars, appliances and buildings than the United States. Its edge in manufacturing plants is even bigger, in part because it has invested so heavily in new factories and equipment over the last three years."[17]

I am not suggesting that the Japanese are models of enlightened environmental responsibility. Their floating fishing factories are doing great damage to marine life around the world. And their callous lumber practices are contributing to the deforestation of very valuable timberlands in Malaysia and throughout the Far East. Nevertheless, their energy policies do show how environmental initiatives can contribute to the overall viability and success of business. "Overall, the Japanese economy is twice as energy-efficient as [North] America's." And this efficiency translates into a considerable competitive advantage.

To embrace the priorities of nature, to nurture a nature-based spiritual sensibility, seem idealistic and dream-like. In fact, it is an imperative, a pragmatic requirement that will increasingly impose its discipline on all companies and all countries.

We've shown the political and commercial will to do so much. Moon-shots, the war in the Persian Gulf, Sony Walkmans, are examples of the incredible will and ingenuity of our species. Applying just a fragment of that will to the issues of the environment will go a long way towards repairing the damage we've done. Governments and companies that take such initiatives to heart will reap the emotional rewards of doing something of value that will benefit the community and future generations. Importantly, these initiatives also hold the basis of a competitive advantage, because countries and companies that are more respectful of nature, and more efficient in their use of resources, are ultimately adding greater value to the products and services they sell. Love for the environment is, finally, good business.

THE GROWING IRRELEVANCE OF BUSINESS

It is almost impossible to escape the influence of business in North American society. Most of us derive our livelihood from participating in business, as owners, managers or workers. The products we use are made by business. Travel, entertainment, and even activities relating to our health and well-being all involve some interaction with a business enterprise. Newspapers contain expanding business sections. More importantly, business news also spills into other sections of the newspaper: the stratospheric salaries paid to baseball players, reported in the sports section, are explained in the business context of the league's profitability from its billion-dollar network agreement with CBS.

Despite the pervasiveness of business, its relevance as an institution is waning. This may seem to be an outrageous statement but, in reality, business is undergoing the same crisis of relevance that traditional religions like the Catholic church have been going through for the last generation.

Business enjoyed special status in the Reagan-Thatcher-Mulroney conservatism of the 1980s. It was the preferred institution of these politicians, for channeling the energy and resources of society, for creating wealth, jobs, innovations and security. Supported by a dogma of free enterprise, business boomed, resulting in the longest peacetime expansion of the economy ever achieved. We are now at the end of that cycle. Many who participated in the boom are now questioning its validity, and whether the price paid for this expansion is morally justifiable. It is through this process of taking stock that the shortcomings and growing irrelevance of business are finally evident.

As a starting point, it is obvious that the flagships of North American business have lost much of their lustre.

General Motors, with its two-decade-long decline in domestic market-share, no longer seems the unassailable force it once was. Today, Toyota is accorded the highest rating for quality, by customers. And it is Toyota that earns the status of a cover story in *Fortune* magazine, entitled "Why It Keeps Getting Better and Better and Better."

As in cars, so in computers. For the first time in its history, IBM was beaten to the punch by Fujitsu. The Japanese company introduced a new mainframe only one day before IBM unveiled its new, state-of-the-art model. Until now, IBM set the standard, which other manufacturers emulated. "IBM-compatible" has been the mantra of this fast-changing industry. While IBM will continue to be a potent force in computers, it must, nevertheless, be dislocating to have its primacy challenged so successfully.

North Americans have always dominated super-computers, with wizards like Stephen Cray producing marvelously complex machines, capable of incredible feats of processing. That domination is over. For the first time since the original Univac processed data through its discombobulating stream of wires and vacuum tubes, a non-American computer is the fastest, most powerful machine on the planet. The leading edge of such computer development is important, because it provides the innovations that cascade down and revitalize the whole industry. Today, that leading edge belongs to a Japanese company.

Banks have always had a profound influence on the health of the business sector, and many North American banks are seriously sick. Citicorp, like many other North American banks, suffered some major set-backs, as it dealt with defaults on loans it made to developing countries during the 1970s. After financing the real-estate developers and junk-bond marketers who fuelled the expansion of the 1980s, this leading bank finds itself in a very precarious position. As Citicorp and other leading banks lick their wounds and consolidate, the capital that business needs to renew itself and remain competitive becomes scarcer, harder to qualify for, and more expensive to pay back.

The problems and set-backs that have stymied the corporate flagships of North America have fostered a growing sense within society that "businesses over there do it better than businesses over here." In his book about the Mercury space programme, Tom Wolfe talked about the cycle of insecurity and second-guessing that took root during the early failures of American rockets. As rocket after rocket exploded on the launch pad, or just seconds after take-off, the Americans began to believe that "ours always blow up." It took a huge investment of resources and money, and some very dramatic achievements, to reverse the widespread perception that America could not successfully compete with the Soviets in space.

The psyche of our society is again questioning its ability, only now wondering whether its domestic business institutions and their corporate leaders have the wherewithal to compete internationally. This questioning is profoundly disconcerting because, for several generations, North Americans have operated as if business were their exclusive domain. We exported mass-production techniques, pioneered in the North American auto plants. We also exported the management theory of people like A.J. Taylor, which evolved from our mass-production expertise.

North Americans produced more, and generally made it better than anyone else. The confidence that resulted from this leadership helped fuel the entrepreneurs and innovators who have so shaped our modern society. Now, as we grapple with the reality of productivity declines and business failures, the growing attitude towards business is that, like the early Mercury rockets, "ours always blow up."

Chrysler's recent advertising proclaims its advantages, versus Honda. The Chrysler car has more features, a larger engine, more interior room, and a lower price than its Honda equivalent. Yet Honda's model continues to be the best-selling in Canada, while Chrysler struggles under the grinding pressure of competition and the recession. Even though its products may have improved in quality, Chrysler's message is dissonant with the prevailing attitude that Japanese cars are superior. In attributing superiority to the Japanese, car customers are not only effecting a shift in market-share, they are also indicating, through their actions, the irrelevance of the North American company to them.

The growing irrelevance of North American business is expressed in countless ways. The joy of a Walkman is conferred by Sony. The wizardry of a laptop computer is provided by Toshiba. The gut-wrenching adrenalin surge of a state-of-the-art sports car is stimulated by Acura. The self-assurance of a statement suit is expressed by Armani. The artistry of beautifully formed, highly functional kitchen appliances is engineered by Braun. The emotions people bring to the products they use provide a gauge for the relevance of the businesses that provide them. Increasingly, our society is looking elsewhere for the emotional connection between people and products.

North American companies, caught in a cycle of producing goods of uninspiring quality at low prices, are often excluded from the highpoints of this emotional interchange. If its products aren't loved by the customers, then the company producing those products quickly ceases being relevant to them.

An article in *The Economist*, in 1989, discussed the importance and value of a brand. Several major acquisitions, such as that of R.J.R. Nabisco, were sweeping through Wall Street. The sale prices for these companies were significantly higher than the value of assets. In large part, the higher prices were the result of brand equity—the awareness and imagery that brands like Oreos and DelMonte had created over many years and countless millions of dollars in advertising and promotional investment.

The Economist observed that most great North American brands were older ones, created at the turn of the century or in the 1920s. Since World War Two, the more fertile source of new brands has been Japan. To contrast the R&D emphasis between the two cultures, the article pointed out that Japan was creating world-wide awareness and appreciation for brands like Sony and Honda, at the same time that U.S. companies were creating awareness for brands like the Trident submarine and the Patriot missile. While the comparison is admittedly tongue-in-cheek, brands remain important vehicles for creating relevance between customers and companies and, once again, North America's business is coming up short.

With the loss of leadership as manufacturers and innovators comes a gradual erosion in authority. The management practices of North American companies are no longer setting the standards for business. The world that used to come exclusively to North America's business schools now studies the techniques and principles of business leaders in Japan and Germany.

Structural innovations in the process of business, such as the "just-in-time" practice of inventory management, are imported by the whole world from Japan. The assumption that management innovation is being led by Japan is so strong that we attribute practices to them that were originally developed in the U.S.. Thomas J. Watson implemented lifetime employment and quality-control circles at IBM in 1935; enlightened management practices that most people in business and in society think of as ideas we are importing from Japan.[1]

The Costly Consequences of Irrelevance

As business loses its relevance, not only customers but also employees are disaffected. A recent issue of *Fortune* documented the departure of many senior and mid-level managers from North American companies. These people were often looking for an equilibrium in their lives, which their devotion to their companies did not provide. Some of the departing people were the very innovators and entrepreneurs whom modern business so desperately needs. The generation that had devoted itself to making it in business is coming to the sobering realization that career is not enough, and the growing irrelevance of business is compounding the sense of frustration and dislocation that many people feel in their jobs.

This dislocation is happening at a time when business is undergoing a massive restructuring, and especially needs the devotion and commitment of its people. A society's wealth has, to date, been primarily related to resources and the manufacture of large quantities of hard goods. The global economy is increasingly becoming one of ideas, rather than goods. As George Gilder points out in his book, *Microcosm: The Quantum Revolution in Economics and Technology*, high tech and the software that runs it require relatively little in hard resources, but rely heavily on the grey matter of people.

Gilder writes, "Today, the ascendant nations and corporations are masters not of land and material resources, but of ideas and technologies. Japan and other barren Asian islands have become the world's fastest-growing economies. Electronics is the fastest-growing major industry. Computer software, a pure product of the mind, is the chief resource of added value in world commerce. The global network of telecommunications carries more valuable goods than all the world's supertankers. Today, wealth comes not to the rulers of slave labour but to the liberators of human creativity, not to the conquerors of land but to the emancipators of mind."[2]

The economics of ideas have yet to be formalized. While new plant investment shows up on a company's balance sheet, the value of its employees' knowledge and training does not yet get an assigned value. Most corporate leaders, whose performance is usually measured by "return-on assets" formulas, have neither the tools nor the sensitivity to lead, reward and manage knowledge workers.

These human assets are being undervalued, at a time when they are also underdeveloped. Virgil Barry, of the U.S. consulting firm A.T. Kearney, says, "Brainpower is in dangerously short supply—at a time when business advances are being made by people who out-think others, not people who buy twice as many machines."

The loss of authority and respect facing North American business has obvious adverse effects on the employees and managers who make up its companies. Confidence in the direction set by management is negated by the experiences of staff cut-backs and plant closings, which have accompanied other management missteps. Empathy for the competitive intensity of the global marketplace is modified by the need to look outside the company for fulfilment, security, and intellectual stimulation. So, without the bond of relevance, business is finding it harder and harder to fully engage the brainpower of its critically important human resources.

The cooling attitude of our society towards business has tangible political implications, as well. If people feel disconnected from the goals of business, it logically becomes harder and harder to galvanize public opinion to support the policies and programmes that our companies need, to be successful in the demanding years ahead. Again, this is a severe disadvantage in the new world marketplace. The growing economies of the Pacific Rim have shown the importance of cooperation between business and the political institutions that regulate investment, taxation and education.

Stephen Schlosstein, in his 1990 book, *The End of the American Century*, examines the many factors propelling the growth not only of Japan, but also of Korea, Singapore, Hong Kong and Taiwan. Schlosstein characterizes these economies as examples of "turbocharged capitalism."[3] The goals of business are closely integrated with those of society. Infrastructure is developed to help business realize specific goals, which provide the most benefit to the society as a whole. Taxation is structured to induce investments in the most important strategic industries, and education is calibrated to provide the knowledge and skills that businesses can use to sharpen their competitive advantage.

The Ministry of International Trade and Industry in Japan is the most widely known government institution that intimately interplays with business in the Pacific Rim, to achieve mutually advancing goals. MITI has spearheaded Japan's export drive. Through its policies, MITI has helped Japan's economy migrate from the heavy industries of a traditional economy to the advanced, higher-value-added industries of electronics, computers and telecommunications, which represent the leading edge of the idea-based economy of the future.

Naohiro Amaya, the recently retired vice-minister for international affairs at MITI, views the interrelationship between business and the other institutions in society as essential.

"People tend to think that Japan is vulnerable because it is isolated and lacks natural resources, but natural resources are the software of the past and are becoming less relevant, especially in an information-intensive age that depends more on knowledge than on raw materials for progress and development. So, if human resources are tomorrow's software, then countries like America, which are rich in natural resources, may be at a disadvantage in comparison with countries like Japan, which have put a greater priority on development of human resources through education."[4]

While North Americans debate the philosophy of government involvement in the affairs of business, the competitive economies of the Far East and Europe are already applying the inter-institutional cooperation that is yielding them a significant advantage. The Reagan-Thatcher-Mulroney brand of economics simplistically assumed that unfettering business, deregulating it, would unleash the full benefits of free enterprise. But free enterprise, as they conceived it, is an obsolete notion. Government, and society in general, are too dependent on business to not influence its strategic development. And business is too fragile, without the full support of its domestic institutions, to weather the difficult storms of global competition.

The issue of whether business is relevant within society is, therefore, not a soft issue, but one that has serious implications. How well we organize ourselves for the challenges of global competition depends on the relationship that we foster between society and business. Without a spirit of trust and reciprocity, we will continue to undermine our economic effectiveness. And, unless we develop a shared mission, we cannot apply the focus that our economy will need to renew itself. North Americans need a sincere commitment between business and society, or we risk dropping to a tier-two or tier-three economy, with ever decreasing opportunities for our people, and an ever more menial industrial base.

Filling Up the Empathy Vacuum

Fostering relevance is an important obligation of business leaders. While it may not yet appear in the formal job description of a CEO, the need to create and nurture relevance will be the true test of the leadership ability of the North American managerial class. Relevance cannot be dictated by inter-company memo. Nor can it be advertised. Relevance does not appear on the bottom line. However, without relevance, without the deep emotional bond of empathy for its activities, business in North America will continue to lose currency with the employees, managers, customers and society from which it draws its resources and opportunities.

Recreating relevance will take innumerable small steps, great patience and consistency. None of these attributes is commonly associated with North American business practice. Our predilection is to hit home runs—new products, new breakthroughs, to quickly win big slices of the market. We also move fast, placing a premium on fast-trackers and fast decision makers. The orientation to the bottom line, with its quarterly pressure points, dissuades managers from making the correct long-term decisions that may adversely affect financial performance over the short-term.

A first step in breaking this cycle, and perhaps the most important in re-establishing the relevance of business within our society, is for CEOs to re-enter the real world. Once the insulation of management reports and research studies has been removed, the leaders of our companies can experience for themselves the dislocation and dissatisfaction that large sectors of our society feel towards business. Relating to this pain, frustration and sense of impotence as a human being will provide the personal connection that CEOs can draw on to make the difficult decisions needed to revitalize our business institutions.

In his award-winning, low-budget film, *Roger & Me*, director Michael Moore poignantly shows what happened to his hometown, Flint, Michigan, after G.M. closed several plants, leaving thirty thousand people unemployed. The movie is a psuedo-documentary, and follows Moore's efforts to get Roger Smith, then chairman of G.M., to talk about the plant closings and the human dislocation they caused.

The film is admittedly biased against G.M., looking at the situation from the point of view of the men and women on the street. Nevertheless, Smith's haughtiness, his refusal to respond to Moore, his following the corporate line and denying the human pain caused by the closings, reinforced the widely held perception that the leadership of business is out of step with the broader social community.

Smith has taken a lot of flack in the business press, much of it deserved. The plant closings depicted in Moore's movie, and the many others G.M. was forced to make during the 1980s, were not the fault of the workers. Management miscalculations about the types of cars customers wanted, about the degree of quality that customers expected, are at the root of G.M.'s ongoing problems.

These miscalculations reflect the great distance that exists between the managers who make product decisions and the real people who buy and use those products. The sad irony is that the people who paid for this miscalculation were those who least influenced the decision. Smith retired with great fanfare and a substantial, multi-million-dollar yearly pension, despite having overseen G.M.'s decline from the pinnacle of the car industry.

Such distancing of the leaders of business from the human community must be eliminated, both to engage the full resources of our society in the crusades of business, and to compete effectively. Look at the example provided by Shoichiro Toyoda, the president of Toyota.

Under Toyoda's tutelage, Toyota has grown to the point of challenging Ford for the number-two position in the worldwide car market. With his guidance, Toyota has applied its "continuous improvement" philosophy with such consistency that its cars have earned a wonderful reputation for quality, around the world. With focus and determination, Toyoda led his company to launch the highly successful Lexus line of luxury automobiles—cars of such precision that they've outscored Mercedes, BMW and Jaguar in customer-satisfaction surveys, in only their first year of availability.

All of this success, all of the hard work that went into it, would justify some smugness. Yet Toyoda remains dissatisfied. He worried that Toyota was growing too big and too removed from its customers. In 1990, he reorganized the company, reassigning managers to new roles, which put them closer to the products being made and the customers being served. Toyoda himself took on the functional task of leading product development. He explains. "We felt we suffered from large-corporation disease. It had become extremely difficult for top executives to convey their feelings to our workers. So we embarked on a cure. We wanted to recertify that customer satisfaction is our first priority."[5]

Toyota's workers would not simply read about the commitment to customers in a memo, they would also see it in the personal involvement of senior management, including Toyoda, in the difficult, day-to-day grind of making their business work. Personal commitment begets personal commitment.

North Americans must learn that the process of reigniting relevance involves more than "management by walking around." It requires genuine human interchange between the people who lead companies and those who make and buy their products and services.

Too often, the needs of customers are brought to management in the form of a comprehensive research study. The needs and attitudes of customers are quantified, categorized and clustered. What is impossible to gain through this filter of numbers is any real insight into the true human dynamics of the market. We end up with a decision process that lacks the real language, the real anguish, the real priorities, of the people who make up the marketplace. We end up with products that miss their marks, factories that close their doors, and a society that is suspicious of business, if not disenfranchised by it.

Relevance is only achieved through genuine empathy and understanding. And it is now imperative for business leaders to step down from their thrones and rebuild the channels for shared interaction with employees, and with the broader community.

From personal experience, I know how hard this is to do. I've worked long hours and have made considerable sacrifices to earn the title and privilege of president. The power and authority of that position are very gratifying to me. To surrender that which I've worked so hard to earn is irrational and feels counter-intuitive. Yet, as I ask for greater commitment from my people, I can only extend to them more of the authority and responsibility that they need to express this greater commitment. While I've learned to share power, I've not yet mastered the discipline of releasing it and not seizing it back.

Operating with empathy does not mean that management forsakes its duties and avoids the sometimes-necessary decisions to close plants or lay off employees. Rather, it means that company leaders must make the effort to personally engage the people involved, to share as human beings in their pain, explaining the necessity, and accepting accountability to the community for the company's action. Extending such dignity is the prerequisite for invoking it.

This, too, is a lesson I'm still learning. After bungling several situations that required painful employee firings and layoffs, I finally learned to see the human being in the situation. When, as the result of a client loss, we were forced to lay off four employees, my managers and I took the time to explain the circumstances in greater detail, to the people affected. We respected their right to know, their need to understand, and their sense of loss.

I also called an all-staff meeting and explained the situation in some detail to the rest of our people. After reviewing the financial rationale for the decision, I asked people to think about those who lost their jobs, and not deny the sense of loss and mourning that we all naturally felt.

Previously, in such situations, I tried to be the objective corporate officer, doing the "right thing" for the company. In opening myself to the people affected, as well as to the rest of our staff, I was able to maintain respect and human dignity in circumstances that are usually destructive to both. Three of the four employees who lost their jobs came back later and thanked me for my candour. One parted, saying this was the best company she had ever worked for. Many of the other members of our staff fed back comments that, although they didn't like what happened, they understood its necessity, and respected how we handled this never-comfortable situation.

While I may have personally advanced in extending empathy to the people who work in our company, I still face the challenge, on a daily basis, of constructing greater relevance for them. As the Catholic church struggled with the issue of relevance, its prescient leader, Pope John XXIII, called a Vatican Council. The Council initiated many reforms, some successful, most, even though well-intentioned, ultimately diluted. The documents of the Vatican Council open each chapter with the injunction that the cardinals and bishops who lead the Church are "the servants of the servants of Christ."

This wording acknowledges that the very hierarchy of the Church had grown distant from the people it was intended to serve. Business leaders have fallen into the same hierarchical trap, and are now experiencing the same disconnection with the very constituents they rely on for the achievement of their business objectives.

The process of training people for managerial positions must be rethought, to create a foundation for building relevance. Professor Mintzberg writes, "How do we train managers, the leaders of our organizations, where products are hammered out in messy factories and then sold in busy marketplaces? We lock bright and inexperienced people up in austere buildings and inundate them with paper. They never set foot in a factory, never meet a customer. Cases do it for them..."[6]

In this sterile environment, the pulse of a business is muffled. The handiwork of craftsmen, the inspiration of innovators, the sweat of labourers, all the human components of making a business work and integrating it within the community are distant and disembodied. For these managers-in-training, the mind is tuned to make business decisions without consulting the heart.

Immersing MBA students in the real-life circumstances of business is one way to foster relevance. Another is to encourage a much more interdisciplinary approach to the academic accreditation for business. Studying history, philosophy, psychology and art can help create a wider awareness of our interconnection as humans, and of our broader interconnection with nature. With a generalist view, it is easier for managers and business people to open themselves to the concerns, worries and needs of the customers they serve, and the employees they must support to fulfil their aims.

E.F. Schumacher challenges us to consider creating businesses that give back to society as much as they take out. The evidence shows that the current model of business is much more exploitive than compensating. The incredible quantities of non-renewable resources that go into maintaining our business structures are but one example. The pollution and waste spewed out by our businesses is a second.

Evolving business to a more responsible use of resources, to cleaner operations, represents an important step in achieving the reciprocity upon which its relevance for society can finally be re-established. Applying this reciprocity to the human factors involved in business is the second critical step. As companies extend pride and support to employees, those employees will respond with greater pride and personal commitment to the jobs they're doing. As managers earnestly demonstrate their desire to listen, employees and customers will respond with greater confidence and loyalty for the products that business is producing.

There is little magic in this concept of relevance. It requires that business acknowledge its interdependence with people, with society, and with our planetary home. Out of this awareness will emerge the sense of wholeness that allows for constructive interchange between business and its various constituents.

Without the participation and endorsement of people, and of our social institutions, North American business risks falling further and further behind its international competitors. And, as that happens, our society is deprived of the capital and opportunity for technological development upon which its future vitality hinges.

This mutuality of interest needs to be led by business. Once they are positively engaged, once people feel the emotional connection of relevance with the companies and leaders who constitute our business assets, we will be able to find the motivation and inspiration to secure our society's place in the global economy.

The Business Success That Flows From Relevance

Some very progressive, highly successful companies are already putting this mutuality to work, building profits by working hard at delivering not only value, but also relevance. Wal-Mart is now the number-one retailer in North America, having surpassed Sears in just the last year. This is a remarkable accomplishment, given that Wal-Mart was only founded in the 1960s, and that it has achieved the status of number one in absolute volume while currently operating in mostly southern and western U.S. markets, with no presence to speak of in major cities throughout the north-east and the west coast.

Wal-Mart has displaced Sears and K-Mart by adhering to the very simple gospel of self-effacing founder, Sam Walton. "Be an agent for consumers, find out what they want and sell it to them for the lowest possible price." The management of

Wal-Mart stays close to customers by actually working in the stores. While Sears corporate officers plotted innumerable, ineffective defensive strategies during the last decade, from their hundred-storey office tower in Chicago, the executives from Wal-Mart, working out of a warehouse in Bentonville, Arkansas, built their enormous franchise by meeting and talking to customers.

The CEO, David Glass, and his senior managers spend an incredible two days a week in stores, watching shoppers, greeting them at the door, talking to them about what they need and what they like, and demonstrating personally how much the company values their custom. The needs of people, the issues and priorities that are relevant to them, are determined face to face, rather than via the distorting, depersonalizing documentation of a research report.

Not only customer relevance is enhanced by this rather humble, hands-on management approach. Employees, too, are better trained and more motivated to deliver the product and service mission of Wal-Mart. This in-store presence by senior executives is not a symbolic formality, but rather genuinely demonstrates "management by example." Through this frequent contact, management develops an empathy for the problems and needs of employees. As they bond with sales and service people, they realize not only greater productivity, but also the heightened emotional commitment that so helps to deliver meaningful customer service. Such human interaction and wide participation yields significant, tangible benefits. Glass stated, in a recent article in *Fortune*, that "99% of the best ideas we ever had came from our employees."[7]

Wal-Mart is a financial success. Although it is a discounter, and delivers the lowest cost to consumers, its profit margins are the highest in the industry. High technology, shrewed buying, and "staying glued to the customer" have helped it win not only the battle for market-share, but also the war for profitability. While retailers generally have maintained adversarial relationships with suppliers, Wal-Mart has worked to include them as partners. By opening its culture to suppliers, Wal-Mart has helped both companies realize cost improvements in distribution and warehousing, which has resulted in still lower costs for the consumer, and higher margins for both the retailer and the manufacturer.

The fostering of relevance by Wal-Mart goes beyond traditional customer, supplier and employee relations. The company commits itself to causes that it believes are important to its wider community. A *Buy USA* programme is credited with creating or retaining "over 100,000 jobs," in the beleaguered American economy.

For the 1990s, Wal-Mart is renewing its relevance by dedicating itself to the environment. CEO Glass believes that "environmental problems are ten times as bad as have been reported." *Fortune* reports that Wal-Mart "will communicate directly with consumers via store signs and advertisements, telling them which suppliers are making packaging and products friendly to the environment."

To study Wal-Mart is to appreciate the power of relevance. While many companies talk about being customer-driven, Wal-Mart is one of the few that engages its consumers on a human level. It provides value based not only on low price, but also on service. A Wal-Mart employee greets customers as they come in the door of the store, demonstrating up-front the company's commitment to serve, and its dedication to listening.

Wal-Mart's executives build and renew relevance by being in the selling environment with their employees and customers. They show service by example. And, while they have among the most sophisticated networks of computers and technology to ease the information flow of their immense operations, this gadgetry never displaces human contact. Communication is eye-to-eye, ear-to-ear, and not computer-to-computer.

Importantly, the great momentum of the company is not exclusively directed to its corporate interests. In a spirit of concern, responsibility and sharing, Wal-Mart is extending its considerable influence to positively affect causes that are non-commercial, but of growing importance to its customers. Its work in the area of the environment connects Wal-Mart to its customers on the the deep, visceral level that is attained when a connection is based on emotional, as well as intellectual, relevance.

Many companies in North America, including many clients of our agency, spent the last decade fighting competitive battles with parity products. Creating "added value" became a widespread objective, as competitors tried to break out of the price spiral that logically spins around products that are too similar. Building relevance into the products and services that we sell is, in fact, a means of developing competitive advantage. Relevance aligns the values of customers, as well as their usage needs, to the brands they are selecting. As common sense tells us, values cannot be added on. They must flow from within, and permeate all aspects of a company's operations.

Relevance, ultimately, comes from caring, from joining one's interest sincerely to another's. Despite our efforts during the last decade, it has become obvious that a marketing strategy alone cannot create values, nor express care. As companies such as Wal-Mart have shown, relevance is the consequence of a heartfelt attitude of caring. It emanates from deep within the corporate culture, and it affects the behaviour of the organization from the CEO on up to those employees serving clients.

It's as if we needed reminding that the Golden Rule works in business, as well as in life. Finally, we seem to be learning that making a profit and "doing unto others as you would have them do unto you" are really very compatible, very complementary, precepts for doing business.

THE DEHUMANIZING VOCABULARY OF BUSINESS

If business is to confer more meaning on the lives of the people it touches, then the language business uses to communicate must be modified to carry new messages, new priorities, new understanding. This is harder than it seems. More than simply adopting a new vocabulary, it requires reworking the beliefs structure upon which the language of business is built.

Language is easy to overlook. We use it every day. We use it on different levels, and in an endless variety of circumstances. Our facility with language makes it instinctive and spontaneous. But language is incredibly complicated. Its meaning is based on more than words. Language draws from an underlying system of thinking. This system contains the cultural beliefs and philosophy that are shared by the people who are sharing the language. The reason so many words don't readily translate into other languages is that the actual systems of thinking within different cultures vary.

In their book, *Einstein's Space & Van Gogh's Sky*, Lawrence Leshan and Henry Margenau explore perception, and our different ways of seeing and experiencing reality. They observe that, "We do not realize the extent to which we have been *taught* how to see the world. We have been taught how to *organize* our perceptions and relate them to each other. Even the see-touch realm, which is so "obvious" and "clear" to our perceptions that we are absolutely certain of the truth of what we see, is largely what we have been taught."[1]

Language is the conduit for creating understanding, and for establishing the context of what we perceive. Northrop Frye, our great Canadian literary scholar, said that we don't have an idea until we can express it. Language gives expression to ideas. Language allows information to be shared. That we live in an era called the Information Age suggests the indispensable role that language plays in the functioning of our society. In our modern world, information, and the knowledge it bestows, is power. Language, therefore, plays a very important role in how power is amassed and how it is extended.

Much of the power of business is derived from language. The incredible resources of information that are intrinsic to the modern corporation are but one example of the leverage that language provides to business. The expression of commercial ideas through the media, both in advertising and in public relations, are another.

During the takeover frenzy of the 1980s, companies were selling for amounts that greatly exceeded the physical value of the plants and assets that the corporate entity represented. The additional value was, in great part, assigned to the knowledge contained within the company. Wall Street views these information resources as equity, because of the difficulty in duplicating them, and because knowledge has become the true competitive differentiator in the marketplace. Such information is given its form and strategic substance through language.

While most of us don't stop to think about it, that we live in an information age at all is largely the result of the technological revolution brought about by business and the military. The microchips that power our computers and telecommunications were designed and developed in the R&D labs of North American corporations such as Texas Instruments, IBM and Northern Telecom. Many of these products, like the first functioning computer put in service by Univac, were subsidized by the military. Satellites, which make international communication instantaneous and commonplace, are the products of corporations such as Hughes Aerospace. And again, the original applications for this new, society-transforming technology were military.

The media that transmit information are, first and foremost, businesses. Media moguls, such as Rupert Murdoch and Canada's Lord Thomson of Fleet, control a wide pool of media properties, including newspaper, magazine and broadcasting interests. The dissemination of information is managed, for substantial profit, by an ever-shrinking group of internationally competing media conglomerates. These vast media machines have turned information into a consumer product, and the raw material for this product is language.

So, while we perceive ourselves as living in an information age, we are, more correctly, living in an age dominated by business. We are surrounded by the objectives of business. We are immersed in its messages. And, while we may be impervious to it, we are, in many ways, being shaped by the language of business.

How much this language, and the the concepts and ideas that it encodes, guides our behaviour is evident when we break down the activities that make up a "normal" day. When we use Crest toothpaste to clean our teeth during our morning ritual, we are responding to the concept of fluoride, and to the endorsement of the Canadian Dental Association, which P&G has communicated to us. The Special K cereal from Kellogg's satisfys our breakfast appetite, and carries with it the assurance that we are receiving nutrients without costly calories. The Ford Taurus we get into to drive to work has convinced us that it provides a unique combination of function and image, which matches comfortably with our own needs and self-perception. The Apple computer we use in the office, the Xerox copier we process our documents through, the Bell phones that carry our conversations, all satisfy a particular need, and connote a certain set of values.

Each of the hundreds of products and services that we encounter every day is infused with meaning by the language of business. The conveniences we expect in a modern lifestyle are expectations created by business. The standards for hygiene, transportation, and social acceptance are, for the most part, standards set by business. How we perceive the refreshment of beverages, how we savour the taste of hamburgers, how we evaluate the softness of tissue paper, are conditioned by the pervasive language of business.

Despite its considerable power, the language of business is largely overlooked. While there has been some debate about advertising, which is the most visible expression of its language, there is little public scrutiny of the overall vocabulary of business, and the values and beliefs that underpin its usage.

Self-Defeating Military Lingo

Having adopted the organizational structure of the military, it is not surprising that business has also borrowed many of the words and concepts of military language. The regimentation of business begins with a *plan*. This plan contains basic *objectives*, and a *strategy* for achieving that objective. Each strategic component will also include certain *tactics*, to facilitate the implementation of the strategy. The most important values for achieving the intended results of the plan are *focus* and *consistency*.

The military origins of this language were made obvious during the highly televised coverage of what the media called the War in the Gulf. The objective of removing Iraq from Kuwait was clearly established, and reinforced at every presidential press conference and military briefing. The strategy of imposing superior air power was applied consistently. Any attempts by Iraq to engage the coalition forces on alternative terms were avoided, since they represented a dilution of focus. The tactical activities of the military exercise were single-mindedly dedicated to fulfilling the strategy of pushing Saddam Hussein out of the emirate he had invaded.

This is language of great precision. It is also language that is devoid of emotion. Such clarity suits the military, for, although the process of war is chaotic, unpredictable, and quintessentially surprising, the language provides the false assurance that things are under control. Such illusion is necessary to retain authority. We forget that losing generals, even those whose tragic follies have been made into movies and poems, were all operating with a basic military plan, with specific objectives and a deliberate strategy.

The illusion of this language has had its affect on business, as well. The process of strategic planning, with its military precision, has given many in business a false sense of control over their own destinies. Well-constructed strategic documents are in the desk drawers of virtually every major company in North America, yet this has not mitigated the incredible impact of ever-more-able international competitors invading our market, to take business from us.

In many ways, the concepts of this language defeat the flexibility and innovation that the modern business environment demands. Plans impose an order, when the marketplace increasingly requires unorthodox responses to provide ever greater service and customization. Plans also set rational, manageable objectives, robbing companies of the inspiration of more ethereal goals, such as dreams.

The process of planning is one that objectifies, creating a distance between the planner and the doer, and between the planner and the final customer for a company's products. This distance denies business leaders the personal interaction, the subjective perspective, that companies need to anticipate the needs of their clients and provide the over-service demanded by global competition.

Dreamers Beat Generals

Kazuo Inamori, the founder and head of Kyocera, is an example of a successful leader of a multi-national corporation who runs his business, not from some abstract business plan, but from the shop floor. Kyocera is a ceramic company that has become the world leader in high-tech applications for its products.

In a recent poll in the *Nihin Keizai Shimbun*, the "*Wall Street Journal* of Japan," Kyocera emerged as the most-admired company among Japanese business executives. It is so respected, because it has managed to combine Japanese manufacturing skills and attention to quality with the entrepreneurship and innovation generally associated with North American companies.

Ceramics are integral ingredients in the construction of semiconductors. Kyocera has emerged as the highest-quality producer in this exploding field. David Halberstam, the author and Pulitzer-Prize-winning journalist, has written about this remarkable company in his 1991 book, *The Next Century*.

Halberstam writes, "The high quality and originality of Kyocera's techniques resulted, as Inamori likes to point out, because unlike the heads of competing American and West German companies, he himself was always on the floor, overseeing the kilns and varying the mixes."[2]

Inamori is a dreamer. He says of himself, "Most industrialists don't dream, and most dreamers don't manufacture things, so I am very lucky." In a business that requires both high-tech facility and the art and patience of craftsmanship, Kyocera has excelled because the people who direct the corporation are never removed from the doing. "I realized," says Inamori, "that if I was above mixing, I should not be in a ceramics company."

The passion Inamori demonstrates to his employees and customers goes beyond even that achieved by those who practice MBWA (Management By Walking Around), which was preached in Waterman and Peters' *In Search of Excellence*. Inamori accords greater respect and importance to craftsmanship than to management. The doing, the trying, the failing, the learning, are as important to Inamori as succeeding, and certainly, they are far more important to him than the planning. Working through a particularly difficult production process, which involved long-long hours, Inamori says, "I told those who stayed and worked with me that we were doing something creative and beautiful."

The zen-like dedication to the practitioner is also evident in how Inamori is handling his succession at Kyocera. The company is now run by what Inamori calls "the top technologist of the next generation." His conviction about having the company led by another person who would work to mix the materials and man the kiln was, in part, arrived at by watching his major American competitor deteriorate badly. After being bought and sold several times, the U.S. company simply slipped further and further behind, until it was no longer competitive.

The financiers and professional managers who acquired and divested themselves of the American ceramics company no doubt had strong enough business plans to win the support of bankers and investors. But they did not have the heart to get their hands dirty, and keep it viable, vibrant, and on the cutting edge of a major growth industry of the future.

This ability to lead by doing is also evident in North American companies, but usually, it is only associated with the particular zeal and drive of an entrepreneur. We tend to applaud these people for their innovation, and reward them for their gumption. But we also operate with the fairly ingrained bias that entrepreneurs eventually become risks to their own organizations. We look for professional managers, with their strong business disciplines and sound planning credentials, to impose their skills and bring order to entrepreneurial companies. While the discipline is often important, the process just as often squeezes the "heart" out of such companies. And, with that loss of heart, goes the innovation, inspiration, and competitive reason for being that motivated the enterprise in the first place.

Inamori, by contrast, does not see himself as an entrepreneur, nor as a manager, nor as a CEO. In his language, he is a dreamer who loves to do. In his language, business is a dynamic process, too fragile, too surprising, too unpredictable, to be regulated by intensive strategizing and planning.

It is telling to juxtapose Inamori's vocabulary for quality with that of most North American companies. In our modern corporate vernacular, the quality goal is often defined as *zero defects*. For Inamori, the challenge is *perfection*. He exhorts his people to strive in their mixing and baking, for "a perfect day," and from that "perfect day to a perfect week," and on again "to a perfect year."

While the North American wording sets the goal of minimizing the negative, Kyocera's sets out to optimize the positive. The first is anchored in avoiding defeat, the latter in ascending to an ideal level of achievement and accomplishment. The words *zero defects* are quantitative and rational. *Perfection*, on the other hand, is qualitative, emotional and essentially spiritual. Such are the nuances of language that an entire philosophy of business, employee relations, and commitment to quality can be compressed into one or two words.

Miscommunication and Misunderstanding

What Kyocera is to Japan, Apple Computers had the possibility of becoming for North America. Both are in very promising, high-tech, leading-edge industries. Both are also indelibly stamped by the vision and passion of the founding entrepreneurs. But, while Kyocera advanced with remarkable steadiness for over thirty years, Apple has gone from boom to bust in regular two-year cycles for most of its twelve-year history.

In part, the story of Apple is one of getting caught in a language warp. Steven Jobs, the co-founder and brilliant visionary who led Apple for most of its history, spoke in a New-Age California-Code, which was indecipherable to most business people. John Sculley, the master marketer Jobs hired from Pepsi, brought his own vocabulary of professional management to Apple. Sculley spoke primarily through strategic plans, organization charts and spread sheets, each of which was as alien to Apple as Jobs's Californiaspeak was to him.

Jobs's language inspired the techno-magicians at Apple to incredible feats of wizardry, but it also left the financial types from the investment community perplexed and unconvinced about Apple's management ability. Sculley's language had the opposite effect, inspiring confidence on Wall Street, while confusing and sometimes alienating the innovators who conceived and made Apple's products.

While they tried to work as a team, and initially succeeded in co-managing Apple, the conceptual views of business held by Jobs and Sculley were so different that they were finally irreconcilable. Jobs lost his company. And, with Jobs's departure, Apple lost its soul. Sculley has continued reorganizing, but his vaunted professional management techniques have not prevented Apple from going to the brink and back several times. Apple and Sculley came up short with the overweight and uninspired Macintosh portable. Then Apple and Sculley regained momentum with the recent introduction of a lower-priced computer, which has the soft-drink-sounding name, Mac Classic.

The language barrier between Jobs and Sculley is symptomatic of a larger meaning-conflict between *entrepreneur* and *manager*, which is endemic in North American business. These words have come to represent contrasting shortfalls.

The entrepreneur creates and starts a business, but lacks the wherewithal to sustain it. The manager maintains a business, but lacks the passion to innovate and, therefore, renew it.

As we come to the startling realization that North American business no longer sets the standards for innovation or management, it is obvious that we need new words and concepts to guide our commercial activities. We need a vocabulary that captures the spirit of corporate leaders who express their vision, not on static pieces of paper in static business plans, but rather, like Inamori, by "mixing and waiting at the kiln."

Many corporations have tried to recreate themselves to be more competitive, and many have adopted new language to express these changes. The mission statements that were the corporate vogue in the 1980s are filled with well-meaning words about commitment to people and customers but, too often, these statements were products of the existing management process, and they failed to actuate a change in values.

Canada Packers, one of our agency's original clients and one of Canada's largest food companies, underwent a process of strategic renewal several years before it was finally sold to Hillsdown Holdings, of the United Kingdom. The company had been slipping for many years, marketing outdated products, such as meat, lard and butter, which were out of step with the nutritional needs and health-consciousness of the general public. The vast size of Canada Packers hid, for many years, the deep problems within both the organization and its product mix. After a long period of poor profitability and failed investment in new ventures, a new management team was brought in to effect a turnaround.

The first step in the "turnaround" involved bringing in a team of consultants, to diagnose the problems and help formulate the strategy. After six months of study, the consultants helped management issue a new mission statement to guide the corporation. The mission dedicated CP to excellence in all its operations. It also committed the company to people—the shareholders, employees, customers and suppliers upon whom its excellence would depend.

Despite the lofty language, the intent of the mission was never achieved. Management persisted in viewing labour as "bastards," who needed to be brought into line. Deprived of heartfelt conviction, the turnaround failed, leading to the eventual sale of the company to Hillsdown.

The Canada Packers experience mirrors those of many other companies that have committed themselves to excellence, and borrowed concepts for achieving it. The words don't reach far enough into the psyche of the organization to effect a meaningful values-change. The process inevitably defeats itself, hampering further efforts at reform by adding the cynicism that results from actions having failed to live up to words.

The reliance on consultants for a diagnosis, and for an action plan that was fairly self-evident, reinforced the perception that the managers at CP were incapable of effecting the business renewal themselves. Confidence and conviction, two critical ingredients for renewal, evaporated. The mission and subsequent efforts at change were imposed top-down, with the same heavy-handedness that had been a part of the company's operating history as a meat packer.

Infusing Words With Meaning

The words of renewal, the words of mission, are very attractive to managers, because they are emotive and ennobling. Yet the process of management remains largely unchanged, so that the spirit of those noble words is often violated. The words do not become meaningless, but rather come to mean the opposite of what they intend. We forget, as managers, how attentive our employees are to our every word, and to the nuances of those words. We forget how fragile is our credibility with them. And we especially forget that action speaks louder than words.

In his much-heralded renewal of Scandinavian Airlines during the mid-1980s, CEO Jan Carlzon not only adopted a new language focused on delivering superior service to the business traveller, but he also implemented actions to give meaning to the new words. Business travellers want more schedule flexibility, which means more flights. So Carlzon cancelled orders for some wide-body planes, and bought and refurbished smaller planes. This action alone spoke volumes about his commitment to business travellers.

In the vocabulary of airline management, *wide-body* meant greater efficiency, higher payloads with fewer flights, fewer crews. Carlzon rejected concepts that were meaningful for the industry, to create a value that was more meaningful for his customers.

The power of actualized language is especially evident in the personal dimension of the service that SAS provides its customers. Carlzon coined the phrase "moments of truth," to define the points of actual contact between the airline and its customers. These were the moments during which SAS's promise of superior service to business travellers would be realized. The phone call for a reservation, the check-in, the proximity of gates, the intricacies of schedule interconnection, inflight reading materials, food, and the countless other operation details that demonstrated the SAS dedication to business travellers.

Delivery of the service promise during these "moments of truth" relied, not on Carlzon, but on the thousands of employees throughout the company. Carlzon not only adopted a new vocabulary for his company, he also reorganized its structure so that the people providing direct service to customers were accorded priority within the operational hierarchy. Carlzon intentionally "flattened the pyramid." He and his managers were, in a sense, at the bottom of the organization, providing support and ensuring that the tools were available, to help the people on the front lines deliver the promised service to the customer.

SAS won numerous awards throughout the late 1980s as the airline preferred by business people. And it has been at the cutting edge, forming international alliances with other airlines to ensure that it has the network in place to serve its business customers in the increasingly global business environment. Importantly, its people, everyone from unionized baggage-handlers to senior executives, understand the focus of the company. They share a language for communicating that focus, for settling the inevitable conflicts that emerge in any operation, and for measuring their effectiveness.[3]

New words have slipped in and out of the vocabularies of modern business managers. *Quality* has become the new obsession of North American business. What is ludicrous about this focus on quality is that it suggests that its absence is even an option. "Quality control programmes" and "quality circles" have, no doubt, helped many North American companies to improve their products, better satisfying customers and improving their overall competitiveness. But the more fundamental issue is whether we have exorcised the attitude that created the circumstances that required this renewed need for quality.

The managerial imperative in North America has historically been cost-control. The language of this discipline is necessarily quantitative. Managers are measured by their return on net assets deployed. Productivity is measured by cost-per-unit equations of varying complexity. The priority in selling a product is, most often, to deliver the lowest price. Quality is programmed into this process as another variable to be measured and controlled, and it is this very scientific imposition of control on quality that usually defeats its achievement.

Akio Morita, a co-founder of Sony, explained in a recent interview the difference in business attitude between North Americans and his company. "[North] Americans tend to think of competitiveness in terms of pricing—if something is a good bargain, it will sell. But I think this approach is not the complete picture. If you look at Sony products, they are loved all over the world, not only for their price, but for their quality and reliability as well."[4]

True quality elicits, in Morita's words, "love." Such emotional reactions from customers are possible only when similar emotional energy is dedicated to the design and manufacture of the products and services they are buying. This is where the pursuit of quality engages the spiritual potential of the humans involved in every step of the business process. Managers intrinsically concerned about quality must become the sources of love; love for customers, love for the product that serves those customers, and love for the employees who produce those products.

Love enriches life, providing satisfaction to both its source and its object. Love is often expressed by putting the interests of another before our own. Love requires nurturing and near-constant attention. Love involves sacrifice and a large degree of selflessness. Such language and spiritual context are, admittedly, uncomfortable for most business people, but they are essential to creating the pervasive attitude towards quality that North American business needs, to produce products and provide services to compete in ever-more-discriminating world markets.

Claude Levi-Strauss, a French anthropologist speaking at the 1983 International Symposium on Productivity in Japan, noted, "The concern of the symposium should be less improvement of the productivity of products than improvement of the productivity of systems...In order to produce better systems, a society should be less concerned with producing material goods in increasing quantities than with producing people of a better quality—in other words, beings capable of producing these systems."

To assign the priority for quality among people, rather than within products, is a spiritually fulfilling objective, which also leads to improvements that are genuine, lasting and effective competitively. The quantitative approach of our management must be renewed with the qualitative language of creativity, inspiration and love, if we are to make this transition in priorities.

Empowerment is to the 1990s what *quality* has been in the 1980s. Finally acknowledging that the archaic management structures of control are ill-suited to a marketplace that demands greater flexibility and heightened personal service, North American managers are "empowering" their employees. People on the front lines, making products, delivering the service, are now granted the power to make the decisions necessary to achieve quality. In car-assembly plants, workers can stop the whole line to address quality problems. At airports, service personnel can immediately upgrade passengers to address any dissatisfaction. While such empowerment has wrought positive changes in customer service, the word carries with it the seeds of its own undoing.

The concept of *empowerment* suggests that the power, and its control, are management's to give. This is flawed thinking. The only power that counts within a company is that of the customer. Power within a company should reside with those closest to the customer, those who most directly influence the satisfaction of that customer. The more removed a manager is from providing that customer satisfaction, the less power there is to be wielded, and the more that managerial role should be one of supporting the people who are closest to the client.

By *empowering*, business leaders are confirming themselves as the ultimate source of authority. They remain the bestowers of power, the governors of its application, the rulers who judge its results. So, the fallacy of this concept is that it perpetuates the traditional structure of power that it pretends to overcome. Empowerment without the spiritual renewal that acknowledges the true potency of the individual serves to actually *disempower*.

Procter & Gamble, one of the most sophisticated marketers in the world, has undergone a process of *empowerment*. Management layers have been "compressed," and decision-making has been "passed down," in order to make the company more "market-driven." This process has, over the last few years, helped P&G become more competitive and more responsive, but, in many ways, the company remains a captive of its own vocabulary.

"Compressing" management levels tries to conceal the bureaucracy that stultified the company, and the human dislocation that any elimination of levels brings with it. "Passing down" serves to reinforce the existing hierarchy, and implicitly denigrates those in the "down" ranks now making the decision. (Presumably this means that managers aspire to be promoted to non-decision-making roles.) "Market-driven" assumes a degree of control over the behaviour of the market, which can lead to an imperviousness to the human needs and competitive grit that make a market dynamic.

The spirit of *empowerment* has a hard time taking root in such an environment. P&G is not alone. In many other companies, the sense of accountability is muffled by the onerous checks and balances that are in place to minimize risk. And absent are the joy, the exhilaration, the personal expression, that typically characterize the exercise of power.

It is facile to assume that words like *empowerment* automatically overcome the rigidity, the orientation to control, the bias towards the quantitative, that are so deeply embedded in the philosophy of North American business. True empowerment is only possible (and, therefore, redundant) when it embraces the full human reality, when it respects the power and motivation that reside within each person, and when it accepts that it cannot be bestowed, but only nurtured and inspired.

Too Much Advertising With Too Little Meaning

Perhaps the most damaging aspect of the language used by business is that it distances the leaders and managers of a company from the very constituents they must serve to be successful. Nowhere is this distancing more apparent than in the language and devices of marketing and advertising.

This is ironic, because these are the very disciplines that companies rely on to translate understanding of the customer into more effective selling of a company's products or services. Marketing and advertising are intended to build a bridge between the self-interest of the customer and that of the company. Yet the language and devices of these disciplines often undermine these very goals.

Marketers often refer to the purchaser or user of a product as a *consumer*. This word, although seemingly innocuous, demeans the very person whose custom the company is trying to win. It implies that the sole value of this human being is his or her capacity to use up the products manufactured by a company. Such simplistic categorization removes the human being from the selling equation. It depersonalizes the relationship between a company and the people who buy its products, creating the often-repeated situation where the convenience of the manufacturer takes precedence over the benefit to the customer.

To attract loyal purchasers for their products, businesses are finally learning to approach their prospects with deep respect. This respect is based on a broad understanding of the pressures, needs, attitudes, and beliefs of the people companies are striving to engage. Consumption is but one dimension of the prospects, and, with the growing environmental concern, it is one that has less validity in defining them. The concept of the consumer was first developed as mass markets were developed, to use up the goods of mass production. Manufacturing and its marketing focused on quantity. With the intensification of competition, the mass market has been fragmented and segmented. Business success now relies on customization. What is important about the prospects today is not that they *consume* products, but how they differentiate between one product and another, how they assign value and accord loyalty.

Relating to prospects only as *consumers* renders them abstract, and assumes them to be far more malleable than they really are. By implication, *consumers* are passive users. In reality, they are active discriminators, whose savvy and sophistication are often underappreciated by marketers. The diversity of humans, the complexity of their needs, the unpredictability of their motives, are denied when the sights of marketing are set simply on consumption.

The vocabulary of marketing contains other self-defeating jargon, which demeans customers and distances the practitioners of marketing from the intimate understanding of the people they are spending so much time, effort and money trying to reach. By defining prospects as a *target group,* marketers are implicitly accepting an adversarial relationship with their potential customers. They wage a one-sided war, scheming and strategizing to win dollars from the pockets of the prospect. This "targeting" abstracts the customer. Just as flying from a great height serves to desensitize pilots about the targets they bomb, so, too, does viewing prospects from such a great distance that a connection of relevance becomes almost impossible.

In his essay, "Management as a Liberal Art," Peter Drucker challenges the conventional view of business. He posits that "the end of business is not to make money. Money is a necessity of survival...but the purpose of business is to create and satisfy a customer."[5] To see a prospect through the viewfinder of target marketing is to fail to see the full humanity and the full potential of that customer.

The research and technology that make "targeting" an ever more precise science have also given marketers a false sense of effectiveness and control. Despite our effectiveness in reaching our "targets," most potential customers remain perplexingly unaffected. Some are bored, having weathered the many false promises and facile advertisements that are addressed to them. Many others are cynical, having mastered the devices and tactics of marketing, to the point of building up a subconscious immunity to them. So, while marketers have worked hard during the last decade to draw "closer to customers," the very concept of "targeting" results in a distancing that makes it impossible to achieve any intimacy, or insight based on real human discovery.

The dehumanization inherent in the language of marketing is largely responsible for the mediocre state of North American advertising. Commercials are generally regarded as nuisances and intrusions. Armed with new technology, viewers are fast becoming their own programmers. They use remote controls to zap from one station to another. Or they use the fast-forward feature on their VCRs to accelerate past uninvolving commercials and uninspired programming, to select only those segments that interest them. Hitachi has, alarmingly for advertisers, announced a new VCR with fuzzy logic, which is actually programmed to automatically edit out commercials.

These technological reasons for declining commercial viewership conceal the more serious issue—people are frustrated with most advertising, and they react with, at best insouciance, and often with contempt towards the quality of advertising messages that are, in the marketers' own words, "targeted to them."

A viewing of the average evening of commercials explains why so many people react negatively to messages that are, by strategy, intended to engage them. Too many advertisements talk down to the people they are trying to convince. Too many also speak in a monologue, representing the interest of the company so exclusively that they fail to connect with any of the deeper interests of the people exposed to the advertising.

Marketers and advertisers spend considerable funds to prepare ads, and to ensure that they are seen with sufficient frequency to make the intended impression on the "target audience." While, in theory, the people who control these expenditures, as the initiators, are in control of the communications process, the reality is that the audience, with its growing selectivity, really has the power in the communications equation. They, and not the transmitters of the message, regulate what is let in, what is absorbed, and what is responded to.

Words Grow Their Meaning From Action

Defying many of the conclusions deduced by market research, people remain unpredictable. The rational inducements provided by most marketers often fail to connect with the largely emotional motivations that underpin most purchases of products and services. With their scientific calipers, North American marketers have sought to demystify the workings of the market, to predict its behaviour and to forecast the outcome of their initiatives. Such deliberate attempts to eliminate the risk of the market have led to the still riskier situation of being irrelevant, slow to innovate, and slow to respond to customer needs and competitive activities.

A recent article in *The Economist* contrasted the North American approach to new-product development to that of the Japanese. While we tend to "test-market" new products to determine their potential, Japanese companies go straight to production, and use the flexibility of the manufacturing and engineering disciplines to adjust the product in countless ways, as it goes through the acid test of real market acceptance. The North American approach is compared to a "rifle shot," one product against one target. The Japanese use a broader "shotgun," introducing an array of new products to let the market itself decide which should survive and be further developed.

The Japanese market by doing, rather than by the exhaustive analysis characteristic of North Americans. According to a study by McKinsey, "Japanese companies develop new products in a third to half the time spent by their Western counterparts, at a quarter to a tenth of the cost." This bias towards action has achieved a remarkable competitive advantage.

The language of marketing, and that of business in general, assumes too much control and precision within the interchange between company and customer. It's important to understand the meaning of our words, for as long as the language of business abstracts the customer, North American business will continue to lose share in the global marketplace. As long as the language of business confers a false sense of power and control to its practitioners, North American business will continue to lose currency with the people who are its customers.

The companies that are building dynamic business franchises often lead by creating a new vocabulary. Their words are usually simpler, more humanistic, expressing values that are genuinely part of the overall corporate culture. Business-babble and its novelty-concepts are avoided, as these companies strive for clarity of communication and dignity in all aspects of their organization.

Pepsico, for example, is among the most-admired companies in America, winning the accolades of business executives, as well as its battle for market-share against giants like Coke in beverages, and McDonald's in food service. Pepsico has a reputation for being tough on its people and expecting a lot from them. It also balances these high expectations with above-average financial compensation.

Pepsico's people are regarded as more than employees. Wayne Galloway, the company's CEO, calls his people "the stewards of Pepsico's assets." To prove his conviction about the importance of his people, and to show his commitment to rewarding them for their efforts, Pepsico, since 1989, has been offering stock options to every one of its over 100,000 employees, worth ten percent of their salaries.[6]

The concept of stewardship, while seemingly unruly, elevates all the people within the company to positions of shared ownership. Even though the corporation is huge, management is using language and concepts that underscore the importance of individual contributions. The greater dignity the company invests in these people is returned in the form of greater commitment, heightened performance, and stronger loyalty.

Disney is another company that has won the hearts of customers, as well as the respect of Wall Street. As you would expect of a company that calls itself "the Magic Kingdom," Disney has its own distinctive corporate style. And much of that style is expressed in a distinct, not very business-like, vocabulary.

At Disney, there are no customers, only *guests*. And there are no employees, only *cast members*. The intent of these words is to convey to the people visiting Disney, and the people serving those visitors, that the relationship, the entertainment, and not only the custom, matter a lot. The psychology of a guest is to feel special, to expect to be accorded special privileges and treatment. And the psychology of a cast member is to feel a participation, and the exhilarating duty to always be on, providing treatment to guests that supports the theatrical illusion of the Disney experience.

Disney's work-force is largely teenagers. By training and by example, the company develops in its people the instincts and sensitivities to make it one of the best service companies in America. It accommodates millions of guests a year, yet manages to make virtually everyone feel special, one at a time. It works every day to fulfil its corporate maxim "to promise high, and then over-deliver." All of this attention to the human needs of its guests, and to the skills and motivation of its people, has helped Disney achieve staggering dollar and profitability growth, throughout the last decade.

The enviable business success, and the joyful quality of the Disney experience, are the results of a unique collaboration between its two most senior executives, Michael Eisner and Frank Wells. The two represent very different business skills: Eisner is the creative spark-plug of the company, who oversees the product, and Wells is the lawyer-by-training, who manages the complex details of execution for a company that includes movie studios, the Disney Channel, theme parks in the U.S., Japan, and a new one being built in France, real estate, construction, hotels, restaurants, corporate sponsorships, consumer products—including mail-order and retailing, publishing and a new record company.

Many companies are in businesses that involve balancing the often-disparate demands of creativity and management, yet very few seem to nurture a culture that accommodates and values both. The genuine partnership between Disney's senior managers signals the indispensability and equality of both of these values. Their respect for each other sets the tone for collaboration, teamwork and results throughout the organization.[7]

Obviously, improving service or employee morale requires more than a vocabulary change—the heart of the company must be totally behind the concepts upon which it bases its business, and the values it preaches. More companies are adopting new terminology for their employees, calling them associates, or stakeholders. Yet few go the distance to invest the full power in those associates that their titles deserve. More companies are setting their sights on better serving their customers. Yet few genuinely have the courage to put the interests of those customers ahead of their own.

The words and concepts that are renewing companies throughout North America are warmer, more emotive, less quantifiable than those they are replacing. *Research* is giving way to *listening*. *Department* is giving way to *teamwork*. *Training* is giving way to *learning*. Companies are stressing *dialogue* between management and employees, and between company and customers. The issues of the heart are finally as preoccupying to senior management as those of the head.

As we re-humanize the language of business, infuse it with the respect and dignity that human beings deserve in their endeavours, we will find that companies will grow in their capacity to provide value and meaning to their customers and employees. Being human-centred, rather than production-centred or profit-centred, does not mean lower productivity or profits. It means that the spiritual aspects of people—their capacity for joy, commitment, surprise, and duty, their expectations for involvement, reward, and inspiration—are accessible as resources, for the companies that nurture and respect them.

Customers, too, are people first. That they purchase a product is but one, usually very small, dimension of their lives. Respecting that sense of proportion, and relating to people in their totality, requires a new, more subtle, more sensitive vocabulary for both defining and addressing them. Clearly, the balance of power in the business equation has shifted from the company doing the marketing to the customer making the final purchase decision. For most companies, a new philosophy of doing business must be evolved, one that respects the primacy and full humanity of the customer, one that engages people across the full spectrum of their needs, desires, dreams, weaknesses and loves.

As Drucker points out, marketing, as a technique, must be embedded in "the ethics of mutual relationships. A sale to a customer thus creates a 'relationship,' and with it a permanent commitment."[8] As managers, we must find the words to give expression to this relationship with customers, to evoke the commitment of the people who work with us, and to encode the reciprocity that is the basis of this new business ethic.

THE CRUMBLING MYTHOLOGY OF BUSINESS

Business, like every other human institution, has its own mythology, its own icons and superstructures, which provide a context for the people who interact with it. This mythology encodes the beliefs that guide our thinking about business, and our behaviour as business people. To renew business for its contemporary challenges, to find a paradigm for business that again makes it relevant, the mythology must be understood and reconstructed.

Mythology is important. With our notions of modern progress, we tend to dismiss mythology as old stories, fantastic tales, which may have had some spiritual significance for ancient cultures, but are largely meaningless in today's more sophisticated society. The attitude that dismisses the importance of myth is the rational one, the *prove-it* mentality that Professor Mintzberg sees as one of the flaws of current MBA training. The intuitive aspects of human judgement are denigrated by the rational mind. And it is our intuition that most responds to the influences of mythology. It is our intuition that draws wisdom and nourishment from the archetypal lessons that mythology provides.

The breakdown in our society's mythological connections is the stuff of psychologists and poets. Psychologist Carl Jung was among those who explored the need and capacity of the human psyche to connect to the broad communal web of mythological imagery. In his book, *Man And His Symbols*, Jung wrote, "Modern man does not understand how much his 'rationalism' [that has destroyed his capacity to numinous symbols and ideas] has put him at the mercy of the psychic 'underworld.' He has freed himself from 'superstition' [or so he believes], but in the process he has lost his spiritual values to a positively dangerous degree. His moral and spiritual tradition has disintegrated, and he is now paying the price for this break-up in world-wide disorientation and dissociation."[1]

Jung believed that the dislocation so many people experience in their lives, a dislocation that has affected the whole of society, was the result of our losing intimate contact with nature. Urban, technological humans have lost their personal unity with nature, and in that loss, we've also surrendered the sense of meaning and continuity that that intimacy provided.

Business is superficially rational. Its practices and activities have contributed greatly to our society's divorce from nature. And it has imposed a new, less-fulfilling construct of meaning on our materialistically rich, spiritually impoverished society. The relationship between business and mythology is, therefore, not incidental, but critically important if we are to renew business, if we are to channel it to serve the aspirations of a human race that is integrated with its planet.

The mythology of business, like any other mythology, has been used to unify people to a cause, creating common understanding and common values to make interchange possible. Myths are like telegrams, providing a shorthand for issuing instructions or directions, for setting aspirations, for regulating behaviour. Business has used the power of myth to extend its control, influencing employees, customers and politicians with it's view of the universe.

The Growth Myth

One of the basic principles of the mythology of business is that growth is good. More than that, growth is imperative. Without growth, business is seen to fail, to cease being vital.

CEOs are evaluated by the growth they achieve for their companies. The valuation criteria of stock analysts include factors that measure growth. Growth versus previous years. Growth versus assets deployed. Growth versus capital expended. The folklore of business includes the injunction to "grow or die." For employees, growth means that the expanding company will provide greater opportunity for advancement. For managers, growth means more power and control over their own destinies.

The concept of growth inevitably clashes with the now-dawning, inescapable realization that our businesses must operate within a finite world. Since 1950, the world's "gross national product" has increased fourfold. Electricity consumption has also quadrupled. The number of cars and trucks on the road has increased by double that level, with over eight times the number of combustion-powered vehicles burning precious fuel and adding their exhaust to our already-sick environment. Only one-fourth of the world's population can be described as developed. For the remainder, quality-of-life improvement only seems possible through their own industrial development. It doesn't take very sophisticated analysis to pro-rate the possible impact of more and accelerating industrialization. Our planet can neither afford nor sustain it. We and other species simply can't survive it.

So strong is the mythic pull of this concept that an alternative to growth, for most business people, is unimaginable. Professor Mintzberg writes, "What operational goals enable an organization to serve itself...? The most obvious answer is growth. Survival may be an indispensable goal and efficiency a necessary one, but what really matters here is making the system larger. Growth serves the system by providing greater rewards for its insiders—bigger empires for managers to run or fancier private jets to fly, greater programmes for analysts to design, even more power for unions to wield by virtue of having more members."[2]

Growth is addictive. Its achievement provides a jolt of satisfaction and the reinforcement of reward, but basically, growth stimulates the need for still more growth. While a degree of growth is both vital and healthy, it is the compulsion to grow that causes much of the environmental and social damage attributed to business.

Activist and eco-economist Hazel Henderson explains that, "in a finite environment, there has to be a dynamic balance between growth and decline."[3] Henderson uses the analogy of nature, which needs the decay of one year's growth to provide the humus for new growth. Compulsive, incessant growth is unbalanced, leading to the trauma and displacement that accompanies any other addictive human behaviour.

The Big Myth

With growth as a major pillar in the mythology of business, it is only logical that another imposing pillar be based on the principle that "bigger is better." The size of corporations, and the concentration of power that they represent, have been disconcerting to our North American society. Anti-trust laws were put in place in the U.S. during the Robber Baron era, to protect society from the abuses of the railroad czars, and later, the oil kings, who had such a dominant influence on the commercial transactions of their time. Suspicion of the "big" has worked to counter-balance the predilection of business to grow and control its markets. Yet there remains an uneasy truce between the huge corporate organizations that cast such a long shadow across the landscape of the global economy, and the human beings who make up the corporate work-force and marketplace.

The justification for size within the mythological framework of modern business is self-evident. Size provides leverage, the ability to expend considerable resources and exert significant pressure to exploit opportunities in the marketplace. Size also provides protection from competitors, enabling companies to withstand the ebb and flow of innovation, and the up-and-down cycles of economic activity. This gospel of size is based on faith in the notion of "economies of scale." The more quantities a company produces, the more discounts it can earn in purchasing raw materials, the more utilization it can achieve out of capital investments in plant, the more efficiency it can realize out of manufacturing and distribution. All the incremental benefits achieved yield better profit, which, in turn, can be reinvested to push the advantages of "more" even further.

Jack Welch, the much-admired CEO of General Electric, added another dimension to the mythology of size, when he adopted the strategy that his multi-divisional company must be Number One or Two in each of the industries it operates within. His premise that profitability is highest among market-leaders, a concept supported by lots of economic data, led Welch to drastically reorganize GE, shedding divisions and companies that did not meet the "One or Two" criterion. GE sold its small-appliances division to Black & Decker, and expanded its investment in jet-engine development. It also swapped businesses with the French electronics group, Thompson, giving up its TV business to take over Thompson's medical-imaging technology. The new GE is a more formidable competitor.

The concentration of being "One or Two" provides GE with the resources to take on the huge multinationals that it faces in each of its market segments. Many other corporations followed Welch's formula, and the strategic reorganization, to concentrate resources and achieve critical mass, was one of the reasons for the merger-and-acquisition frenzy of the 1980s.

The mythology of "bigger is better" has taken on new currency, as North Americans look to Japan for new management lessons and models. The business press, which spent the last decade dissecting the manufacturing and quality tactics of Japanese companies, is now turning its attention to the overall management structure and philosophy that powers their economic machine. An important feature of Japan's success, particularly its export prowess, is the much-written-about formation of *keiretsus*.

These industrial groups knit together a web of companies through cross-ownership, interlocking directorships, and long-term business relationships. Each company is autonomous, and often competes with other members of the *keiretsu*, but they are made stronger by their "insider" status, and by the heft and scale of the whole group they are partnered with. Chalmers Johnson, a professor at the University of California, and an expert on Japan who has written numerous books on its economy and corporations, calls the *keiretsu* Japan's "most important contribution to modern capitalism."

Mitsubishi, the largest industrial group in Japan, with total yearly sales of $175 billion (U.S.), was the recent subject of a cover story in *BusinessWeek*. The Mitsubishi *keiretsu* includes twenty-eight "core members," companies that compete in a wide array of distinct markets. The family includes paper-mills, petrochemical, steel, oil, car manufacturing, construction and other companies under the Mitsubishi moniker. Through a maze of cross-ownership, the *keiretsu* also includes companies such as Nikon Corporation and Kirin Brewery.[4]

The *keiretsu* does not necessarily operate with a cohesive central strategy, but it does afford its members many advantages and benefits. Working with a family bank provides more flexibility and a more ready access to capital, which can help accelerate investment in new plant. Buying supplies from family members provides subtle but significant efficiency. "Mitsubishi executives argue that being able to equip a factory with mostly Mitsubishi equipment makes it more efficient than using one set of machines from manufacturer X and another from manufacturer Y. Because Mitsubishi's machines are made to function smoothly together, fewer operators are needed, and the company gains a cost advantage."

The glue that holds the *keiretsu* together is not simply inter-company business, which is usually no more than fifteen to twenty percent of any given company's sales. Rather, it is the personal relationships, the familiarity and friendships that develop within the confines of the larger corporation. Minouro Makihara, president of Mitsubishi International Corporation in New York, said in the *BusinessWeek* interview, "If a deal comes up, and you can do business with two people, you tend to pick the person you know better." A colleague from Mitsubishi Heavy Industries America Inc. adds, "We don't have to exchange business cards."

North Americans are only superficially aware of the true power agglomerated in such industrial families. Mitsubishi spent almost a billion dollars to buy that landmark of American capitalism, the Rockefeller Center. While politicians, the press, and the general public have been preoccupied by the symbolism of the real-estate purchase, very little debate has been applied to understanding the real economic implications of the *keiretsu*. A new microchip factory costs hundreds of millions of dollars to construct. The technology to make such products, and the materials that go into microchip manufacturing, require many more millions of dollars investment, on the part of supplier companies.

Through family cooperation, such investments can be mutually supported, and can be made to pay back through long-term business contracts. The *keiretsu* allows Mitsubishi to make its own chips for its own computers. This means that it can be the first to apply advances in its microchips to its own computer technology. This integration, with its obvious competitive benefits, is beyond even giant IBM's ability.

The obvious success of the *keiretsu* is pressuring North Americans to consider still-larger concentrations of corporate power within our own society. Some of the cynicism and suspicion that held large companies in check, leading to the break-up of AT&T, and the long anti-trust suit against IBM, are now abating. Previously unthinkable linkages between industry and banks are now being considered, in order to offset the emerging advantages of similar cross-ownerships in Japan and Germany. Even co-operation among competitors, which has been anathema to North Americans, has been accepted, to try and mount an effective response to the growing lead in electronics achieved by Japan. In both microchips and high-definition television, American companies have pooled resources and R&D, to try and win slices of these incredibly lucrative markets, which, alone and individually, they would not have the wherewithal to compete in.

With the momentum of increasing globalization, the myth of "bigger is better" continues to get bigger. But there is a considerable price to be paid for size. As a society, we've not yet fully measured that price. Nor have we determined, within the broader accounting of human fulfilment, whether that price is worth paying. As business people, we remain mesmerized by the power that accompanies size, without tallying up the true costs to the creativity, effectiveness, and renewability of our enterprises.

In their study of large corporations, entitled *Beyond Human Scale*, Eli Ginzberg and George Vojta reveal some of the flaws and built-in impediments to success that hamper big companies. The significant financial resources of large corporations are as often a liability as they are an asset, because they can actually cushion senior management from the harsh reality of the marketplace.

RCA spent hundreds of millions of dollars in the 1970s, in a failed attempt to compete with IBM in computers. It spent millions more to develop laser-disc technology in the 1980s, only to be overwhelmed in the home-entertainment market by videotape technology. RCA was one of the premier electronics companies of the early and mid-twentieth century. Even with all its research and capital resources, it was unable to move quickly and with precision. Start-ups, such as Digital in computers and Sony in electronics, have won the markets that RCA believed were its legacy.[5]

The very financial base that is their strength can also blind and bind management. Not only are investment decisions made at a numbing distance from the actual marketplace, but such investments often go to protect the assets that the company already has in place. The daily business press is filled with references to companies writing off millions for bad acquisitions, or taking quarterly losses of still more millions for products that didn't sell, factories that didn't work, and partnerships that didn't gel. Some of these losses are the results of inevitable and healthy risk-taking, upon which all commerce is based. The point is that the scale of companies works to conceal the overall effectiveness of these investments. The size of companies hides whether their leaders made smart or stupid decisions.

No one knows the cumulative price we've paid for the imprudent risks that only large companies can afford to take, and that only large corporations can camouflage within broader financial statements. Presumably, with examples like RCA, billions and billions of dollars have been squandered. The price to those companies has been lost competitiveness. The price to society has been lost jobs, lost opportunities, and lost taxation revenues to apply back to improve infrastructure and education.

Size not only numbs companies to the investment risks they face, it also often numbs them to the needs of the customers they are serving. The examples of large companies that have lost touch with the customers who made them large in the first place are legion. What is particularly humbling is how many of our best-managed companies have fallen into this trap.

McDonald's, which built the company by "doing it all for you," missed the seriousness of the environmental concern felt by its customers, and was slow in adopting more recyclable packaging. With its predominantly fried menu,

McDonald's is in the uncomfortable position of having a product mix out of step with an aging, more health-conscious customer group. Even value, which was a founding principle of McDonald's, has been surrendered to fast-growing competitors such as Taco Bell.[6]

McDonald's remains a formidable competitor and a successful company, but these disconnections with its customers point to the difficulties that even the savviest of our large corporations have in remaining vital within their marketplaces.

Large corporations generally fail to actualize the true and full potential of the human beings who work within them. In their study, Ginzberg and Vojta note that, "the modern corporation has evolved structures that are dysfunctional for utilizing the abilities of its managerial personnel. [As well] these structures impede the CEO from effectively discharging his multiple duties, which include oversight of the corporation's human resources."[7]

The tendency of bureaucracy to stifle innovation is a conundrum that many managers have struggled with. Despite the many prescriptions that are flogged in the business press, North American corporations continue to be slow to respond to either competition or the customer. Xerox and IBM have both tried to break away chunks of their respective companies, both to facilitate innovation, and to foster entrepreneurial action among their managers. This is one of those ironic expenditures of great amounts of energy that E.F. Schumacher noted when he wrote that, "as soon as great size has been created there is often a strenuous attempt to attain smallness within bigness."

Some of these efforts have succeeded but, by and large, as happened with both Xerox and IBM, the dominant corporate culture of the large organization brings these breakaways back into the orbit of the parent company. IBM can't be Apple, even though it tried, and spent countless millions trying, to make its PC as "friendly" as the Mac. It finally took another entrepreneur, Bill Gates of Microsoft, to create the *Windows* software that made the IBM machine look and work more like Apple's.

In a time when it is crucial for management to have the passionate commitment of its employees, large companies, with their shrinking management levels and profitability, are finding it difficult to provide the motivation to elicit the needed dedication. At a point where the marketplace is demanding innovation, large organizations are struggling to unleash the creativity and ingenuity of their people. McGill's Henry Mintzberg warns that, "every form of organization sows the seeds of its own destruction in machine bureaucracy devoid of human commitment, which manifests itself as politicization."[8] Politics preoccupies people, consuming precious time that should be spent addressing the needs of customers. Politics also demotivates, because the self-interest of individuals overtakes the genuine priorities of the business. Politics, most damningly, squashes creativity.

The myth of "bigger is better" is part of the illusion of permanence that large companies strive so hard to project. This illusion is comforting to bankers and reassuring to investors. The illusion also helps reinforce management's authority, providing them with the justification for taking steps that may hurt an individual, or a community, but assure the permanence of the organization.

Ultimately, this is only an illusion. Ginzberg and Vojta studied the rankings of corporations, made by both *Forbes* and *Fortune* magazines. There has been considerable turnover in those rankings: only one company that was on the *Forbes* top-ten list in 1917 remains there today (Exxon, the descendant of Standard Oil). Only half of the companies on *Fortune's* 500 ranking from 1955 were still on the list in 1980. The merger-and-acquisition activity of the 1980s saw the purchase and dismemberment of many seemingly immortal companies. When RJR Nabisco was bought by KKR for $24 billion in 1989, the chilling message to every CEO in North America was that no company was too big to be a takeover candidate.

Part of the value of big companies to society is the number of jobs they create, but the complexion of this benefit is changing. Countries, provinces and states, even municipalities, are now competing to attract the companies that provide the jobs. This intense competition can involve providing many millions of dollars in tax benefits and in improvements in infrastructure. While the community sometimes benefits, there is evidence that the balance of advantages may have swung too far in favour of the employing corporation. Mel Hurtig, a publisher, has tabulated corporate contributions to overall tax revenue in Canada. While companies paid 46.4% of all taxes collected in 1950, that number today stands at 13.1%.

The concentration of power in the hands of a very few companies is even more pronounced in Canada than in the United States. One one-hundredth of the companies in Canada control fifty percent of our nation's economic assets. One percent of all the companies control a staggering eighty-six percent of Canadian corporate assets. The fundamental issue is whether this incredible concentration of corporate power provides reciprocal benefits to society. We must ask ourselves, has our competitiveness in the global marketplace improved as a result of the corporate giants we nurture? Has our work-force benefited with more of the added-value and knowledge jobs that the global economy rewards most highly? Has taxation been sufficient to renew our education systems and infrastructure, securing a competitive advantage for our society in the future?

The evidence is not very encouraging, particularly as we measure the losses resulting from free trade, and as Canada falls further behind in R&D expenditures and patent submissions, relative to other industrialized countries.

The Entrepreneur Myth

Our collective intuition worries about the possibility of abuse and corruption, which, historically, have accompanied such accumulations of power. Much like classic mythology, which contains counter-balancing figures and forces, the mythology of business includes the inspirational notion of *entrepreneur*, to offset these darker associations of big business.

The entrepreneur is the spark-plug for business, the individual innovator who uses brainpower and quickness to out-manoeuvre bigger companies. The entrepreneur embodies all the positive elements that we normally believe big corporations lack; a closeness to customers, passion for service, an aptitude for risk-taking, creativity, and closer realization of reward, commensurate to contribution. Entrepreneurs like Stephen Jobs and Ken Olsen in computers, Bill Gates in software, Fred Smith in delivery service, have won the accolades of society for their daring. They are the dreamers who became fabulously wealthy by beating the big guys, with guts, innovation and speed. They are the Davids who beat the corporate Goliaths.

Entrepreneurs have also come to represent the great hope of North American business, the secret weapon for winning the competitive battles in the global marketplace. Europeans seem too staid, lacking the frontier culture and Wild-West mentality that stimulates entrepreneurs and tolerates their idiosyncrasies. Asians seem too bound by consensus to foster the sense of independence and drive that fuels entrepreneurs. So, while big North American corporations may be losing ground, we, as a society, are sustained by our belief in the entrepreneur. These are the business leaders who will help keep us one step ahead, or at least even, in the race for global markets.

As with the other basic beliefs of growth and bigness, the myth of the entrepreneur is crumbling. Throughout the last decade, Europeans and Asians have shown themselves to be as clever and as quick, in bringing innovation to the marketplace, as North Americans. The miraculous miniaturization of laptop computers came from Japan's Toshiba. The sensible and inspiring green practices of The Body Shop toiletries chain came from Britain. Just like our larger commercial institutions, our entrepreneurs suddenly seem flat-footed, less cocky, less capable of conquering the world than they were a decade ago. Even Silicon Valley, the hotbed of entrepreneurial achievement, the centre of North American high-tech innovation, has cooled as the symbolic centre of North America's business creativity, and remains in a prolonged slump.

In part. the decline of the entrepreneur is attributable to the growing business savvy of other cultures. In part, it also reflects a major shift in the business skills and resources that are needed to bring innovation to the marketplace. In his book about Apple Computers, *West of Eden*, journalist Frank Rose describes the "crash-and-burn" syndrome that has affected Silicon Valley. A decade ago, microchip innovations required extensive brainpower to design, but relatively modest investment to produce.

Venture capitalists, sometimes called vulture capitalists, provided seed money for the scientists and engineers who concocted the technological improvements in microchips. Many of these investment backers, and the entrepreneurs, won huge fortunes very quickly, as their technology broke new boundaries. Many more "crashed and burned," as their original invention was leapfrogged by yet another entrepreneurial start-up.

In the frenzied euphoria of entrepreneurial competition, the whole North American microchip industry missed a fundamental shift in the development cycle. Each generation of microchip required exponentially greater investment in plant and equipment. So much greater is the manufacturing and technological complexity of new chips that current production facilities cost several hundreds of millions of dollars to build—far beyond the reach of any entrepreneur, a severe financing challenge for even the largest U.S. computer companies.

After dominating chip production, accounting for almost sixty percent of the world market in the early 1980s, North Americans watched as their leadership of this cutting-edge technology declined to the point where we now produce less than thirty-five percent of the world's microchips. The "crash-and-burn" of Silicon Valley, as a symbol of North American entrepreneurial ingenuity, was underscored in a recent article in the business section of *The New York Times*, which described the migration of American research labs to Japan. Kodak, IBM, Dow Corning, Texas Instruments and Hewlett-Packard are among the companies that have set up serious R&D operations in Japan. High-tech companies without a research base in Japan are at risk because, as Nobuo Mii of IBM Japan explains, with understatement, "It presumes that the best technology is in the United States. Oftentimes, that is not the case."[9]

Entrepreneurs remain vital elements within our business culture, and their achievements provide critically important regeneration to our economy. But, increasingly, global competition is showing up cracks in the entrepreneurial myth, and what we believed to be a North American strength. The broader management skills to lead a company beyond its start-up seem to be missing in the genetic code of the entrepreneur. The capitalization to tackle international markets is also beyond the reach of entrepreneurs. Consequently, the risk-taking and the achievement of the entrepreneur seem to be on a diminished scale. Our "Davids" seem suddenly very small, very vulnerable.

The crumbling of so many of the important pillars of our business mythology is unsettling. As Joseph Campbell has said, "myths offer life models." They encode a collective wisdom that provides meaning, sense of purpose, and sense of commitment to individuals. When a society ceases to believe in its mythology, when it no longer relates to the wisdom that the myths contain, there is an inevitable loss of ethos. Without a mythology to unify them, people operate in an emotional vacuum. Without a mythology that they can relate to, people put their self-interest first. Without a mythology to inspire them, people have no reason to accept sacrifice or make commitments. These are the very dislocations and disconnections that are hampering the effectiveness and competitiveness of North American companies.

Constructing a new mythology is not a process that is easily understood, nor is it one that rates a very high priority with business leaders. The more concrete pressures of day-to-day management are challenging enough. To look beyond the scope of an individual business, or the industry in which the company competes, is a distraction for most of us who lead companies. But, unless we address the broader framework of beliefs about business, we may find ourselves increasingly unable to engage the full human potential of our employees. If, as business leaders, we also fail to recapture the hearts and imagination of our society, we will continue to lose appreciation for the quality of our products, the abilities of our managers, and the relevance of our business institutions to society as a whole.

Throughout history, myths have provided people with a connection to the rhythms and cycles of their own lives. The stories and rituals of mythology relate a meaning for life's important transition points; the mystery of birth, the trauma of passage from adolescence to adulthood, the celebration of unity through marriage, the gift of wisdom in old age, the fear and hope of death. Interaction with the myths allows individuals to measure their own lives' progress.

A Post-Adolescent Mythology For Business

Institutions, like human beings, go through cycles of development, growth, maturity and stagnation. If we view business through the lens of history, we see that it is a relatively new institution, one that formalized its structures only in the last century. In comparison to its political, religious, artistic, academic and scientific counterparts, the institution of business is in fact, in human terms, only an adolescent. Such anthropomorphization of business is useful, because it provides a context for what is needed, what mythological direction and guidance can most benefit business as it makes the transition from adolescent to adult.

Like any other teenager, business is self-centred, to the point of self-consumption. It seeks the instant gratification of short-term profits, without the sensible, more adult regard for the longer-term implications of its actions. Business also displays adolescent aggressiveness. It is very strong, sometimes brutal. Yet, because business "doesn't know its own strength," it remains irresponsible, extending its considerable power without the maturity in judgement to modulate its potentially destructive acts. The plunder of the planet is the result of such adolescent behaviour. The disregard for other people, for other human institutions, and the inability to balance non-business pressures with those of profit, are characteristic of the selfishness and insecurity of adolescence.

This metaphor of business as adolescent is not to be taken lightly. In fact, it's uncannily accurate. Like many teens, business has been alienated, operating with a feeling of separateness, and with a general disregard for the other dimensions of human society. The single-minded focus on profit parallels the self-absorption and painful self-centredness that so many of us experienced as teens. Traumas of pain, of loss, of the unfairness of life, force humans to grow up. Similarly, the traumas of limitation and imminent self-destruction are forcing business to make the painful transition to young adulthood.

With business developing to become the dominant institution of our time, it's obvious that we can no longer tolerate its adolescent behaviour. Our environment cannot accept much more callous harassment. Our employees, customers and suppliers cannot be engaged any more through bullying. For its own long-term health, as well as for that of our society, it is important for business to accept the responsibilities, challenges and obligations of adulthood.

An adult mythology to inspire adult behaviour is desperately needed. Firstly, such an adult mythology will be based on a regard for others. Just as people assume responsibility for their families, communities and countries as adults, so, too, business must adopt a broader sensitivity to how its actions affect the world around it. Adolescent principles of uncontrolled growth and irresponsible size must give way to new priorities of long-term sustainability, environmental protection, and deeper human enrichment for all.

Towards A More Human Scale

One of the pillars of this more adult mythology may be the notion, first espoused by E.F. Schumacher, that "small is beautiful." In Schumacher's view, the scale of big business has served to dehumanize it, to distance the people in power, who make decisions, from the real world that their decisions so dramatically affect. He also argued that large business entities are inefficient, because so much of their energy goes into maintaining the machinery of the corporation itself.

An economy based on a more human scale is both more efficient and more equitable. Schumacher envisioned small enterprises interacting within closely-knit communities, to render that city or market nearly self-sufficient. He argued that the closer people are to their own production, the more intimate they are with the sources of the foods they eat and the products they consume, the more value they ascribe to the resources and work that went into meeting their needs. The resulting heightened appreciation would inspire more responsible industrial practices, and greater regard for the environment.

Schumacher characterizes his views as "Buddhist economics."[10] Modern industry has been "shifting the emphasis from the worker to the product of the work, that is from the human to the sub-human." From Schumacher's perspective, goods can never be more important than people, and consumption can never be more important than creativity. By returning industry to a smaller, more manageable scale, the preeminence of human beings is restored.

While seemingly idealistic and quaint, Schumacher's model is, in fact, one that has pragmatic benefits for modern business. Smaller business units have already proven themselves to be more entrepreneurial, more innovative and more accountable for results than large, corporate bureaucracies. Professor Mintzberg, in a recent address to a group of Eastern European business people, suggested that "the best way to learn how to manage their unshackled economies...was by learning how to manage organizations with a more intimate scale." He admonished them to learn to *feel* what's going on, and not fall into the trap of a "planning mentality."[11]

This advice obviously has considerable application in North America. In his book, *Rebirth of The Corporation*, Harvard business professor D. Quinn Mills details the advantages that accrue to companies that eschew the structures of size and, instead, operate with what he calls "clusters."

Through clusters, large companies de-layer themselves and create units that operate with the spirit and drive of small companies. British Petroleum and IBM Canada are among the companies that Mills reports have adopted cluster-based organizations. "Groups of professionals across the firm with a common interest will link informally, avoiding the bureaucracy and rigidity of traditional departmental and committee structures. The teams are small, some permanent and some temporary, and are activity-oriented [rather than turf protective] and fully interconnected internally."[12]

Whereas in large groups, considerable energy is naturally expended on managing the group, smaller clusters focus the attention and commitment of team members on the problem to be solved or opportunity to be met. There are fewer titles, fewer reports to write, and decision-making is in the hands of the team itself. People who work in clusters generally feel greater participation, and are more cognizant of the contributions they are making to the team. Both personal satisfaction and accountability are heightened.

The process of eliminating titles, reducing bureaucracy, and delegating decision-making to clusters is not a panacea. New problems emerge, as people struggle with newly irrelevant, but deeply embedded, questions like, "Who do I report to?" In my own experience, people are so used to the framework and security of a hierarchy that workers themselves sometimes resist taking it down. To help clusters work, people need a new mythology. This mythology, unlike the control-emphasis of traditional business, will be based on principles of human support.

Mills establishes that the most significant tasks within a cluster-based organization are those of facilitation, communication and co-ordination. While adolescent business has believed exclusively in the need to supervise and monitor, in its more mature iterations business is according others the dignity and space to fulfil themselves while doing the work.

Fortune reported on a team of workers at General Mills that has achieved a forty percent increase in productivity, since clustering was introduced. The team largely self-manages, and even runs completely without supervision during the overnight shift. The manager responsible for the team does not supervise, in the conventional sense, but rather supports his group, and links them with the goals of head office. They maintain their own machinery, and come up with ideas to solve their own problems. Strikingly, they are thriving with the added responsibility. One worker said, "I work a lot harder than I used to. You have to worry about the numbers."

In clusters, people spend less time planning and more time doing. The distinction between strategy and execution blurs, because every action by every team member is of strategic importance. The understanding of strategy is more intuitive, because people live it with every decision they make, every product they produce. In this way, clusters approximate the way Japanese companies use strategies—not to set out a plan, but to act and learn in the marketplace.

A growing number of progressive, highly successful North American companies, such as Federal Express, Corning Glass and Levi-Strauss are using clusters and super-teams to sharpen their operations and enhance their competitiveness. Such new structures reflect a maturing, a coming of age of business. As that happens, the mythology and models that sustained it during its adolescence will have less and less currency with business. New myths, new models, are needed. These will provide guidance for achieving the new goals of business, those based on co-operation, interdependence, and sincere concern for the long-term.

This commitment to the future is of paramount importance. Unlike teenagers, adults are concerned with their legacies. With a growing sense of their own mortality, adults look to the future and feel responsibility for the structures and opportunities that they will be creating and leaving for their children. Through such reflection, some adults achieve that rare inspiration and insight that we call wisdom. Now, as business assumes its own adulthood, we can only hope that it finds wisdom at a faster pace than it left adolescence.

SEARCHING FOR THE NEW HEROES OF BUSINESS

One of the more frivolous consequences of *glasnost*, and the rapprochement between East and West, is that communism is no longer the black-hatted bad guy in popular culture. That role now, more often than not, belongs to business. In movies—high drama such as *Crossover*, science-fiction such as *Robocop*, and comedy such as *Uncle Buck*—the villain is less often a political or military adversary, and increasingly a corporate one.

The hyperbolic business of Hollywood is corrupt and menacing, its power a threat to the unsuspecting public, to the innocent individual. In Stephen Spielberg's *Who Framed Roger Rabbit?*, the human detective and the animated rabbit are being framed by a menacing villain whose real intent is to buy up the Los Angeles transit system, and build freeways to promote both the purchase of cars and the development of the oil industry. People cheered, as this corrupt business villain was foiled.

Obscured by the humour and incredible special effects of this movie is the fact that Los Angeles did have a great transit system in the 1920s. As happened in other cities at that time, the L.A. transit system was bought up, and largely destroyed, by none other than General Motors, in partnership with the Socal oil company and Firestone Tires.[1]

In this case, the fiction was based on truth, which the public didn't recognize. In others, the fiction is outrageous, which the public also may not recognize. In either case, the credibility and trustworthiness of business is strained. A stereotype is reinforced, of business amorally focused on profit. The suspicion and cynicism provoked by such movies inevitably gain momentum in real life, when companies fail in their public responsibilities, as Exxon did with its clumsy response to the oil spill in Prince William Sound.

This is not to suggest that business does not deserve the scrutiny and critical view that many in society and the arts community cast upon it. Business has been abusive and irresponsible. We shouldn't forget that, without the blood and toil of labour unions, big business would not have reformed its inhuman labour practices. Nor that the automobile companies implemented life-saving design changes to their cars only after consumer advocates like Ralph Nader made the public pressure on them so acute as to be unbearable. The larger point is that North American business needs the emotional support of the public. Movies are showing with their storylines that we in business are not doing a very convincing job of earning it.

The reason public support is so important, and why something as seemingly frivolous as imagery in movies counts, is that many of the countries we compete against in the global economy operate differently than we do. Business in Japan, Korea, Singapore and the many countries that are emulating their success, is handled like public policy. In these economies, business is too important to be left in the hands of business people. Politicians and business people work together to make their industries as competitive as possible on the world market, even if that means burdening the population in the home market.

Professor Bruce Scott, the economics professor at Harvard who taught my OPM class, characterizes the developing economies of the Pacific Rim as "production-focused," versus

North America's, which is "consumption-focused." In the production economies, industrial policy is geared towards exports. This is a top-down process, in that taxation, labour policies and domestic market conditions are managed, to produce a worldwide competitive advantage in a target industry. By contrast, consumption economies operate much more at the grass-roots level, with both business and government setting as their general aim the satisfaction of the needs of the domestic market.

Production economies do not have a very strong democratic tradition. The well-being of the entire country is understood to be based upon success in business. That's why these nations are run more like companies than countries. And that's why the concept of Japan Inc. is so appropriate.

The general population in these economies is viewed primarily as a resource for production. Savings are "encouraged," through banking policies that require individuals to make prohibitive down-payments of up to fifty percent on home or car purchases. The "encouraged" savings are then channeled back to business, to provide capital for plant improvements and further development of exports. In North America, the emphasis on the "consumer" promotes banking practices that make it easier to own a home or car, with down-payments of ten percent or less. The pool of savings available for business is considerably smaller, requiring many North American companies to seek more expensive capital abroad.

In a market geared to production, the goals of government and business are homogeneous, the relationship between ministers and managers understandably cooperative. In markets where the "consumer is king," politicians and business must address the often-conflicting needs of quite different constituents. The electorate of the politician and the shareholders of the business person have differing priorities. This fragmentation of interests makes it very difficult to develop cohesive policies, to compete against the very focused industrial strategies of the production-oriented economies.

Naohiro Amaya, retired deputy minister of Japan's MITI, asks, "How can you hunt without a target?" He believes strongly that the new, more relevant economic model will be based on forging focused industrial policy. "When you go hunting, you have to shoot at a target. But your [North American] neoclassical school of economics says you can fire in all directions at once and the 'market' will ensure you hit the target. Well, we don't accept that line of reasoning, and our economic model will probably be stronger in the future, and have a greater demonstration for effect for developing countries than either the American model, which has become weak and less relevant, or the Soviet central-command model, which will probably cease to exist as a practical alternative early in the twenty-first century, or before."[2]

Focusing on, and hitting, the targets of industrial strategy are admittedly much easier in a country where the social customs are based on consensus, and that doesn't have our tradition of democracy and freedom of the individual. That production-centred economies have realized this advantage underscores the dangerous fallacy of our society's general acceptance of the concept of "free trade." There is only smart trade and, while we argue economic theory, Japan, Germany, and Korea pursue their industrial strategies with remarkable success, often at our expense.

The North American focus on free trade is a distraction. We've expended considerable energy of our ministers and business people to get Japan and Korea to open their markets for rice, beef and coal. Freer access for such commodities will hardly enrich North Americans. Nor will it contribute to our global competitiveness, by helping us to develop the electronic and intelligence products of the economy of the future.

The real challenge for North Americans is to develop the collective will, within our tradition of democracy, to make the strategic decisions about business that are necessary for us to compete. Developing such a consensus cannot be done heavy-handedly. Business cannot, and should not, impose its will on society. Rather, we should engage the tools of our democratic traditions to win the grass-roots support for business.

The responsibility is not only government's. Business leaders have to make our companies so aspirational in their goals, so reciprocal in their achievement, that the will of our society will gel around the broader cause of international industrial competitiveness.

A recent poll, published in *Newsweek*, underscores the importance of this responsibility. The survey, which included almost 200,000 college students, shows that "interest in business careers is in steep decline now that the 80s are over." One-third fewer college students are choosing business for their careers than in 1988. This suggests that the opportunity for fulfilment that business represents to students has dropped. For companies, it means that fewer people with the educational skills demanded by the global marketplace will be accessible to them. The more limited the talent pool, the more limited the opportunities.

The Wounded Heroes Of The '80s

The 1980s afforded business a rare window of opportunity to effect a positive change in its standing within society. The hellish inflation of the 1970s had sapped the energy of society, and the government expenditures that had contributed to that inflation were understood to be largely wasted. Out of this exasperation came the electoral support for deregulating business, for unfettering its investment potential, for releasing it from its restrictive tax burden. This renewed faith in business also caused popular support, for the first time in generations, to shift away from unions, which had themselves become anachronistic.

With its initiative and creativity, business flourished. Entrepreneurs jumped at new opportunities. Large companies streamlined themselves, to be more responsive in the superheated marketplace. And the result was the longest peace-time economic expansion ever recorded in history. During the height of the economic expansion, business enjoyed an unusually positive reassessment by society. Books about business became popular best-sellers. The dramatic turnaround of Chrysler by Lee Iacocca earned him such widespread support that there was even discussion in the press of his suitability as a possible presidential candidate. Of course, Iacocca's book was a best-seller.

Business seemed to have the resourcefulness and energy to get things done. It's efficiency and productivity accomplished projects that various levels of governments seemed incapable of doing. Donald Trump won the admiration of the men and women on the streets of New York, for taking on and completing quickly repairs to the skating rink in Central Park—a project that had foiled the city's parks people for years. Trump's book, too, was a best-seller.

The exploits of business people became fascinating for a wide audience, as the realization grew that so many of the changes in society are driven by business. Stephen Jobs became the celebrated guru of computers. His was the quintessential success story. He and Steve Wozniak started Apple in a garage, and the popular press tracked them as they made their dream, grew their company, and realized great wealth, at the crest of the personal computer wave. Jobs came to represent the visionary, the New-Age business person, who elicited zen-like devotion from the engineers and designers who worked so frenziedly for him. Stephen Jobs rekindled North America's faith in the entrepreneur, and he became one of the brightest lights in entrepreneurial heaven.

Iacocca, Trump and Jobs became heroes to many in business, and to many in society. Their accomplishments were significant. Their ability to innovate, to overcome sometimes impossible circumstances, inspired many. They also seemed to lead by example, taking on the challenges of their respective situations, and putting themselves on the line to get results. The "can-do" spirit, which had been missing in government since John Kennedy, seemed to have a found a new home in the hands of the very capable business people who were leading the economic regeneration of North America.

But history moves in cycles, and it was perhaps inevitable that society's infatuation with business would eventually grow thin. The inevitable slowing of the economy would naturally demystify business and show up its shortcomings. While it's understandable that business would lose its appeal, its star status, many of the people who were business's most visible lights ended up contributing to the erosion.

Iacocca remains charming and popular, but the perception of his leadership ability has waned as Chrysler, saved from the brink, continues to design and build cars that do not represent leadership in quality and vision. That he has also engaged in Japan-bashing in Chrysler's advertising, and in many of his speeches, has made Iacocca seem desperate, trying to assign blame to competitors, rather than owning up to the quality challenge of the modern marketplace. Chrysler's prospects in the more difficult economy of the early 1990s has again raised questions about its ability, not only to compete, but to survive.

Trump has become a lightening rod for much of the cynicism and revulsion that people came to feel for the excesses of the 1980s. His pretentious lifestyle combined with a growing arrogance to turn many people off. The greed of dealmakers like Trump and Drexel Burnham's Michael Milken made it easy to accept their demises as a form of social "poetic justice." Trump's latest book had the dubious distinction of being the poorest seller on a CNN poll, during the high-volume Christmas selling period.

Jobs, too, has dropped from consciousness. His last two years at Apple were nearly catastrophic for the company. He treated all but the few who worked with him on his own special projects with derision, creating an environment within Apple that was both divisive and very political. Self-indulgence eventually overtook both Jobs's business and new product judgement, and he became a liability to the very company he founded.

Frank Rose, in his book, *West of Eden*, describes Jobs's arrogant behaviour during an important trip to Japan. They were visiting companies such as Sony, Epson and Hitachi, to look at available disk drives and monitor technology for new Apple computers. "By the time they reached Epson it was almost noon and nobody had prepared lunch for them. Steve was furious. He was rude to everyone."[3]

The next day at Hitachi, Jobs continued his insensitive behaviour. He challenged the Japanese engineers who were explaining product features to him, and he usually dismissed them by saying he already knew what they were telling him. "Finally Steve announced that he wanted some cookies, so everybody had to scurry around looking for cookies for him." The paragon of entrepreneurial achievement was, in fact, a petulant child, and his very visible break with Apple tarnished him and the wonderful company he had helped to create.

Iacocca, Trump and Jobs were but the more visible business heroes who fell from their pedestals. In many ways they were also among the more innocent, and there were many others who had moments of infamy in the public eye. Frank Lorenzo, for a time the "most-hated boss in business," led hostile takeovers of Continental and Eastern Airlines. To force concessions from unions and effect streamlining of the bloated operations of the airlines, Lorenzo led first, Continental, and then, Eastern through bankruptcy.

After reorganizing both companies and emerging from bankruptcy court, Lorenzo led both airlines back to the brink of failure, until both were again in bankruptcy, a tailspin from which Eastern never recovered. It finally went out of business. Lorenzo's callous, ultimately inept management style had a ripple effect, dislocating thousands of employees, frustrating and under-serving hundreds of thousands of travellers, and disaffecting millions of people who followed the dramatic disintegration of these once-proud airlines in the popular news.

What Lorenzo achieved in the airlines industry, the Saatchi brothers of England did for advertising. After rapidly acquiring a group of international advertising agencies, the Saatchis faced the nearly impossible challenge of repaying the very large debt they had taken on to complete their purchases. Several of the agencies purchased, including the huge Ted Bates agency, represented business philosophies that were very different from that of the Saatchis, so managers also faced the even more onerous task of integrating very different, sometimes totally alien, corporate cultures.

A few senior managers, such as Bates president Bob Jacoby, walked out with millions and millions. Long-time clients like Warner-Lambert and Colgate-Palmolive were so dislocated that they fired Bates. Hundreds of employees lost their jobs, to help cover the costs of paying-down debt, paying-out senior managers, and shrinking the payrolls of companies affected by the departure of disgruntled clients.

The massive reorganization of business that occurred during the 1980s brought about innumerable such failures. The cumulative ripple effects—job losses, factory closings, asset fire-sales—did much to destroy the confidence of the general public in the people who lead its business institutions.

Appropriately, the man credited with sparking the decade-long binge of acquisition, Michael Milken, recently received a ten-year sentence, after a much-publicized trial for insider trading. Milken is famous for making the junk bond the premier corporate-financing instrument of the 1980s. He is also famous for the billions he earned—in 1988 alone, Milken's salary and bonuses totalled more than $500 million. Such fabulous wealth was created by convincing investors to purchase high-risk shares in companies that "the chief credit-rating agencies, Moody's and Standard and Poor's, deemed to be unable to repay their debts."

Milken has become a sinister figure in society's consciousness, a financial alchemist who mesmerized clients and created gold out of lead. But, in fact, he was only doing in finance what Ronald Reagan had done in politics—promising people immediate rewards, without regard for the future price.

Milken was not alone. As Michael Lewis chronicles, in his best-selling book about Wall Street, *Liar's Poker*, thousands of traders and MBA students aspired to be Milken. Thousands more corporate officers and stock speculators were eager to participate in his magic. Lewis writes, "Milken drowned his people in money." People earning millions of dollars in individual bonuses were loyal to Milken and his junk-bond philosophy. Others seeking such quick wealth jumped into junk-bond financing. The ever-widening spiral of high-risk debt took on a destructive momentum of its own.

This is not to dismiss some of the restructuring that occurred in the 1980s. Business always involves risk, and some of the junk bonds actually helped companies reorganize and make significant investments in plant and technology, to improve their competitive position. However, for the most part, junk bonds lived up to their name, having undermined the integrity and competitiveness of North American business.

A very few shareholders, and the market traders who managed their transactions, grew rich. The managers with debt-loaded companies have been hard-pressed to make the nearly extortionate payments demanded by the junk bonds. Many companies have failed. Many others are unable to make investments in the plant and equipment that they require to be competitive, because they are so strapped to pay back debt. The failure of the savings and loan industry in the U.S. is, in great part, attributable to the abuses of junk bonds, which many of those fragile institutions used to back imprudent real estate investment.

The immediate price of leveraging the economy with junk bonds has been the loss of jobs. Not unusually, the people most traumatically affected had little to do with the decisions that led to the circumstances requiring the elimination of hundreds of thousands of jobs. Longer-term, the side effects of the junk-bond binge are even more ominous. With our economy addicted to debt, there is much less capital available to regenerate business.

While we borrowed to buy and sell companies, global competitors like the Japanese were investing profits in new plant and technology. Steven Schlosstein writes, "The success of Japanese industrial policy has meant that there is hardly a factory in Japan that has not been built, rebuilt, or refurbished since the late 1970s, with every Japanese worker supported by more than twice the value of plant and equipment than supports his American counterpart."[4]

These new factories are still coming on stream. The new equipment and training of employees in Japan and Europe is proceeding. And, while the competition gets stronger and more sophisticated, many North American companies are handcuffed by their debt burdens. In this way, junk bonds have directly debilitated our competitiveness. The huge bill for government's bailouts of failed companies like S&Ls also penalizes the North American economy, draining capital from future-benefitting investment to pay off past mistakes and abuses.

In his book, *Day of Reckoning*, Harvard economist Benjamin M. Friedman provides a sobering assessment of the future cost of North America's decade of debt financing. "The cost of the economic policy we have pursued in the 1980s is no more than what any society pays for eating its seed corn rather than planting it. Our rate of investment in business plant and equipment has fallen beneath that of any previous sustained period since World War II. So has our investment in roads, bridges, airports, harbours, and other kinds of government-owned infrastructure.

"Perhaps most ominously, the investment in education has also shrunk compared to our total income, despite the urgent need to train a work force whose opportunities will arise more than ever before from industries oriented to technologically advanced production and the processing of information."[5]

Friedman views the economic policy of the last decade as "a violation of a basic moral principle," that each generation is responsible for seeding the well-being and potential enrichment of future ones. The business leaders who oversaw this debt-based restructuring, people like Ross Johnson of RJR

Nabisco and H. Ross Perot of EDS, have generally escaped their abandoned companies with their personal wealth intact.

The legacy of this generation of business leadership is to have alienated many segments of society with their excesses. They've squandered whatever trust and enthusiasm people had for business, raising suspicion and cynicism about the role of business in North America. The trust of clients and customers has been stretched, often to the point of irreparable damage. The loyalty and commitment of employees has also been sapped.

The Heroic Challenge

To reverse this spiral of ever-diminishing competitiveness, the leadership of our economy must again engage the imaginations of the public. A new pantheon of heroes must emerge, to reconnect the goals of business to the broader needs and aspirations of our society.

The men and women who will make up this pantheon will operate very differently from past business heroes. The achievement of corporate goals, no matter how significant, will not be enough. Instead, the new heroes will provide examples of how the needs and achievements of business are compatible with those of society. They will show, through the performances of the companies they manage, how the benefits of an enlightened, mature business establishment can be reciprocal, enriching society, its workers, customers and the environment, to the same degree that the enterprise itself is being enriched.

This heroic reformation of business, this quest for reciprocity, is necessary, not only for the sake of society, but especially for the competitiveness and vitality of our companies. A recent article in The Economist reported on a study carried out by the Boston Consulting Group for the European Commission. The study examined the very large car-component manufacturing industries, to assess their readiness for the expected competitive onslaught from Japan and North America.

Even though European companies have adopted many of the most progressive manufacturing techniques, and have invested billions in the latest manufacturing technology, they remain dangerously inefficient, relative to their Japanese and American counterparts. The European car-parts companies have spent more in R&D than even the Japanese, yet the labour productivity of the Japanese worker is up to 2.5 times that of the Europeans, and improving twice as fast.[6]

In exploring the causes of this productivity lag, BCG contrasted the implementation of such modern manufacturing practices as "just-in-time" stock management, between Europe and Japan. "Just-in-time" is the principle, pioneered by Toyota, of *synchronous manufacturing*, meaning that parts suppliers produce and deliver their components to the manufacturing facility just as they are needed for production. This practice eliminates the very expensive, unproductive process of stockpiling and warehousing. While about two hundred European car-parts companies claimed to be following "just in time," BCG only found nine examples of it. The rest had merely transplanted the stockpiling and warehousing process, so that it had become an internalized cost.

The inability to realize the full benefits of "just-in-time" is essentially due to a failure in achieving reciprocity. *The Economist* concludes, "The biggest obstacle is the relationship between Western car firms and the car firms they supply. "Just-in-time" calls for co-operation; in the West, the relationship between supplier and supplied is still often adversarial, despite efforts in recent years to forge closer ties." The BCG study shows that Japanese companies integrate their suppliers much more closely into their operations, including them in the actual process of initial design and engineering, and affording them longer-term contracts.

This begins a circle of reciprocal advantage. Because of this intimate involvement, suppliers are committed to making considerable investments to customize and improve the parts they are supplying. This improves the quality of the finished product, and enhances productivity for the manufacturer. The customer wins with better products. The manufacturer wins with better sales and better margins. And the supplier wins with more sales, and the security to invest to achieve future competitiveness.

As with classical heroes, the new business heroes will break down the exclusive self-interest of their individual organizations, and will strive to serve a broader interest, which includes our human society and our natural environment, as well as the enterprises they lead. The whole will be enriched by creating circles of reciprocity; vital, imaginative companies made stronger by vital, imaginative employees, made stronger by a vital, imaginative society, made stronger by vital, imaginative companies, and on and on.

The new heroes of business will bring a sense of deeper meaning, a potential for personal fulfilment, to the companies they lead. Employees will be inspired by such leadership. Their creativity will have expression, their commitment will be rewarded. Because of their genuine concern for community and planet, these heroes will be celebrated by society, earning widespread trust and admiration. The positive energy of employees, the trust of society, will, in turn, provide the emotional capital for North American companies to thrive in the world economy.

Such heroic leadership cannot be mass-produced in conventional business schools, nor will they emerge easily from traditional training programmes. The new heroes will necessarily be much more interdisciplinary, combining a passion for business with that for humanity and for nature. Out of the balance of their own humanity will come the balanced practices, the reciprocity, that will be the paradigm of the enlightened business enterprise of the future.

There are many obstacles to overcome in achieving such unorthodox business structures, some of them seemingly insurmountable. But it is the very scale of this challenge that invites the participation of the soul, that inspires those who view the heroic deed.

E.F. Schumacher writes, "The true problems of living— in politics, economics, education, marriage, etc.—are always problems of overcoming or reconciling opposites. They are divergent problems and have no solution in the ordinary sense of the word. They demand of man not merely the employment of his reasoning powers but the commitment of his whole personality."[7]

The heroic often seems, initially, to be foolish, idealistic, and naïve. From the point of view of the comfortable and the conventional, the heroic often seems pointless, if not hopeless. In his book about heroic archetypes, entitled *The Hero*

With a Thousand Faces, Joseph Campbell wrote, "It has always been the prime function of mythology and rite to supply the symbols that carry the human spirit forward, in counteraction to those other constant human fantasies that tend to tie it back."[8] The current philosophy of business, which fails to see its integration with nature, and which fails to acknowledge its wider responsibilities to the human family, is based on regressive fantasies.

The new heroes of business will "carry the human spirit forward," by providing business models that integrate and enrich on all levels, including, but no longer exclusively, profit. Such aspirations are counter-intuitive for traditional business thinkers, so the new business heroes, as all heroes do, will have to overcome the skepticism of the very people whom they will eventually come to lead. Operating largely without precedent, such heroes, as all heroes do, will have to rely on their own instincts and heartfelt convictions, to see them through the lonely process of creating a new paradigm.

In the end, heroes are put on pedestals because their heroic deeds served an unselfish, public good. This is the essence of heroism. It may seem to be asking too much to expect the managers and leaders of companies to strive for the heroic. Yet, we who lead companies are, in so many ways, the privileged within society. We have the power to direct the considerable energy and resources of our enterprises. We also have the network to influence others beyond the walls of our companies. So, if we don't rise to the challenge, who will? If we, who benefit so much from business and society, don't lead this transformation, who should?

THE FEMININE AND MASCULINE IN DISEQUILIBRIUM

After seven years in the male-dominated world of a Roman Catholic seminary, I found the transition to the male-dominated world of business to be an easy one. The patriarchy that dominates both the religious and commercial institutions has been long established. And, while the goals were different, success in either vocation was based on established masculine traditions of aggressiveness and competitiveness.

Ironically, business is now suffering much the same constriction and loss of relevance that has so negatively affected the Church. And among the causes of this erosion of meaning are the same domination of masculine energy, and the same deprivation of the feminine, that also characterize the Roman Church.

The feminine and masculine energy I'm referring to is not based on sex, although there are obvious overlaps. Instead, I'm focusing on the combination of energy that, in differing weightings, all human beings have within themselves.

The Inner Duality

The notion of the duality of masculine and feminine has been a part of our mythic traditions for centuries. The ancient forces of Yin and Yang, which even appear on the national flag of Korea, are examples of this duality, from the culture of the Orient. In Western thought, Carl Jung, one of the founders of modern psychology, gave the notion of feminine and masculine energy its clinical credibility.

Although so much of our natural and human world is defined by these principles, modern business has largely ignored the duality and, like the Church and other religious and political institutions, has been slow to grasp the consequences of the bias for the masculine.

Again, I'm not talking about sexuality. Nor am I attempting to delve into the unfair exclusion and abuse of women that has marked human history. My point is that the duality of feminine and masculine exists, and that, in supporting one influence while suppressing the other, institutions, particularly business, are depriving themselves of a good portion of the energy and vitality that they need to renew themselves and find currency in our modern world.

As Jung and his followers suggest, every person has aspects of his or her personality that are generally associated with the opposite sex. Psychologists argue that mental health and a vital personality are in fact, dependent on the complementary interaction between these masculine and feminine dimensions.

The Masculine

Not surprisingly, institutions created by humans contain not only the dimensions of masculinity and femininity, but also any imbalance that history or culture has tolerated. Although it's often explained as a consequence of biology, business has evolved almost exclusively as a masculine force, because of the domination, sometimes destructive, of the patriarchy. The aggressiveness of business, sometimes ugly, its strong goal-orientation, sometimes fanatical, its discipline and decisiveness, sometimes constrictive, are some of the expressions of this masculine bias.

As with other aspects of our human and natural lives, imbalance produces problems commensurate with its achievements. The tragic misuse of natural resources, the subjugation of all other human priorities to profit, the inability to nurture creativity and innovation, are some of the consequences of this imbalance.

The pervasiveness of the masculine force in politics, religion and business has meant that all of us, in both Eastern and Western societies, are brought up to accept this bias, and not immediately see its distortions. The current model of business, with its traditions of power, profit and performance, seems immutable, even though any logical and sensitive human being can see that its practices are on a fatal collision course with the natural world that sustains us.

While we accept the moral imperative of business to seek profit, many of us remain uncomfortable with the power it wields in the process. Corporations rarely talk about power, because it is so intimidating. But these organizations are essentially concentrations of power; resources of people and capital bonded together to achieve goals that are of priority to the corporations. When the corporation is imbalanced, when its culture is dominated by masculine energy, the application of its considerable power has the devastating effects that we've witnessed throughout our society.

In this context, business is expressing the same imbalance that has affected institutions like the Roman Catholic Church. The Church has a very rigid hierarchy, dominated by men, with women relegated to positions of service, with little power and authority. Although the Church preaches equality, maintaining, as a point of doctrine, that the soul is asexual, it continues to discriminate against women, denying them the possibility of ordination to the priesthood.

The Church's sermons and teachings about gentleness and love have become hollow, undermined by the hypocrisy of its own conduct. It has disenfranchised many in society, ultimately losing many of the strong, spiritual women who could have been a source of future strength for the Church.

These discrepancies apply with alarming accuracy to business. And for business, as it has been for the Church, the price for maintaining an ethos based only on the masculine can be the calamitous loss of the very resource it needs for its renewal.

This issue of masculine and feminine balance is not simply about sexual politics, nor about the domination of one sex by the other. Men, as well as women, have been demeaned by traditional business practices, their spirits impoverished, or their creativity crushed. And bringing more women into positions of power within business will not automatically correct the masculine imbalance. The quest for balance must begin personally, by developing the individual capacity to give expression to the feminine principles within each of us. Only as whole and balanced human beings can we create whole and balanced institutions, and within them, whole and balanced companies.

The Feminine

Striving for such equilibrium is important, both to integrate business within the totality of human need, and to regenerate business to be more successful. Theodore Levitt, professor at the Harvard Business School and, until recently, the editor of the *Harvard Business Review*, has published a series of essays, entitled *Thinking About Management*. He writes, "A business is about only two things—money and customers. It takes money to get started, and customers to keep going..."[1]

This is the business we know, that which has been promulgated by business schools and codified by countless corporations. But Levitt has another lesson to teach. "Little else matters by comparison [to money and customers], except one thing. It matters how people feel about the moral legitimacy and social worth of what they do, and about the people with whom they are associated." People are more motivated when they work in a company that acknowledges the higher values and goals of life. They make their fullest contributions when the fullness of their humanity is involved. And this can only happen in companies that operate with a balance of masculine and feminine energy.

The imbalance of energy not only distorts the impact, but also deprives business of the positive, enriching qualities of the feminine. We know the principles of the feminine to be as strong as the masculine, but with a greater capacity for nurturing and creativity. And, while our inner masculine dimension is combative, our feminine can win and let others win too.

These may be dangerous assertions to make, in the context of business. Women will rightly argue that they can compete and win against anyone. And men will argue that they are too smart, maybe too sensitive, to ignore lessons of a "win-win" approach to business. These objections are valid, proving the point that aspects of the feminine and aspects of the masculine are intrinsic to all human beings. Each of us express a different balance, or a unique imbalance, between the two. The goal in business, as it is in life, is to achieve the most constructive partnership between these two, very different forces.

By tradition, we identify the drive to achieve, with its personal measures and individual satisfactions, as flowing from our masculine dimension. And our inner feminine dimension is that which allows us to love, to include others and participate in a life of intimacy. Both of these are strong, vital forces, and the individual who has access to both has the attributes that will be indispensable to any enterprise that seeks to build and maintain a competitive advantage in the marketplace of the 1990s.

In his essay, *The Changed World Economy*, Peter Drucker notes, "In all developed countries, knowledge workers have already become the centre of gravity of the labour force, even in numbers. Even in manufacturing they will outnumber blue collar workers within fewer than ten years."[2] Unlike traditional labour, who provided the power of their bodies and the nimbleness of their hands to business, knowledge workers contribute with their thoughts and ideas.

The masculine forces of drive and control, which have developed in the factory, are largely inappropriate in managing the ephemeral process of human thought. Renting bodies for production is much easier than engaging the mind. Business, with its masculine-biased construct, is currently ill-suited to achieving the white-collar productivity gains it so urgently needs.

Knowledge workers, everyone from accountants to journalists, from CAD engineers to CAM plant people, use information to produce value. Information cannot be manufactured to specification. It relies on interpretation, on interconnection, to finally create understanding. Such creative judgement cannot be achieved in the straight line of masculine deduction. Rather, it requires nurturing, the inspiration and support that we so strongly associate with the spirit of the feminine.

A knowledge environment also requires clear communication. The feminine dimension of human nature is that which shares, that which thrives on interchange. Without a strong social sense, supported by a caring feminine spirit, it is easy for companies to break down into compartments and components. These units often view knowledge as power, and use it for competitive leverage within a company. This resistance to extending knowledge and to sharing power works to defeat the common corporate good.

Tracey Kidder, In his book, *The Soul of a New Machine*, docu-ments the self-defeating competitiveness of various groups of engineers at Data General, who were vying to create the next generation of faster, more powerful data processors. Operating with ruthless competitive drive, teams destroyed themselves while trying to destroy their internal competition. Many innovative ideas were squandered, many brilliant minds "crashed and burned."

Management failed to understand the lonely, oppressive pressure of being engaged in an act of creation. They pushed for more output without replenishing the diluted, damaged human spirit. While this approach at Data General produced some initial successes, such internal rivalry for information, and such disregard for the needs of people in a creative act, eventually undermined the company's efforts, and destroyed its competit-iveness. Data General has since fallen into a cycle of mediocrity and financial crisis.[3]

This is an extreme example of knowledge workers corrupted, and finally defeated, by the unbridled masculine drive to compete. Even such enlightened companies as Apple have been through cycles where internal co-operation and communication have run into barriers of possessiveness and drive. In such environments, the corporate goal is subjugated to that of a small group. Missing, in these circumstances, are our more feminine capacities to nurture, to bond together, to include and to share.

The capacities to nurture and share should not be mistaken for passive attributes, nor are they soft issues for companies. Increasingly, these are acknowledged as very important assets, requiring drive and determination, along with strength and courage, to implement well. The evidence suggests that sharing companies are strong companies.

How The Partnership Works

One of the structural innovations that Ford used, during the development of its company-saving Taurus-Sable models, was the formation of an inter-disciplinary task force to lead the project. Previous Ford models were designed in a linear fashion—design conceived the overall concept for a car, engineering worked out the specifications, production implemented the manufacturing, and marketing developed selling strategies.

Each group worked independently. The internal rivalry and competitiveness inevitably hampered a new model's development. Engineers developed concepts that production could not implement. Designs were made without reference to the customer-understanding that the marketing people embodied. The result of this internal wastage was that it took Ford twice as long as Japanese competitors to develop new cars, and these cars, once complete, were so far removed from the concept of what the customer wanted that they propelled the company towards disaster.

Ford was sufficiently on the ropes that its executives now admit that, with the Taurus-Sable, they "were betting the company." Donald Petersen, then president of Ford, needed not only a new model, but a new way of doing business. He needed products that met the higher quality-expectations of customers, and a process that was radically more efficient, to compete with the cost structures of foreign automakers. Petersen restructured the Ford organization. Most important, he went beyond its structure to modify the very culture at Ford.

Quality can only be achieved when all those responsible for a product or service work co-operatively to meet the set standard. A lapse in design, a shortcut in engineering, sloppiness on the shop floor—each of these can short-circuit the delivery of quality. The interdependence of the group to achieve its final goals led Petersen to form the interdisciplinary task force. The group, sharing both the mandate and the accountability for its successful completion, hunkered down.

The Taurus-Sable was developed in two years less than it had previously taken Ford to introduce a totally new model. Customers were included in every step of the process, so that the Taurus-Sables included many small but important features that demonstrated quality to its buyers. Importantly, its then-radical "jelly-bean" styling evoked a strong emotive response from buyers, which showed that Ford met the psychic, as well as functional, needs of its customers.

The changes at Ford led to a major turnaround in sales, and profits in the billions of dollars during the mid and late 1980s. Business results were so impressive that Ford actually achieved greater absolute profits than GM, for the first time since it lost market leadership to Alfred Sloane's company in the mid-1920s. These staggering financial results were directly attributable to the new spirit at Ford, a spirit dedicated to cooperation, to sharing information to better serve the customer, and to surrendering individual authority to engender accountability in the whole group.

The dynamics of the Taurus-Sable programme at Ford illustrate, in another dimension, the potential success of a working partnership between feminine and masculine energies. The group was both driven and, atypically, open to new input and change. The combination of planning and doing, of working alone with accountability or in a group with respect, reflects a balance, a partnership of the dual energies.

Other attributes we associate with the feminine are also in evidence at General Motors. A new advertising campaign for GM claims that it's "Putting Quality On The Road." As discussed in an article in *BusinessWeek*, this advertising implicitly acknowledges that, "for years, GM's cars fell short of its customers expectations." Such honesty, although still muted, reflects a major breakthrough on GM's part in listening to its customers.

The person directly responsible for "this unorthodox sales pitch" is Shirley Young, the vice president for consumer market development. Young has used what she calls "persistent evangelism" to push through the strong marketing strategy expressed in the $40 million advertising campaign. Using an incentive study to better understand how consumers go from "thinking about a product to actually buying one," Young has built her strategy, and her case to GM's executives, by listening, and responding honestly to what she's heard.[4]

Information will continue to grow in importance as a strategic tool in most companies. This means that communication will be among the most critical activities affecting the productivity of an enterprise. Many companies are overcome by data, and seem incapable of, or too slow in, translating that abundant information into understanding. The primary cause for this endemic misunderstanding is the failure to listen.

Many books, articles and training programmes have been dedicated to the art of listening, to improving internal communication and efficiency, and to heightening a company's sensitivity to its customers. Listening is basically about opening oneself to the ideas and needs of others. It requires suspending that inner voice that we all have, which is ready to respond, react and enter into a dialogue with what is coming in. It requires honouring the person being listened to with attention, intelligence and empathy. These social skills are generally ascribed by psychologists to the feminine capacity within each of us.

Canadian Business magazine recently included a short article that explained the formation of a six-member advisory board of directors at Nestlé Enterprises Inc. The board performs a different function than that of traditional directors. As Nestlé CEO Ian Murray explained, the advisory board will primarily be involved in issues relating to the environment, nutrition, and global marketing. Half of the board is made up of women. While this makes sense, relative to the makeup of our population, this is an unusually high ratio, in comparison to other, more traditional boards.

Nestlé has made some big mistakes in the past, suffering a long, world-wide boycott, for promoting water-mixable baby formula in developing countries, where often "the water is so contaminated it kills." The advisory board will be a tool for challenging management to look beyond the bottom line, to prevent the narrow thinking that previously hampered Nestlé. Its counsel will be based on greater listening and more openness to the needs of consumers. In effect, this board represents an attempt to formalize feminine disciplines within the decision-making structure of a big corporation.[5]

Again, it is important to underscore that the issue of masculine-feminine balance is not about sex, but about realizing the fullness of our human potential. Whether male or female, we each embody this duality. We know from experience in our personal lives that imbalance in these forces is ultimately unhealthy. My own overdrive as a workaholic stemmed, in part, from such an imbalance. Only when my other personal needs assumed their rightful priorities was I able to achieve a balance. And exercising that balance at work has contributed to a more stable, satisfying and creative work environment.

Creativity

The global marketplace is demanding an unprecedented degree of innovation in the products and services created and produced by North American enterprises. Yet the skills of innovation are, most often, at odds with those conducive to innovation. Theodore Levitt, in his book, *Thinking About Management*, explains that "innovation is an axial characteristic of management. But because organizations evolve to do predictable work, they create procedures and routines that also tend to stifle innovation. Innovation may be systematically fostered by organized R&D and managed change, but mostly fixed procedures and set routines impede change."[6]

While slow to take hold, North American companies are finally realizing that a new skill-set is required to achieve the creativity and innovation that will promote their renewal and competitiveness. As *creativity* replaces productivity as the mantra of business, more companies find themselves fostering, consciously or not, their more feminine dimensions.

Creativity defies logical assessment: it stands apart from the regimentation and measurement that the rational bias of business so admires. The act of creation cannot be programmed, processed, nor standardized. It cannot be categorized, nor arrived at through the traditional business contrivance of specialization. As such, creativity is often regarded with suspicion, or viewed through a filter that stereotypes and demystifies it. Managers and those who are to provide "creativity" usually end up in conflict, shaking their heads in puzzlement and frustration over the inability of each to understand and relate to the other.

To integrate creativity into the basic culture of an organization requires evolving those skills and conditions that are most conducive to its inspiration. These skills spring primarily from our inner feminine force. While creativity requires hard work and intense concentration, it involves, not the linear focus of the rational mind, but rather the amorphous trusting of intuition.

Arthur Koestler, in his masterful book, *The Act of Creation*, writes that "the moment of truth, the sudden emergence of a new insight, is an act of intuition." Intuition is that which connects us to a subconscious wisdom that is not apparent to our rational knowledge base. Intuition operates laterally, reaching outside the conventional and the expected to, in Koestler's words, "uncover, select, re-shuffle, combine and synthesize" what we know into new, innovative combinations.[7]

For a long time, our society has assumed intuition to be female—an inner voice peculiar to women, which usually provided some premonition. In fact, intuition is a feminine skill that fuels creativity in both women and men. Most business people already know and respect intuition, but they disguise it in the masculine phraseology of "gut feeling."

Frenetic activity, no matter how productive, defeats creativity. In the act of creation, *being* is far more important than *doing*, because it allows for the random swirling, mixing and nurturing of the ideas, notions and questions that finally interconnect to ignite inspiration. As "human doings," we too often define ourselves by our activities, and measure our worth through productivity and accomplishment.

The drive to produce and achieve sustains one of the core precepts of business, that "time is money." From this perspective, the notion of *being* is devalued, rendered inadequate and meaningless for not producing something measurable or saleable. Deprived of the right and knowledge to simply be, we are denied the opportunity to explore who we are *essentially*, without the job titles and possessions that superficially define us. As *doings*, we can only relate to other people based on what they do, and not in the fuller terms of who they are, and how they express their humanity. As *doings*, we are also incapable of revering nature simply for what it is, rather than valuing it for what it could be worth in manufacturing and trading terms. So the "doing" not only prevents us from experience the fullness of life, but it also blinds us to the true price of our activities in the currency of natural degradation and loss of human dignity.

Respect For Nature

Throughout history, the feminine energy has been understood to be more intimate with nature, closer to its rhythms and mysteries than the aspects of humanity that are masculine. Psychologists link this unity with nature to the female's own participation in the process of giving life, and nurturing it.

Charlene Spretnak, in her book, *The Politics of Women's Spirituality*, explores this "experience of connectedness." In Spretnak's view, this deep, intuitive awareness of "the oneness of all life" provides the core of a feminine spirituality. Such spirituality is holistic, embracing, rather than excluding or seeking to dominate, the natural world. It also underpins an emerging new movement, which Spretnak terms "eco-feminism."

The linkage between ecology and feminism is very uncomfortable for business, which has not been very open towards, nor respectful, of, either influence. Yet it is this very eco-feminism that can provide the new framework for conducting commerce in a world of limitation and interdependence. Anita Rodrick's highly successful Body Shop toiletries chain is one of the most visible examples of ecologically responsible companies.

The Body Shop has won a very loyal franchise, by offering products that are natural and of high quality, which are developed and manufactured with no animal testing, and packaged in the least damaging format possible. This philosophy enriches in more than monetary ways. The customers, the people who own and manage Body Shop stores, the employees who sell its products and stock its shelves, all share a sense of contributing, in however small a way, to the greater whole.

Despite the logic of such a business approach, eco-feminism remains a threatening concept to mainstream business managers. It will likely have the same destabilizing effects on the institutions of society that Copernicus and Galileo had, because, once again, humans will be displaced from their assumed position at the centre of the universe. Thomas Berry, the mystic who is studying the inherent spirituality of nature, explains. "One of the main characteristics of the emerging ecological or eco-feminist period is the move from a human-centred norm of reality and value to a nature-centred norm. We cannot expect life, the earth, or the universe to fit into our rational human designs of how life, the earth or the universe should function. We must fit our thinking and our actions within the larger process."[8]

The formal movement of eco-feminism is being led by women, but its relevance cuts across the boundaries of sex. Its principles are essentially human, and its lessons have application for even the most masculine of institutions, including politics, religion and business.

Theologian Matthew Fox writes that we must "encourage those who man the upper echelons of the ladder [business establishment] to join the rest of the human race and to start combining love with work, rather than dichotomizing the two spheres of energy. In overcoming this dualism between work and love, action and feeling, it is hoped that some holiness and compassion might re-enter the spheres of economic and political influences..."[9]

By developing our capacity for compassion in business, we are engaging in the process of strengthening the feminine influence, counter-balancing the now-dominant masculine. However, the goal is balance, since the compassion of our feminine dimension will only realize change if it is matched by the drive, ambition and action-orientation of the masculine. Achieving a business paradigm that operates with respect for the interdependence we all share with nature will require both creativity and discipline, both imagination and steadfastness, both the capacity to love and to do.

As women advance through the corporate ranks, the task of achieving this balance in business will get easier. However, the critical need remains, for each of us to develop within ourselves the partnership between the two complimentary, synergistic forces of masculine and feminine. Strengthened by this inner balance, we can then begin to take on the daunting task of building a society and building business institutions that respect and value the two forces equally. The companies that promote and achieve this balance will be stronger, more creative, and better able to withstand the pressures of future competition.

Although business is but one of many institutions that has operated with, and perpetuated, a pronounced male bias, it is important that it use its great and growing influence within our society to effect a new equilibrium. Just as the feminine within each of us has been stifled by the masculine, so, too, females within our society have been generally dominated by males. Sometimes—too often—this domination has been expressed through hostility and violence towards women.

The issue is complex, and obviously beyond the scope of this essay. Nevertheless, it is important to acknowledge that business, because it is essentially based on a meritocracy, probably has the most potential of any current human institution for freeing us all from this debilitating bias against the feminine.

BUSINESS IS SERIOUS BUT ITS PRACTICE DOESN'T HAVE TO BE

Business essentially involves money and power. These tend to be fairly serious pursuits. With the demands of the current competitive marketplace, the seriousness of business has increased considerably. There is greater pressure than ever to perform, to be more productive, more creative, more risk-taking. All of this within business circumstances that are more demanding, less forgiving, and ever more serious.

Seriousness has become a significant burden on many of the managers and leaders of our business enterprises. It should be obvious that such intensity cannot be maintained, that people ultimately burn out or disconnect from such pressures. Just as people become callous to crises that are too frequent, or just as they become immune to urgency that is unrelenting, so, too, are they now tiring of all the seriousness that our society continues to invest in business.

Growing Pressures

The sources of the compounding seriousness are so integral to the way we do business that we've come to assume that they are a natural part of doing business. The very advances in technology and information transfer that have increased productivity, have also become new expressions of the seriousness of business. Cellular phones make us all accessible, nearly everywhere, nearly all the time. People interrupt their walks on the sidewalk, or their meals in a restaurant, or their weekend in the garden, to connect with the office, or a client, or a colleague. The *beep* of beepers is ubiquitous, connecting more people to more messages and more information from the office.

As a society addicted to such technology, it's hard not to be impressed by the achievements of our communications prowess. The cryptic messages that are displayed on beepers have usually bounced off satellites, even if trying to reach people who may be only a few blocks from the source of the transmission. The productivity arsenal is expanding with remarkable products, which, only a few years ago, seemed exotic and rare. Portable fax machines. Portable copiers. Portable computers. Portable VCRs. Impressive technology, which makes it all the easier to keep the serious, urgent, pressing demands of business moving, as we carry our work with us, taking it home, or on the road, or even on vacation.

Most of this technology facilitates the transfer of information. In business, as it has been throughout history, information is power. In an unending quest for power and competitive advantage, our companies have made huge investments in the hardware and software and the training required to collect, sift and summarize vast quantities of data. The explosion of information has created what Saul Wurman calls "information anxiety." There is too much information to know it all. But not to know it is to afford a possible advantage to competitors.

Caught in this dilemma, managers have become information junkies, taking it in as fast as possible, making as much sense as possible of it, before confronting the problems, needs and issues of new information. Not only is there more information, but it is also available faster and faster. The anxiety of knowing too little is multiplied by the reality of not knowing it soon enough. Such anxiety breeds seriousness.

Despite the growth of information, the advances in the technological gadgetry that serves it, and the ever-more-serious attitudes of the work force, much of this information has yet to translate into better understanding of the real problems and issues. Professor Levitt writes, "The more abundant the information, the less meaning it seems to yield. All seems, instead, congestion and confusion."[1]

Ironically, some of the very companies whose business is based on information-processing proved inept at wading through the data to achieve understanding. Xerox, which revolutionized information-processing, lost its market leadership in copiers by failing to understand the specific needs of the business market it dominated. IBM, despite its ability to process copious quantities of data, was so absorbed in what it believed that it failed to learn what the market wanted, first missing the move to PCs, and then missing the move to laptop and notebook portables.

Even the most progressive of customer-driven marketers, including those with the most advanced information systems possible, slip in the transition from processing to understanding. McDonald's exhaustively researches its performance with its customers. It also collects data from its stores on a daily basis, to measure sales and movement of individual products. Yet, for the first time in McDonald's remarkable history, its gears no longer seem to be meshing smoothly with those of the society that it serves. McDonald's has been slow to introduce leaner menu items, despite the growing nutrition sophistication of its franchise. McDonald's has also been slow to adopt the more environmentally benign packaging that society expects today. The misalignment has contributed to a marked slowdown in McDonald's growth.

Packaged-goods marketers have among the richest stores of information available to business. "Usage and Attitude Studies" provide statistical profiles of product performance in the marketplace, yielding important data about who uses which brand, where, why and how, how often, how exclusively, how loyally. Tracking studies quantitatively measure changes in the marketplace wrought by new marketing initiatives of the sponsoring, or of a competing, company. Supermarket scanners can provide daily summaries of which brands sell where, to whom and how often. Warehouse shipment information can pinpoint which products move through the distribution system most quickly and most profitably.

Once again, the companies with the most accurate information are also among those that have made the biggest missteps of recent memory. Coke introduced New Coke because the research data proved that more consumers preferred the new taste. It failed because they did not understand how the hearts of consumers were bound to imagery and tradition, and not just taste.

P&G has a tradition of exhaustive research, and there were, no doubt, ample data supporting the "closer-to-home-made" selling premise of its Duncan Hines cookies. The brand withered and died, in part, because the data did not reveal a real understanding of consumers, who may have judged Duncan Hines to be closer to home-made but, nevertheless, preferred the staler, crunchier texture of Nabisco's "Chips Ahoy."

These companies all take a very serious approach to their information management, yet for them and many others the sophistication of this information-collection technology has not yielded a commensurately more sophisticated understanding of the customer. Often, the opposite has happened. As the conditions of the marketplace have been tracked by ever-more-elaborate and intensive research, the understanding of actual market conditions and factors seems to become more opaque. The more time people spend immersed in the data, the more removed they seem to become from the actual dynamics of the situation they are studying.

The marketing people at IBM launched their latest in a series of assaults on Apple by introducing Microsoft's *Windows 3*, a software programme that allows IBM's PCs to operate with the simplicity and civility of the Macintosh. While the marketing people had lots of research to support their marketing initiatives, incredibly, very few, if any, had ever had actual, hands-on experience with a Mac.

They believed the IBM and *Windows* combination was superior, because the research told them so. From this perspective, actually trying the competitor's machine seemed unnecessary, because the outcome had already been documented by data. It also seemed a bit repugnant, even disloyal, to those immersed in the culture of IBM, to even venture to a Macintosh keyboard to see what the competing experience was like.

IBM has watched as huge, multi-billion-dollar corporations such as Digital and Compaq grow in niches that it miscalculated and undervalued. For the longest time, IBM also chose to ignore Apple, despite that company's growing penetration of the personal-computer segment within the business market. After floundering in its attempts to improve the "user-friendliness" of its PCs, IBM finally teamed with Microsoft to create a software that made IBM machines behave more like Apples. After several false starts, its product seems, finally, to be a match for the easy-to-use Mac, but the marketing people are marching into the marketplace with only faith, and little or no exposure to their competitor's products, or customers.

It seems so obvious. Without intimate experience with a Mac, how can marketing people come to understand the emotional connection Apple users feel with their machines? Without playing with a Mac, how is it possible to understand the joyfulness and creativity that are engendered by its child-like operating format? How effective and how meaningful will the marketing strategies be, if they are created in a vacuum, without understanding the experience that bonds many Mac users to their machines?

It can be assumed that IBM has lots of information supporting its marketing activities, and that it is taking this whole exercise very seriously. However, just as such information may be insulating IBM from the very customers it must try to reach, many other companies are also so immersed in their information-processing and management that they miss the achievement of the fundamental understanding that all this information was geared to in the first place.

Falling Behind While We Sleep

Managers continue to mistake what constitutes true understanding, believing that more scenario-crunching or number-tumbling or report-writing will finally reveal it. A frenetic cycle feeds itself, leading to the "analysis paralysis" that remains so characteristic of North American companies. No wonder the paperless office envisioned only a few years ago has, in fact, become a paper dump.

The anxious drive to absorb and use ever greater amounts of information has been exacerbated by the truly international nature of modern business. On our wired planet, business never stops, never takes a breather. It's disconcerting to realize that we are falling behind, even as we sleep. Over the last few years, CTV, CBC Newsworld, and the American networks have introduced early-morning business news programmes, to help us catch up on what we missed while sleeping. During toast and coffee, in between showering and tooth-brushing, we can track the markets in Asia and Europe, or we can clue in on the latest merger news, or mourn the latest bankruptcy statistics.

Information is the oxygen of business, and we compress and wedge it into stolen moments throughout the day. The commute to work allows for reading the business news, or, increasingly, listening to audio programmes that condense the wisdom of the latest business book onto a sixty-minute cassette. News programming throughout the day updates us on the latest moves on Wall Street or Bay Street, on the price of an ounce of gold or a barrel of oil. Like any other addicts, those of us hooked on information can't get enough, nor can we seem to satisfy the basic need—greater understanding—that is the initial motive for opening ourselves to the information.

Most of this information is important; much of it useful. But without the opportunity for synthesis, reflection, and interconnection, the information itself is of little benefit. While we are very serious about having the information, we don't seem to have the facility or training or self-confidence to explore the meaning behind the data. The more we know we don't know, the greater the potential anxiety.

The global competition of business has added different pressures to the already-frenetic attempts to cope. We are competing with other countries for understanding of the international marketplace, but also, increasingly, we've got to compete on the basis of work ethic. Japan has two percent of the world's population, but it produces ten percent of the world's exports. Its achievements, in large part, are attributable to the deep dedication of its workers and managers.

Jim Impoco wrote about the sometimes-excessive work habits of the Japanese in a "Dateline" feature in a recent issue of *U.S. News & World Report*. "A recent television special said it all: It showed a building in downtown Tokyo with pre-programmed office lights that uniformly shut off at 10:00 p.m.; seconds later, virtually every light in the building came right back on."²

This work ethic has dangerous side-effects, and Impoco's article went on to explore yet another Japanese concept, called *karoshi*. Tetsunojo Uehata, the medical authority who coined the term, defines *karoshi* as "a condition in which psychologically unsound work processes are allowed to continue in a way that disrupts the worker's normal work and life rhythms, leading to a build-up of fatigue in the body and a chronic condition of overwork accompanied by a worsening of pre-existent high blood pressure and a hardening of the arteries, and finally resulting in a fatal breakdown."

Over two thousand cases have been reported in Japan since *karoshi* hot-lines were put in place in 1988. While it's easy to dismiss the extremism of such "death from overwork," the fact remains that the average Japanese clocked-in 2,150 hours of work in 1989, compared to 1,924 for Americans. The mathematics of productivity are very simple. A work force working ten percent more hours produces at least ten percent more. The impact of this ten percent more time compounds considerably, and affords a particularly strong competitive advantage, when the hours spent by those workers are in new plants, with state-of-the-art machinery for design, engineering and manufacture.

For all of their fanaticism in work, the Japanese may not even be the most dedicated of our international competitors. As Stephen Schlosstein points out in *The End of The American Century*, Koreans are devoting themselves to international business development with even greater rigour and discipline than the average Japanese company. Indicative of their pride and work ethic, the Koreans call the Japanese "the lazy Asians."

Malaysians, Chinese and other emerging economies of the Pacific Rim, along with the Spanish and Portugese, Italians and French, are hungrily applying their resources and labour to carve niches in the world's economy. In a such global marketplace, the pace of competition is set by the most avid competitor, and North Americans are increasingly confronting a value system in business that is harsher, more demanding, and even more serious than we've grown accustomed to.

Seriousness Overload

The pressures and seriousness are understandable. Much is at stake for the individual managers, as well as for the companies, communities and countries whose competitiveness is affected by the decisions made by the managers. However, prolonged seriousness and pressure are ultimately debilitating. Like too much of anything, they will hamper rather than enhance performance, and demotivate rather than inspire employees. While it may seem contradictory, the next stage of business success may come from taking business much less seriously. In fact, it may very well be a serious priority for companies to lighten up.

Many of the most talented and creative people at mid-management levels within the North American work force are beginning to recoil from the pressure. This shutting-down of work pressure is partially due to fatigue, but more fundamentally, it reflects a conflict in values between the individuals and the companies they've been dedicated to. People want very much to do well at work. But they increasingly don't want work to become their lives. People want to contribute. But they also need, and now seek, refreshment, renewal and regeneration in other than work activities.

In March 1990, *Fortune* ran a cover story about the growing restlessness of mid-managers. The sweeping restructuring of business during the last decade was intended to get companies closer to customers. Bureaucracies were bashed. Layers were eliminated. While companies improved their responsiveness, those left in companies confronted the difficult challenge of generating more work with fewer people. Personal sacrifice and commitment were expected. The extra hours and intense energy that were traditionally associated with crises or special projects became the everyday norm. The pace of the fast-tracker, the workaholic, became the pace for the majority.

Productivity, for white-collar workers, improved substantially. Now the price for that productivity burst is becoming more apparent, and it seems to be a steep one. People are pulling back, defending themselves emotionally, at a time when we in business need their forward energy and commitment more than ever. "The best people are leading the move away from overwork," argues Robert Kelly, a business professor at Carnegie Mellon University and an expert on corporate restructurings. "It used to be that sixty-hour work-weeks gave you warrior status, but the trend is reversing. People are saying that sixty-hour weeks mean something is wrong with the system or with the person."[3]

Some very bright people are leaving their companies, to take on new jobs that will allow them to better accommodate a balance between their professional and personal goals. Others, like Cathy Cook, who worked with Stephen Jobs, first at Apple and then at Jobs's new company, Next, are walking away from their high-pressure careers and going back to school for additional academic and personal development.

Importantly, those who are staying within companies are also signalling that they've had enough. In a survey by Korn/Ferry International, the large executive-search firm, senior executives at large corporations were shown to be less and less enthusiastic about taking on more work, more responsibility, more pressure. Ten years ago, the poll showed that, among seven hundred senior managers at *Fortune 500* companies, fifty-eight percent wanted more responsibility. Today, only forty-seven percent indicated a willingness to take on the extra pressure that comes with more responsibility.

The exodus of talent, and the withdrawal of commitment by many of those who remain, is a chilling problem confronting business leaders. Yet, for all the thinking and planning that went into the restructuring, surprisingly little attention has been given to the issue of human cost, human adjustment, and human motivation.

The seriousness of the business need has overshadowed the effects and impact on people. And very little in our traditional management training has prepared business leaders for addressing the broader needs of our restive work force. Marilyn Punder-York is a psychologist who counsels executives on Wall Street. She says, "Developing the proper balance is such a fine line and requires so much wisdom. I don't know if enough senior managers have experienced enough trauma in their own personal lives to be that wise."

In attempting to manage the human consequences of all the restructuring that business has been through, managers are scrambling to try new models for alleviating the pressure and rededicating employees. Much of the new thinking involves charging up the culture of an organization to be more supportive of employees, more responsive to customers, more focused on quality. While this notion of culture addresses many of the human needs within companies, the objectives and goals remain very serious.

Hundreds of companies have engaged in the process of writing mission statements, dedicating their respective enterprises to their employees, their customers, and to the pursuit of excellence. Many of these statements have worked to clarify goals and priorities, and to emotionally engage employees. But many of these statements are also so lofty that their achievement is unrealizable, resulting in disappointment and a feeling of inadequacy among employees. Many others, possibly the majority, are simply statements and, because they are not backed by progressive change within companies, employees become disillusioned, frustrated by the apparent gap between what companies preach and what they do. These mission statements, while noble in their intent, have generally served to increase the pressure to perform, and underscore the seriousness of all that has to do with business.

Breaking out of this debilitating spiral of pressure requires new thinking, a new approach to the dilemma of getting not only more work, but also better work out of fewer and fewer people. The conundrum does not have a rational solution, so again we must explore the intuitive dimensions of human nature to discover the possibility of new models for company development.

Strengthening Competitiveness Through Humour

One untapped source of motivation, inspiration and energy may be the human capacity for *humour*.

Most business people, in their business mode of thinking, are highly suspicious of humour. By evoking laughter, humour seems to trivialize, to diminish the importance, the seriousness, of the issue at hand. Humour is seen as a distraction, a time-consuming diversion that is inconsistent with the new priorities of urgency and productivity. People who engage in humour often carry the stigma of not being serious about their careers, of not focusing on the serious demands of their jobs. Everyone likes to laugh, and humour has a place in life but, by and large, it has yet to find a place in the companies and corporations that consume so much of our time and energy.

That's too bad. Humour slips into virtually every human situation, because it is so much a part of our nature, and by maintaining it a distance, business is depriving itself of an important dimension of the human experience. Humour provides release. Laughter is not only an expression of joy, but also a healthy way to relieve the pressures of stress and of the inevitable disappointments we confront every day. The healing power of humour is now being used in progressive health-care institutions, particularly to help seriously ill patients work through the difficult, depressing process of recovery. Unleashed in the work environment, humour can release the built-up anxiety caused by unrelenting deadlines, ever-higher quality expectations, and more intense competitive pressures.

Beyond its therapeutic benefit, humour also exercises the very faculties and skills that contribute to creativity. The mental activity of humour involves surprise, discontinuity, and the gymnastic connection of new conclusions, new realizations. The same thought processes apply to creative thinking in business. Disparate information is synthesized and reconnected, to come to a new conclusion. Humour sets up an expectation, and then surprises with an unexpected resolution. Arthur Koestler, in his book, *The Act of Creation*, calls this process bisociation. Two different thoughts or experiences are interconnected in a surprising way, which reveals a new truth or insight.

The outcome of humour may be very funny, but the process itself provides important, valuable lessons for achieving greater productivity. Koestler says that "when two independent matrices of perception or reasoning interact with the other the result is either a *collision* ending in laughter, or their *fusion* in a new intellectual synthesis, or their *confrontation* in an aesthetic experience."[4]

The same process that makes us laugh is that which also helps us see things in a new way. Ideas for new products, for product improvements, for innovative marketing plans, for proactive service to customers, flow from the same mental faculty that finds humour in incongruous situations.

Koestler defines creativity as "the defeat of habit by originality." Much of the productivity-wastage in companies is the result of habitual thinking and habitual modes of behaviour. With fewer people to do more work, a great fluidity is required. People must be flexible, moving without hesitation into situations that may be beyond their traditional job descriptions, in order to complete a project or satisfy a customer. Such fluidity requires a capacity for making new connections, for embracing the ambivalence of change. A mind that is open to the discontinuous connections of humour will likely be open to the discontinuity of the modern business environment.

The encoding of humour in corporate culture does not mean that business objectives are taken less seriously, or that goals are dismissed in laughter. As Levi's has shown, by acknowledging the human need and capacity for fun, people are ultimately more productive, more loyal, more dedicated to the cause of the company. Business needs are seriously attended to, but within an environment that respects people's need and willingness to have fun, joke around and play, as well as work hard, sweat and achieve. The people in such circumstances are engaged on a deeper level. More of their energy and commitment is available to the companies they work for, because more of their needs are being satisfied.

Humour can play a very important role in bringing people together and bonding them to a cause or project. The team that worked so hard, long hours under excruciating pressure, to create the first Macintosh computer, accepted their difficult assignment because they had so much fun doing it. The Apple environment described by Frank Rose often seems like a college fraternity house. Such collegiate humour will not work for all businesses, but it underscores the degree of sacrifice that employees are willing to undertake when they truly enjoy what they're doing.

As corporations continue to shrink management levels, there will obviously be fewer and fewer opportunities for promotion for many of the senior and mid-level executives within those companies. In a traditional company with a traditional structure, such limitations will result in the frustration, and likely loss, of some very valuable resources for whom there is simply no room for advancement.

To maintain these human assets, with their expensive experience and skills, companies must evolve their culture. The predominant ethic of internal competition cannot be maintained in flatter companies, without damaging many people for the advancement of a few. Therefore, a new ethic, one that blends our natural inclination to compete with the growing need within companies for co-operation, must be evolved.

Humour is a catalyst for co-operation. It breaks down barriers, cutting across the usually rigid boundaries of rank, department and division. Humour smooths interaction. It breaks the ice and builds camaraderie.

Some companies are taking radical steps to inject some humour into their operations. *The Globe and Mail* carried a report about Minneapolis-based National Computer Systems, which has hired what they call an "Elation Strategist," to help lighten up its corporate culture. As the company comic, the Elation Strategist is providing both fun and new methods for interaction, which are helping to improve communication.

"Employing humour in the workplace is not unheard of," says Bob McGarey, director of the Human Potential Center in Austin, Texas, "but it's not widely used, partly because people think that they have to be serious at work, that laughter is inappropriate. But humour enhances creativity, and with Japan breathing down our necks, we need creativity."[5]

The time invested in activating humour within companies is not wasted. The spark it brings to organizations that have it, the greater commitment it engenders, make humour a valid productivity booster. Like everything else, the time devoted to creating a culture of fun must be in balance. It's there to offset pressure and, in excess, humour can create more pressure, by getting in the way of performance. Balancing the drive to do with the ability to laugh may be the formula for business to do both more and better.

The nurturing of humour within companies cannot be dictated. Nor will it be easily measured or evaluated. Humour is, by definition, spontaneous, so all we can do as managers is create an environment that allows it to ignite and combust. People will come to realize that they need not divorce work from fun. They will come to appreciate that the two actually complement each other, producing work that is more satisfying, in a company culture that is more enriching, more humanly fulfilling. It is ultimately liberating to realize that taking our work seriously does not preclude having a good time.

USING HISTORY
TO PLAN THE
FUTURE

Companies, and the business people who run them, are obsessed with the future. Strategic plans try to gaze through the fog of what may happen, building hypotheses on assumptions, to establish likely scenarios for a company, for the coming five- or ten-year period. General managers and marketing people work in smaller increments, extrapolating this year's performance and activities into next year's plan. Economists track broader trends and cycles, studying GNP, exports, employment, and then using complicated theories to try to predict what will happen next quarter, next fiscal year, next decade.

Although it never appears in their job descriptions, clairvoyance is a much-sought-after attribute in CEOs. Knowing what will happen, or at least guessing right, is part of what is expected from business leaders. Investment in R&D, plant and equipment, marketing and sales, are all based on an expectation that they will yield significant return, long into the future. Leaders whose instincts about the future are more often right than wrong are celebrated for their insight, and for the grit it takes to take the educated gamble on what is not yet known. Those who are more often wrong are failures.

To stack the odds in their favour, more and more business people are surrounding themselves with consultants and specialists, who process information about the present to predict the future. Alvin Toffler's *Future Shock* and *Future Stream*, John Naisbett's *Megatrends* and *Megatrends 2000* are examples of popular best-sellers that feed the nearly insatiable need to know what may happen next.

Every year, countless seminars, newsletters and magazines spew out predictions on what will happen next. How the stock market will perform, how consumers will behave, how technology will change operations, how energy shortages will create new opportunities for new products, are among the hundreds of topics covered. These glimpses into the future, however fleeting, are incorporated, with religious fervour, into the plans and activities of virtually every company.

Future-gazing is not restricted to business, but is evident throughout our whole society. Late-night television is filled with half-hour commercial programmes that not only predict the future, but promise consumers great glory and achievement in it. By buying into a system, consumers can turn their dreary present into a dynamic future, with millions to be earned by buying real estate with no money down, with weight to be lost without giving up one's favourite foods, with facial wrinkles to be faded and windows cleaned by magical potions, which may, in fact, be interchangeable. The premise of this programming, and so much other commercial advertising, is that the future can be managed to one's personal advantage.

The Future Is The Past Expressing Itself

All of this future-thinking has obscured a basic lesson of human experience. That lesson is that much of what is to be learned about the future can be found by thinking about the past. History remains largely an academic discipline. Journalists will use it for reference, when commenting on current events, but business people generally avoid the idea of historical study.

The bias towards mastering the future is so strong that reflecting on the past seems quaint and out of step with the gung-ho, "we can take on anything" attitude that is so admired among business managers. History seems to be a passive, regressive preoccupation, while business needs aggressive action to move ahead.

In forsaking history, many people in business are, to paraphrase philosopher George Santayana, "condemned to repeat its mistakes." Yet, while most large corporations have developed economics departments within their structures, none have encoded the valuable knowledge about the company, its market, customers and competitors into company history departments. While major companies, such as banks, stock-brokerage firms, car manufacturers, computer conglomerates, and other manufacturing and service groups have appointed Chief Economists, none have announced a Chief Historian.

This orientation to the future, at the expense of the past, is characteristic of our North American industrial culture. While Europe and Asia have built their industrial institutions on a platform of thousands of years of history, North Americans developed industry at the same time that we forged our countries. In Canada's case, the railroads and phone companies were used to create a nation, not simply connect it.

With no history to ground our culture, we drew from the future to define our national characters. North Americans are the world's optimists, looking ahead, believing for generations that the future will be brighter for anyone who works hard enough to earn it. For generations, the vast frontiers of the American West and the Canadian North fuelled the attitude that ever more was possible, that land, trees, minerals, and fossil fuels were inexhaustible.

Operating on beliefs based on the unlimited potential of the future, without reference to the lessons of history, has created the quagmire that business is in today. The depletion of natural resources, the pollution of our rivers, lakes and air, are examples of business thinking that assumes an unending source of future replenishment. That we continue to pile up spent nuclear fuel, without having mastered its dangerous radiation, is only possible because of our nearly blind faith that some development, some technology in the future, will solve the scientific puzzle of safe disposal.

Such irresponsible behaviour is only possible when a society is detached from the lessons of history, when its naïve beliefs in its future obscure the judgement and wisdom of practical experience. Common sense, which distills collective wisdom from history and experience, is in such short supply in today's business environment that it deserves to be renamed "uncommon sense."

Hidden Lessons

Failure to respect history, to learn its lessons, has seriously weakened North America's economic competitiveness. The savings-and-loan crisis facing our free-trade partner, the United States, will cost at least a half-trillion dollars to contain, and probably more. Large American banks are also in trouble. Some, such as the Bank of New England, have been taken over by the federal deposit insurance, in an attempt to stem the staggering losses.

The dangerous unwinding of the American financial sector is the result of the deregulation imposed during the Reagan era. While the theory of deregulation is desirable for the flexibility and initiative it promotes, the practice of deregulation only works if one remembers the lessons that prompted the regulation in the first place. The irresponsible and unethical practices that so depleted the banking system in the 1980s are very similar to those of the 1920s. In losing our understanding of the lessons of the Great Depression, we've created the circumstances for almost repeating it.

The loans banks made to the Third World in the 1970s were based on optimistic assessments of future economic development. Failure to understand the history of economic and political development in those Third World markets led U.S. and Canadian banks to write off billions in unrecoverable debts. The double jolt of failed loans in the 1970s and disorganized deregulation in the 1980s have drained the American banking system, leaving it exposed, vulnerable, and in need of taxpayer bailouts.

This, in turn, has weakened the overall competitiveness of our economy, since dollars used to make up for past mistakes are unavailable to invest in the research, technology and training that yield real standard-of-living improvements. As capital becomes scarcer and more expensive, our companies face the comparative disadvantage of having to take on debt in more expensive foreign markets. The cumulative effect of squandered billions has been a serious erosion in the competitive position of North American companies.

Banks are not alone in under-appreciating the lessons of history. The advertising industry spent the last ten years in a frenzy of merger-and-acquisition activity. The whole industry was restructured, with buy-outs, sell-outs, and conglomerate-building proceeding at a staggering pace. In less than ten years, only two, of an original eight, Canadian agencies have survived in the top-ten ranking—the rest have been merged or subsumed into larger British or American groups.

The fallacy of conglomeration was revealed during the 1970s, when companies like IT&T, built by Harold Geneen, sputtered and fragmented. History shows that diversification is ultimately a distraction, that it dilutes management attention and impedes focus on the core issues of a single business.

Saatchi & Saatchi and WPP, the biggest conglomerate-builders in advertising, were each so fixed on their future vision of an international communications business, that they failed to heed these lessons. Advertising agencies, PR companies, packaging design, even human-resource companies, were purchased and grafted onto each other, until the two giants had created the two largest communications groups in the world.

As was to be expected in an industry that sells creativity, most of the acquired companies did not share a common vision, process or work ethic. Agency cultures are very much the product of the people who create and manage them. Unlike competing chewing-gum companies, which use the same technology to make their products, and the same trucks to distribute them, the diversity of advertising agencies is genetically encoded.

So, while merging agencies sometimes achieved the economies of scale that justified the financing of the acquisition, more often than not, it neutralized the strengths of the individual agencies. Distinctiveness and corporate personality, fundamental underpinnings of the agency business, vanished. Clients, such as Procter & Gamble, Warner-Lambert, Colgate-Palmolive, Ford, IBM, and many others, rebelled, moving hundreds of millions of dollars in business out of the merged agencies.

The financial plans for the purchases made by Saatchi, WPP, and many other agencies, must have seemed very sound to the banks, brokers and stockholders who backed them. Again, this suggests a failure to absorb the wisdom of history. In the midst of the 1980s expansion, the longest ever recorded, it became almost unpatriotic to question how long the economic boom would extend.

Despite debt, despite junk bonds, despite the chilling mini-crash of October 1987, the herd mentality of the investment community remained convinced that the next year's growth would follow the pattern of the current year. That such assumptions fly in the face of historical cycles did not stem the flow of financing, until companies like Saatchi and WPP hit the hard wall of reality, and began to have trouble meeting their payment obligations.

A report, published in *The Economist* several years ago, showed that the majority of mergers don't work out, and don't fulfil the financial or performance objectives that prompted the acquisition or sell-out. Hundreds of the mergers implemented in the last decade were, therefore, completed on a faulty premise.

The money used for many of those mergers will never be recovered, meaning that, again, the economy is deprived of capital for regeneration. Saddled with so much debt, many companies are only barely making financing payments. Investments in people, plant and technology must be delayed to meet debt obligations, resulting in a further loss of competitiveness. Thousands of divisions have been sold to quench the thirst for cash, of these very dry companies.

Important assets, such as the landmark New York City skyscrapers of Exxon, ABC, Mobil, and Citicorp, were sold. And countless plants in hundreds of communities were closed. While the managers who negotiated these often-unsound transactions landed with "golden parachutes," thousands of displaced workers lost their means of livelihood and their prospects for security.

The disregard for history runs so deep in business that we sometimes don't implement the lessons of our own experience. Much of the pioneering work in statistical quality management was done by General Motors, General Electric, AT&T and IBM. The science of quality was pushed considerably further by Americans such as Dr. Demming and Juran. But, by the mid-sixties, the growth in the economy had caused companies like GM to become complacent about quality. Consumers seemed to buy whatever the manufacturers made.

While Demming was largely ignored in North America throughout the fifties, sixties and seventies, his principles became the impetus for the Japanese practice of "continuous improvement." Applying the principles for quality management defined and developed by North Americans, many Japanese and European companies were to eventually overtake North Americans in setting the standards for quality in products—everything from cars, to cameras, to microwave ovens. North Americans are now scrambling to learn lessons from competitors who have won in the marketplace, using strategies and tactics we developed. Such is the humbling fate of a society or an institution that loses its sense of history.

History And Human Connectedness

Business leaders have become more sensitive to the importance of culture in the management of their operations. Production and productivity define what a company does. Culture defines how. The style, attitude and behaviour of an organization spring from its culture. The values that inspire and regulate how a company conducts itself are encoded in that culture. History, since it has helped mould the attitudes and values that influence the culture's expression, is an important contributor.

Most people who are happy in their work environment are reacting to the company culture, and its receptivity and responsiveness to their individual contributions. Many people are proud of their companies, just as they are proud of their communities and countries. There is an opportunity to make the culture of a company even more vital to its people, by developing a deeper, more passionate understanding of its history.

Max Depree, of Herman Miller, provides anecdotal examples from his company's history, of special people or special circumstances that have helped create corporate character. Herman Miller is famous for the innovation and high quality of its furniture design—many of its office furnishings are on permanent display at the Museum of Modern Art in New York. Depree believes that the creativity in his company comes from "enabling others to reach their potential—both their personal potential and their corporate potential."[1]

This attitude is deeply ingrained in the history of Herman Miller. In the company's early days, a millwright died. While offering condolences to the family, the management of Herman Miller discovered that this man had written poetry, some of it very beautiful and evocative. Depree asks, "In our efforts to understand corporate life, what is it we should learn from this story? In addition to all of the ratios and parameters and bottom lines, it is fundamental that leaders endorse a concept of persons. This begins with an understanding of the diversity of people's gifts and talents and skills."

Herman Miller has the most productive work force in its industry, generating the highest net income per employee. Such tangible business results flow from a workforce that is highly motivated by an innovative compensation structure, one that is also nurtured and supported by a strong corporate culture. A key element in that highly motivating culture is that the lessons of the company's history are applied every day.

That history is honoured, studied, and brought to life, so that it has relevance to all the people in the company. Depree writes, "The simple act of recognizing diversity in corporate life helps us connect to the great variety of gifts that people bring to the work and service of the organization. Diversity allows each of us to contribute in a special way, to make our special gift a part of the corporate effort."

The process of honouring its history is an active one, and it's maintained at Herman Miller by what Depree calls "tribal storytelling." While companies are groups of people who work together to achieve a set of goals, a tribe is a more holistic unit, one that provides enrichment for the individual, as well as for the group.

Tribes are bound together not only by a common interest, but also by shared values. These values are transmitted not via mission statement, but rather by stories—the legends, tall tales, acts of heroism that define the essence of an organization. Unlike mission statements, which appeal mostly to the head, and marginally to the heart, stories engage the imagination, and involve the full range of human emotions in the lessons or principles of the tale being told. In relating to stories, people are acknowledging their relevance to what they themselves are doing. And, through this connection, they are able to feel the added commitment of participating in history's unfolding. As Depree suggests, "Though there may be only a few tribal storytellers, it's everyone's job to see that things as unimportant as manuals and light bulbs don't replace them."

The Overwhelming Of Wisdom By Youth

Creating a corporate culture that is respectful of history is, in many ways, at odds with the pronounced bias within our society for youth. Energy, drive and determination, the characteristics of youth, are highly valued by companies. People with these attributes are promoted quickly, given opportunities to prove themselves, make their marks, and demonstrate their potential leadership abilities.

In weighing ambition versus experience, ambition often wins. Perhaps it is a reflection of our consumer-oriented, highly disposable society, that the new is so widely preferred to the proven. Whatever the reasons, this fixation on the new and the young has deprived many companies of the strength of their own histories, and the wisdom of their most senior executives.

This is not to argue that youth should be penalized. On the contrary, as many companies have been hurt by CEOs who stayed on too long as by the appointment of too youthful a manager. The demands of today's fast-changing business environment are generally more readily met by younger managers, those with the flexibility, openness and energy to respond to its shifting opportunities, new exigencies, and high technology. Companies benefit greatly from this youthfulness, despite, as Theodore Levitt points out, its obvious shortcomings. "Because they are not likely to have the wisdom that only deep experience confers, they may be more easily bamboozled by plausible simplifiers and elegant technocrats, and misled by their own hubris."[2]

Balancing youth with seniority, energy with experience, ambition with wisdom, is the task of every leader. The issue, therefore, is not whether to contain youth or promote it, but how to imbue all managers with a sense of history, a context for making decisions and feeding the living culture of a company.

Using History To Competitive Advantage

In their book, *Thinking in Time*, Richard Neustandt and Ernest May explore how government leaders have used their knowledge of history to help them make decisions. During the Cuban missile crisis of 1962, President John Kennedy and his staff used actual historical materials, and a very strong historical intuition, to manage that very difficult, very dangerous situation.

In the initial stages of the crisis, Kennedy felt that he did not know enough about Russia and Cuba, so he personally ordered "the CIA to produce a detailed review of the history of Soviet military aid to Cuba." This history provided a context, a point of reference, for the Kennedy team to use while evaluating their options. Neustandt and May write that Kennedy also "showed an uncommon interest in the history in the heads of the adversary...He asked, in effect, Why is he doing this to me?"

The brinksmanship displayed by President Kennedy, which led to the successful resolution of the crisis, was, in part, the result of his understanding of the national, political and personal history of his opponent. Neustandt and May conclude, "Kennedy had the wherewithal for reasoned and prudent choice, and resort to history helped produce it."[3]

While the stakes in business are on a very different scale than those faced by President Kennedy, the use of history as an active tool in decision-making has equal validity. To study the histories of competing companies, and to gain an insight into the histories of their leaders, is critically important. For example, many price wars have been waged, often with devastating results for the entire industry affected, because managers in one company underestimated the fortitude and motivations of those in another. With a sense of history, both for competitors and companies they lead, managers can devise strategies that are more precise, more insightful, and ultimately more effective.

Another lesson from *Thinking in Time* is that history is not only about the past, but also about the future. "In unusual degree, Kennedy and Excomm (his executive committee) saw the issues before them as part of a time sequence beginning long before the onset of crisis and continuing into an increasingly indistinct future. The more Kennedy and Excomm deliberated, the more they weighed the consequences, and the more they shifted from the simple question of what to do now to the harder question: How will today's choices appear when they are history?"

For managers, understanding their roles and decisions to be integral parts of a much larger continuity can help develop the longer-term perspective that our companies need to prepare themselves to compete in the coming century. The discipline of understanding the past carries within it the possibility of better understanding the future.

The relevance and immediacy of history to our modern lives was very recently demonstrated by director Ken Burns's documentary, *The Civil War*, which ran, to such critical acclaim, on PBS during the fall of 1990. Burns used very simple images, mostly still photographs, to chronicle the story of the war. The commentary was, for the most part, based on first-person accounts derived from the letters, diaries, and newspaper stories of the day.

The nine episodes turned the theory about television programming upside down. With no video action, and with material from diaries that is usually judged too boring for TV, Burns produced a riveting, highly evocative film. PBS achieved its highest ratings ever. For many viewers, both north and south of the Mason-Dixon Line, and both north and south of the forty-ninth parallel, this was the best television experience ever.

In responding to the unexpected public involvement and acclaim, Burns explained that the history of the Civil War was not only about the past, but about the present as well. The issues of race, of women entering the work force, of families torn apart by divergent beliefs, of the growing dependence of the economy on the military, of revolutionary technological development that changed the face of war, of Wall Street speculation, of corruption in politics, of profiteering by businesses supplying materials to the government, of regional rights, of the powers of the federal government—all of these dimensions of the Civil War period preoccupy, concern and affect us today.

Without a passionate understanding of our history, the issues we face in our countries and in our companies today will seem isolated and disconnected. And without a respect for our history, the solutions we prescribe for these issues will lack the wisdom of the past and, therefore, relevance for the future. Burns speaks about President Lincoln in the present tense, because his love and admiration for that president is real and active today. Similarly, Max Depree speaks of the history of his company in the present tense, because, for him and the people at Herman Miller, who they are is, in so many ways, defined by who they were.

Resorting to history will not diminish the hard work and anguish that accompany most major decisions in business. The intensifying pressures of the competition, and the shifting needs and values of the customers will challenge business executives to keep their focus on the current marketplace. Historical understanding will not replace smartly thought-out market research. Historical wisdom will not automatically solve the puzzle of the future.

But a profound regard for history can be a valuable complement to the other tools of modern business. It provides a context for research, which may help unveil deeper insights, or interconnect information to create a deeper understanding. It also provides a broader sense of purpose, a system of values and beliefs, which, when thoroughly absorbed, can prepare companies for the difficult demands of even the most tumultuous future.

The process of instilling understanding, respect and even love of history can take many forms.

Corporate historians may be appointed, and elevated in importance to the same stature accorded economists, researchers and strategic planners. In this way, the lessons of history can play an active role in company decision-making and planning.

Immersion programmes for new employees and training programmes for employee development can also be embellished with more history of the company, its competitors, and the industry in general. This will help ensure that a historical consciousness is nurtured and embedded throughout the organization.

History can be brought to life and made vital, made current, by paying attention to the traditions that express it. Company birthday parties, yearly awards presentations, "tribal storytelling," company newsletters and annual reports are all vehicles for celebrating history and amplifying its importance to people throughout the company.

A respect for history is ultimately expressed as respect for the people who made it. When Akio Morita, the co-founder of Sony, stepped down as chairman, he assumed a new, less-defined role, which he called Company Philosopher. Morita embodies so much of the creative spirit of Sony, is so wise in the ways of world trade, that a traditional and arbitrary retirement would deprive the company of a very valuable resource. By detaching himself from the day-to-day operation of the company, he is making room for a new generation of executives to take charge. But, as a Company Philosopher, he remains available to the company and its many constituents, to provide ideas and inspiration. Morita is there to provide the wisdom of the past, to help make sense of the opportunities of the future.

Again, it is to be responsible for what is to come, that we in business should hone our understanding of what preceded us. Daniel J. Boorstin, historian and the Librarian of Congress Emeritus, writes, "History should be our cautionary science. Our past is only a little less uncertain than our future, and like the future, it is always changing, always revealing and concealing. We might better think of Prophecy as History in Reverse."[4]

LEADERSHIP THROUGH FOLLOWING

These are times of transition, what John Naisbett, the author of several books about "megatrends," calls a "time of parenthesis." The whole of our society, our world, as we've come to see it, is caught up in a massive, historical shift. Such eras of transition have occurred throughout history, but these usually happened over centuries, sometimes over generations. In our case, the shift is happening, dramatically and irrevocably, within a single lifetime. The unthinkable often becomes almost instantaneously commonplace. The Berlin Wall falls. Syria joins the U.S. to fight Iraq. The United States, the world's largest creditor for generations, becomes the world's largest debtor virtually overnight.

We are so caught up in change, so conditioned to its traumas and surprises, that we've become somewhat complacent about it. Each more outrageous manifestation of change numbs us a little bit more to it. In so many ways, we don't expect constancy anymore, except the constancy of change.

While we've shown remarkable resilience and adaptability, we've been so involved in dealing with the day-to-day priorities of change that we've yet to master an understanding of its full implications. Many of the beliefs and values that provided an anchor for our lives, both personal and professional, have lost their relevance and applicability. Yesterday's certitudes have quickly become today's fallacies. And the new beliefs, new anchors, have yet to be defined, yet to be tested to ensure that they deserve the full weight of our conviction.

The Leadership Crisis

Within this dynamic, often exhilarating, sometimes debilitating environment, we who lead businesses are being challenged to define new models for our enterprises, and new paradigms for the leadership we exercise. The philosophies and structures that supported our companies in the past have shown that they can become the millstones that impede competitive performance in the present.

For example, the pyramidal system of control, so essential to achieving the volumes of the mass market, has become an anachronism and a liability, defeating the innovation and pursuit of quality demanded by the marketplace of diversity and customization. The leaders of business, therefore, face not only the task of maintaining the day-to-day viability and vitality of our companies, but also the formidable challenge of making sense of all this change, to create new systems and new structure to provide meaning and understanding for the people who follow.

Leadership in business, as in politics, religion and academia, is in critically short supply. Many people haven't noticed the shortage, because we've generally come to believe in business that management is a substitute for leadership. How better to wring operational order out of the swirling chaos of change than by applying the discipline of management? The circular process of planning, strategizing, implementing and learning, seems ideally suited for wrestling change, for controlling its effects, for measuring its implications.

After decades of encoding the principles of management, we are encountering circumstances that are showing up its shortcomings in effectively dealing with change. Lost markets, environmental degradation, closed plants, falling market-share, disaffected labour, dwindling productivity, and declining technological achievement are causing us to question the basic tenets of our management dogma.

John P. Kotter, a professor at the Harvard Business School who has researched and written extensively about leadership, characterizes the problem as one of being "over-managed and under-led."

In his book, *The Leadership Factor*, Kotter writes, "It would help greatly if we could take the concept of the professional manager who can manage anything and drive a stake through its ever-so-resilient heart. That concept is still very influential today, despite some people's efforts to demonstrate the problems with it. It haunts MBA education. It influences how managers think about their careers [sometimes in the most destructive ways]. It is used to justify tragic staffing decisions, some of the more outrageous acquisitions by raiders, and many of the least successful diversification efforts seen in the last two decades."[1]

Even as the shortcomings of management become more obvious and more pronounced, we in business persist in adhering to its strictures. We most often struggle to control change, to contain it, rather than embracing it for the new opportunities it will yield. Robert Waterman Jr., the McKinsey consultant and co-author of the landmark business book, *In Search of Excellence*, has studied change and the challenge of corporate renewal. He writes, "Most of us fear change. Even when our minds say change is normal, our stomachs quiver at the prospect. But for leaders and managers today, there is no choice but to change."[2]

We are in a struggle, not only with the fluid circumstances surrounding our companies, but with the institutions of management which, with their rigidity and drive to institutionalize, are inappropriate and ineffective in inducing change. For Waterman, "the complacent manager merely presides," while what we really need is for business people "to engage in a daily effort to fight corporate entropy, to welcome change, to uproot habits, and to use renewal to build the future." Such dynamic participation in change cannot be managed. It can only be realized through leadership.

A Shifting Model For Leadership

Leadership is hard to define, although it is often apparent in those who have it. In simple terms, leadership is about seeing things and encouraging people to accept what's seen. We often confuse charisma and power with leadership and, while both may be present in leaders, the essence of leadership is to create an understanding that others adopt and act upon. These two dimensions of leadership—the ability to see and the ability to draw others forward—involve a rare combination of introspective and outward-directed skills.

As the role of business changes within our society, the role of the leadership of our business institutions is also changing. Communities, cities, and nations themselves, rely on the companies that make up their economy to fuel prosperity and standard-of-living improvements. And the whole ecology of our planet is now affected by the process of business, as it consumes more and more of our resources for raw materials and energy, and as it leaves ever greater quantities of pollutants and toxins in its wake.

So important is business to our modern world that the leadership of individual companies can no longer be viewed in isolation from the whole. We are all affected by decisions made in companies that we don't work for, don't buy products from and, often, don't even know exist.

Thousands of industries, which are invisible to those of us who live along the Great Lakes, spill their waste into what, downstream, becomes our drinking water. We are, therefore, intimately linked with those companies. Our health and well-being is connected to companies far removed from our day-to-day consciousness, and to managers unknown to us. We are deeply and personally affected by their ethics, practices and efficiencies. Although we are not shareholders, we are profoundly dependent on their business acumen, since their ability to generate capital correlates to their ability to make the plant improvements that reduce pollution. We may not know their employees, but we are all touched by their skill, training and commitment.

Such interconnection and interdependence mean that the leaders of companies are accountable to a far wider constituency than traditionally acknowledged. Beyond shareholders and employees, beyond banks and labour unions, the leader of the modern business enterprise is responsible to the broadest community within which the company operates. Whether we are comfortable with this notion or not, the leaders of business have no choice but to accept that business has become too important to our society, with too much impact on our natural environment, to have its authority and responsibility segregated.

Marina Whitman, a vice-president and chief economist at General Motors, is now responsible for its public affairs. She speaks on behalf of the largest corporation in the world, one that has defined many of the structures and procedures of traditional management, and that has frankly stumbled in trying to renew and revitalize itself. Whitman believes that a new balance must be struck between the goals of the corporation and those of its natural and social home. "...profit is the ante. If you don't make profits you can't stay in the game and you can't do anything else useful. But it's also clear that society does not regard that as the only goal. There is a kind of implicit social compact under which the corporation, businesses exist, in which they are expected to do a good deal more than that, and are expected to fulfil a great many goals."[3]

The issue of a social compact is, at this point, only tenuously established. Many companies have dedicated themselves to their communities, and have embarked on a variety of social programmes to give back some of what they take out from communities. But these initiatives remain largely incidental to the primary objectives of profit delivery. During the current recession, even the most generous of businesses have pulled back in their support of charities and social programmes. This is prudent from a business perspective, but it demonstrates how that perspective has yet to evolve to embrace the broader responsibilities of business.

Many of the people who lead companies, and many of the economists, like Milton Friedman, who shape the thinking of our leadership, persist in believing that, "the sole social purpose of a corporation is to make profit." History will judge this view as shallow and dangerous.

One of the telling lessons in Ken Burns's highly evocative film about the American Civil War is that rigid, seemingly immutable beliefs become obsolete and irrelevant, as the moral sensibility of society shifts. The rebel Confederates fought with such tenacity, because they believed they were morally right to perpetuate slavery. Jefferson Davis and Robert E. Lee were learned gentlemen with very educated sensibilities, and they believed God was on their side, in institutionalizing the repression of one race and the elevation of another.

Just as this view has become morally repugnant to our society, future generations will likely regard the segregation of business interests from those of society as simplistic and irresponsible. Just as slavery has become totally unacceptable in human affairs, the slavery our businesses impose on our environment, the mastery we exercise over other species, will probably be as incomprehensible and distasteful to the children from whom, as the people of our First Nations say, "we are borrowing this earth."

The leadership required for a world of interdependence is very different from that which is focused singularly on winning in the competitive marketplace. While drive and determination are the valued attributes of a competitor, empathy and the willingness to share are the principle characteristics of accommodation. While specialization and authority have been the primary vehicles for competing, a much broader, more generalist type of leader must emerge to manage the complex exigencies of interdependence.

Enhancing Performance Through Sharing

This is the crux of our leadership challenge. Control must give way to sharing. Authority must give way to service. So, not only must we manage the new, we must also adopt new ways of managing it.

Forging a leadership based on a more holistic view of business is not a deterrent to effectiveness, and productivity, and profit. On the contrary, it's essential to the continued viability and overall competitiveness of our business organizations. *BusinessWeek* reported recently on the divergent strategies used by companies to manage labour relations. Some companies, like Eastern Airlines and Hormel & Co., followed Ronald Reagan's lead, confronting and busting unions, as he did with the air-traffic controllers in the early 1980s. Others, like Ford, established more co-operative relations with unions, believing that more teamwork would boost productivity. This latter approach shares powers, shares accountability, and shares rewards, to elicit the fuller commitment and participation of the whole employee group.

William Cooke, a Wayne State University professor of industrial relations, surveyed fifty-six unionized manufacturers that took one or the other approach, and he came up with some startling, yet commonsensical conclusions. "Employers that had tried teamwork—about half the sample—reported a 19% increase over the decade in value added per employee. The combative employers reported a 15% decline."[4]

This is a remarkable achievement, providing a significant advantage in terms of competitiveness and profitability. Sharing breaks down the barriers between leaders and managers, between managers and employees, between company and customers, and between company and suppliers. Sharing does more than empower; it equalizes. It makes everyone important. Yet, the results of sharing remain a surprise, and its implications difficult for most companies to accept and implement. Sharing seems altruistic and immeasurable, when, in fact, it is the more sensible and inspiring way of bonding people together to achieve a common goal.

Since leaders have spent their careers working hard to achieve their heightened responsibility, it is emotionally contradictory to relinquish it, and disperse widely the control and power that accompany responsibility. Defeating such deeply ingrained biases and traditions is tough. While the pressures from society, competitors and employees will activate some change, the real transformation of companies will only happen as the leaders themselves undergo personal and profound transformations of values, skills and ambitions.

Joseph Boyett and Henry Conn, who work for the international consulting firm A.T. Kearney, Inc., have written a provocative book, entitled *Workplace 2000*, which details the changes they envision and recommend for North American companies to thrive in the emerging marketplace of tomorrow. The priority in virtually every industry will be to help employees actualize their fullest potential, so that the full spectrum of skills and commitment can be applied to the innovation, quality and service demands of customers.

Boyett and Conn don't believe that today's business schools and training programmes are preparing the types of leaders that companies dedicated to their human capital will need. "The skills required of the *Workplace 2000* leader may be found among the historians, philosophers, and political scientists, and perhaps even among the psychologists, sociologists and English majors with a grounding in the great literature of the world."[5]

What Boyett and Conn are advocating is a generalist, someone with the academic eclecticism to create a new context for business goals within the broader needs, pressures, influences, and history of society. More than that, it is important that this intellectual breadth be matched by an expansiveness of the heart, for this context, this respect for connection, this acknowledgement of interdependency are, in fact, expressions of the spiritual sensibility that business must have to sustain itself, nurture its people, and function in harmony with nature. The people entrusted to lead such organizations will necessarily be expressing more of themselves. Not only their intellects, but their hearts and spirits will be apparent in their attitudes and styles.

Once again, this embracing of the spirit is not idealistic, nor does it represent a softening of business. It is a pragmatic requirement for surviving and thriving in a world that can no longer tolerate isolationist behavior. More and more companies are finding that they can no longer remain competitive, without forging strategic alliances.

IBM and Apple have both been on the fringe of the laptop revolution. Although they come from diametrically different traditions and cultures, both introduced products into this fast-growing, very competitive segment, that were heavy, cumbersome, and on the flat edge of technology. A recent article in *BusinessWeek* reports that both are now pursuing alliances with Japanese companies, to develop their next generation of laptop computers.

As incredible as it seems, Apple and IBM have also joined forces to create compatible systems and products. In such cases, success depends on suspending self-interest and creating common ground for a common goal that is mutually rewarding. Such *entente*, such mutuality, stretches leadership to include those aspects of our humanity that moderate self-interest with genuine concern for others.

As important as these alliances are, it is difficult, if not impossible, to achieve such constructive partnership, while adhering to traditional beliefs about management. As Kenichi Ohmae suggests, "a real alliance compromises the fundamental independence of economic actors, and managers don't like that. For them, management has come to mean total control. Alliances mean sharing control. The one precludes the other."

The dynamics of a leadership geared to sharing control, rather than accumulating it, will build upon, and modify, and add to, our concept of leading. Confidence and communication, so important in the traditional leadership practices of driving and directing, will take on a new meaning, as we adjust to the particular demands of sharing.

Logically, it takes a hyper-confidence, a well-developed and well-integrated sense of self, to surrender absolute control and share responsibility, accountability and rewards. It also takes very clear communication, with frequent reinforcement, to instil those values and customs that make the sharing productive and mutually rewarding. Such clarity of communication is only possible if it carries the deep, personal conviction of purpose.

In addition to these expected qualities of leadership, the people who will set the tone and direction for companies dedicated to sharing will operate with a fundamentally different view of themselves, within their organizations. The authority-based paradigm, with its trappings of power and systems of control, is giving way to one that is service-oriented. In the service paradigm, leadership primarily supports, nurtures and encourages those who provide the service. This new paradigm applies to manufacturers of products, as well as providers of services, because competitive pressures are demanding greater flexibility, accommodation and service from everyone who participates in the marketplace.

Sharing To Deliver Superior Service

Service, while it may have commercial goals and results, is essentially a spiritual capability of humans. Giving service involves suspending self-interest, to advance the needs of another. Genuine service makes the recipient feel important and valued. Service is purest as a consequence of the Golden Rule, since it involves extending courtesy and respect and attentiveness to others, to the same degree that we expect it for ourselves.

The competitive potential of superior service is obvious, and many companies have dedicated themselves to becoming better agents of service in their respective fields. Only a few have sparkled. Disney and Federal Express and American Airlines and Pepsico and American Express are among the handful of companies that set the gold standards of service.

In an article, entitled "Service That Sells," a recent issue of *Fortune* explored the philosophical and structural underpinnings of American Express. James Robinson, the CEO, consistently preaches a dictum that is adhered to by all the notable service organizations: "Promise only what you can deliver, and deliver more than you promise."[6]

While service is a powerful discriminator in the marketplace, most North American customers and consumers remain frustrated, or at best disinterested, about the quality of service they experience. While business has developed a vocabulary for service, we've generally failed to make the attitudinal and structural changes that promote genuine, competitive service.

The principle mistake is that we've tried to manage our way into better service, applying disciplines, norms and measurement with the same dedication to control that has characterized the management of manufacturing. While disciplines, norms and measurement are important, they can only be realized as after-effects of service, and not as the inspiration and catalyst for it. Creating a culture of service cannot be dictated, because imposition crushes the spirit of service. Rather, it must be demonstrated, and nurtured, with the same attention and care as other, more ephemeral human assets, like creativity.

As Jan Carlzon has shown at SAS, a service company gives superior service when the organizational structure is reversed. The customer is at the head of service companies. The most important assets of such companies are the front-line people who actually create and deliver service. These are the employees, the ticket-counter attendants at SAS, the muffler-installers at Speedy Muffler King, the assembly people at Ford, the delivery people at Pepsi. Management elicits greater commitment from these front-line people when it stands behind them, providing the support and tools and training that they need to do a better job. And leaders inspire superior service when they not only set the goals, but also commit themselves personally to "serve the servers" within their organizations.

This is a difficult notion to accept, and a difficult one to activate. The competitive nature of business instils an ethic of wanting to win. And winning has always brought power, prestige, and the spoils and perks of status. These expressions of leadership, which motivated many to aspire to it, have increasingly become the impediments to its effectiveness.

With his typical understated wisdom, Max Depree defines a leader as "one who serves." In his book, *The Art of Leadership*, Dupree writes, "The measure of leadership is not the quality of the head, but the tone of the body. The signs of outstanding leadership appear primarily among the followers. Are the followers reaching their potential? Are they learning? Serving? Do they achieve the required results? Do they change with grace? Manage conflict?"[7]

Service, and the management style that spawns it, must not be mistaken for servility. The stronger and healthier and more balanced the person providing the service, the more value that service has to the customer. So the role of leaders is to help their employees realize their fullest potential, as professionals and as people, so that the breadth and depth of their humanity can be activated through their work. This breadth and depth is then more readily applied to serving the ever broader, deeper needs of customers.

The interdisciplinary grounding argued for by Boyett and Conn is logical, because it promotes breadth and depth in the very leadership of companies. Strategic insights or a genius for numbers are no longer enough to lead companies. Today's leaders must have the breadth of skills to motivate employees psychically, as well as financially. They must themselves be examples of the whole and healthy human being, to provide models for their employees and to embody the ethic that their customers will be attracted to.

If sharing and service are indispensable attributes of the progressive and competitive business—and they are—then it is very important that we understand how to best actualize them. Once again, the inner sources for these new, still-rare attributes, are the more spiritual dimensions of our humanity, which have been largely ignored, if not misunderstood, by business. Genuine, instinctive sharing comes from our spirit of compassion. And genuine, instinctive service comes from our spirit of humility.

Compassion and humility are not words spoken very frequently in boardrooms. The pride, aggressiveness and drive for achievement that we normally associate with the successful business organization are at odds with the more introspective, less assertive values of compassion and humility. Yet both of these attributes are expressions of a whole and healthy humanity. Each is also critically important to helping us create companies that are not only vital and successful, but also integrated within society and nature. Compassion extends our concern to embrace a broader one, and humility provides the context and sense of proportion for how our individual goals fit within the wider social and environmental framework.

Compassion and humility, while noble, seem like quaint concepts for the harsh world of global competition. In reality, both compassion and humility make us better leaders, better managers, better business people.

Competition And Compassion Are Compatible

Compassion is that spirit that allows us to connect with other people on the basis of head, heart and spirit. This goes beyond what we generally qualify as *people skills*, because it gives as much importance to the other as to the self. It is the healthy and essential source of our human capacity for sharing. This sharing, this ability to connect on deep and meaningful terms, is critically important if we are to inspire our employees, and earn their conviction and commitment, to the degree that our companies need to meet ever steeper, ever more demanding, ever more competitive business goals.

Compassion is often misunderstood. It is not pity, for that devalues the other person. Nor is it simply self-sacrifice, for that devalues the self. Instead, compassion is the ability of a whole and healthy individual to achieve what psychologist William Eckhardt calls "the principle of coherence." This coherence, this sense of oneness, allows us to feel intimately and personally the experiences of others; their joy, their pain, the anxiety, concerns and dreams that are experienced individually, but shared universally.

From this position of compassion, we who lead companies can simply do a better job of putting ourselves in the places of our people, in understanding their strengths and weaknesses, in defining their goals and solving the problems that impede their performances.

Companies with a strong ethic of compassion achieve great things, because of the trust and heightened sense of purpose that it engenders. Compassion is the prerequisite for deeply held, intuitively based cooperation, which some companies are now using to advance their competitive performance. The business literature about competition and cooperation has shown consistently that the latter achieves significantly better results.

In an article in *Psychology Today*, author Alfie Kohn explains why. "Success often depends on sharing resources efficiently, and this is nearly impossible when people have to work against each other. Cooperation takes advantage of all the skills represented in a group, as well as the mysterious process by which that group becomes more than the sum of its parts. By contrast, competition makes people suspicious and hostile toward one another and actively discourages this process."[8]

Compassion, as the basis of cooperation, is also the source of excellence. Kohn explains that "competition generally does not promote excellence, because trying to do well and trying to beat others are simply two different things." In these terms, compassion is not a lofty ideal, nor a "nice-to-have" attribute of corporate culture. Rather, it is a "need-to-have," an essential ingredient for heightening the efficiency, competitiveness and cohesion of our modern corporations.

Ron Zemke and Dick Scaff have studied companies across a wide cross-section of industries, to qualify those attributes that produce superior customer satisfaction and superior profitability. In their book, *The Service Edge*, the authors report on "101 companies that profit from customer care." They conclude that "compassion may be the mother lode of all service gold," because it creates a bond of empathy between company and customer.[9]

Empathy involves not just relating to the state of mind or conditions of the other person, but actually having, as defined by *Webster's*, the "capacity for participation in another's feelings or ideas." This deep participation with the customer is like Velcro, providing the hooks of anticipation, gratitude, responsiveness and respect, to secure a long-term relationship.

The empathy that flows from compassion, if genuine, becomes pervasive. It stimulates a spirit of reciprocity, of mutuality, in all things, within and beyond business. In this way, compassion is the wellspring, providing our business institutions with the sensibilities and tools to develop a sustaining relationship with our natural environment.

Without compassion, business will never be able to operate with integrity and respect for nature, because it can never fully value that which it is so widely using and destroying. Without compassion, the gain of the corporation will never achieve a balance with the other needs of our humanity, of our society.

Service Without Humility Is Hollow

Just as companies that share and cooperate are more productive, more satisfying to work for, and ultimately more competitive, so, too, those that have an intrinsic sense of service are forging a powerful competitive advantage. The systems and structures of superior service are now widely publicized and celebrated, to the degree that GM's Cadillac division won the prestigious Malcolm Baldrige Award in 1990, for excellence in quality, not only for the product it makes, but also for its after-sales service innovations. Lexus and Infiniti are now pushing out the boundaries of superior service even farther, as they compete with great determination and long-term resolve against the European luxury badges, Mercedes-Benz and BMW.

This spiral of ever increasing competitiveness, based on service, is being played out in numerous other product categories. Hotels and airlines. Banks, life-insurance companies and accounting firms. Grocery chains, fast-food restaurants and gas retailers. All are sharpening their skills to provide better, faster, cheaper, more courteous, and more consistent service to their customers. Even packaged-goods marketers are moving from a philosophy of "adding value" to a product to one of "adding service," in order to secure competitive differentiation. P&G, for example, has added 1-800 numbers to the packaging of its many brands, to better serve its largely mass-market customers.

As the service factor becomes more critical, company leaders are beginning to look beyond traditional systems for its implementation, measurement and improvement. Unlike quality, which can be standardized and evaluated, service is more amorphous, bending, shaping, and demonstrating itself within each specific encounter that a customer has with a company or its products. So, the models for producing quality, while important, are not necessarily relevant to a company, as it tries to set competitive standards of service. That leaves many of us scratching our heads, trying to define new approaches that will permeate the cultures of our entire companies.

In remodelling companies to provide better service, the attitude and character of the leader must change, as well as that of the organization. Max Depree, in his inspirational chapter, "What Is Leadership?" writes, "The first responsibility of a leader is to define reality. The last is to say *thank you*. In between the two, the leader must become a servant and a debtor. That sums up the progress of an artful leader." To be a servant, to be indebted, are metaphors for being humble.[10]

Humility is not one of the primary descriptions that come to mind, when we think of executives who head companies. Corporate jets, corner offices, company cars, executive assistants, are but a few expressions of the significant responsibility and power vested in the leaders of our large businesses. Even in smaller companies, the status of the CEO is usually apparent.

Some leaders even develop what *BusinessWeek* terms "CEO disease," letting their egos overtake their better business judgement, to the point at which business performance suffers. But most senior executives are already shedding some of the symbols and gestures of power, which have worked to distance them from the customers they must serve and the employees they must motivate. However, very few have adopted the spirit of humility, the attitude and stance of the "servant and debtor," that can be so deep a source of genuine, mutually rewarding service.

Humility is even more misunderstood than compassion. Our society, and certainly our commercial culture, largely involve promotion. Politicians promote themselves through promises and projects. Companies promote themselves through lobbyists and public-relations firms. Products and services are promoted through advertising and contests. So pervasive is this ethic of promotion that individuals themselves are adopting its disciplines, following the advice of countless self-help books on how to promote ourselves for success in business, or in relationships. All of this promotional activity breeds *hype*—the dramatization of what's being promoted, which often stretches to over-promise, and sometimes even goes beyond that to deception. Within our culture of ever present hype, humility, with its spirit of deference, seems like an antiquated, largely undesirable attribute.

In reality, humility is the necessary counterweight to pride. It is that aspect of our humanity that provides some sense of proportion to our individual self-importance. Humility makes it possible for us to coexist within society, making the hundreds of accommodations and adjustments to our individual wants, in order to function within the broader dynamics of our communities. When we suffer because someone's "ego is too big," be that someone a political leader like Saddam Hussein, or a business leader like Michael Milken, we are essentially suffering the absence of humility.

The collective ego of our business institutions has been too big for too long. It is the absence of a sense of proportion that has allowed us to justify the ruinous environmental practices of business for the last two centuries. It is also the absence of a sense of proportion that has tolerated a few thousand fin-anciers and Wall Street brokers growing richer by billions of dollars, while the North American economy sinks into a quagmire of junk-bond debt, which they promoted. Without the antidote of humility, business has fallen victim to the destructive greed that accompanies unbalanced self-importance.

Our own human affairs, throughout history, have shown that humility can be achieved two ways. Often it is imposed, as the ego and pride of a person, company, or country, eventually gets so out of balance that it is crushed by its own arrogance.

Ross Johnson, whose egomaniacal excesses were written about in the best-seller, *Barbarians At The Gate*, is an extreme example of someone whose career, reputation and company were finally lost because of blinding pride. Achieving humility through such humiliation, while it may be deserved, is regressive. The balance is achieved at great price, with the damage caused by the pride usually far outweighing the redress in the humiliation.

The far healthier source for humility is the inner one—the positive capacity that every thinking and sentient human has, to be awed. When we are in awe, we are touched in some deep way that provides not only a sense of proportion, but also some sense of purpose. Such awe-inspired humility is usually derived from nature—the macro-mysteries of outer space and the micro-mysteries of genetics, the redwoods of California, The Rockies of British Columbia, the Great Barrier Reef of Australia, each has the potential to move our spirit.

Many human achievements also inspire awe. The mathematics of Einstein, the music of Mozart, the diversity of Da Vinci, the moon-reaching rockets of Von Braun, touch that part of our humanity that can be dazzled and amazed. Out of this awe, whether of natural or human creation, springs a humility of respect, the healthy recognition that we are important, but not central to the vastness around us. Such humility does not demean us, but rather involves us as participants in the expansive grandeur or achievement or artistry we are responding to.

In broad terms, our choice as business leaders is to nurture this healthy humility, both as individuals and within our companies, or face the certainty that either nature or society will impose a much harsher humiliation upon us.

The inner development is obviously preferable, yet, in many ways, far more difficult. While enthusiasm is appreciated as a business asset, humility is viewed as passive, and, by implication, a liability. Furthermore, while optimism is valued, to be in awe suggests an absence of control that is anathema to what business leadership is supposed to be about. Overcoming these biases, even if it will be in the best interests of the institutions they are leading, is tough for CEOs.

Practising What They Preach

Some have started the process. Sam Walton has built the highly successful Wal-Mart retail chain into a powerhouse that is challenging Sears for leadership in mass merchandising. Mr. Sam, as he is known by employees and customers, is a billionaire, but he still drives himself to work in a pickup truck. He preaches a service philosophy, to the over 185,000 people who work for Wal-Mart, which is as simple as it is effective. "Treat customers like neighbours."

To promote such neighbourliness, Mr. Sam treats his own people with the same deference. They are called *associates*, rather than employees, because, in Walton's view, they, and not just he, are the expression of Wal-Mart to its customers. This attitude towards his people is demonstrated through a far-reaching profit-sharing scheme, which involves all the Wal-Mart associates who have worked there for over a thousand hours.[11]

The spirit of humility Walton has shown is genuine, but it is also very smart business. All managers at Wal-Mart give up their supervisory roles for at least one week a year, and go to work doing an hourly job in one of the company's stores. This getting behind the counter and serving customers reminds executives that they are, in the vernacular of the church, the "servers of the servers" of customers. Walton has even switched the jobs of his most senior executives, flipping the reporting roles, in order to promote a sense of personal proportion within his company.

Other executives are taking similar steps to close the gap between themselves, the people they lead, and the customers they rely on to stay in business. Robert Crandall, the highly effective and very successful CEO of American Airlines, makes it a point to stop off at executive and staff lounges at airports he's travelling through, to talk to customers and employees.

Roy Vagelos, chief executive of pharmaceutical giant Merek & Company, eats as often as he can in the company cafeteria, so that he can talk informally with the scientists and engineers who are working on new products. This accessibility keeps him connected to promising new developments, or the inevitable bottlenecks that slow development. The results of this leadership style have been impressive. Merek is not only highly profitable, but it has also come out consistently, during the past five years, as the number one or two most-admired company in North America, in a poll that *Fortune* has conducted annually among senior executives.

Humility at the top cascades down throughout an organization. People work more cooperatively, with less energy being drained away by activities that promote self-interest. Ultimately, the values of humility help companies serve their customers better. How many times have you walked out of a restaurant, or car-service bay, or department store, and wondered why you were made to feel so little when you were the one spending the money? Humility reverses this frustration, putting the interests of the company behind those of the customer. So, in this sense, humility is not passive. It is very active, a strength that can build the loyalty of customers and provide a powerful competitive plus.

It takes a strong person to be humble. It takes a strong person to accept that his success and well-being comes from displacing his self-interest. Ray Kroch, the founder of McDonald's, revolutionized franchising, because he decided not to get rich by franchising, but to make his franchisees rich first. In the early years, he was well paid, but significantly less wealthy than the millionaires he created by franchising his concept. This attracted the number and quality of new franchisees who fuelled McDonald's explosive world-wide growth.[12]

Kroch also turned the relationship with suppliers upside-down. While suppliers are often regarded as disposable, and are generally pitted against one another to deliver the lowest price, Kroch made them participants in the McDonald's adventure. Rather than following the master-slave dynamics that characterized most supplier-customer relationships in the food-service industry, Kroch had the common sense and humility to treat these supplying companies with respect. He promoted partnership, helping the companies that supplied McDonald's to grow and prosper. This encouraged much greater commitment, so much so that many new products, including the Big Mac and the Hot Apple Pie came, not from McDonald's, but from its suppliers.

Humility, like compassion, can significantly strengthen those companies that have the courage to live by its principles and values. Importantly, the humility cannot be cosmetic. It must be deep and genuine, a part of the behavior of not only those employees who touch customers, but also the managers who supervise them, and the leaders who direct them. We who lead companies must, in the words of the unorthodox economist Hazel Henderson, "walk what we talk." This means living service, and showing humility by example.

Honda is one of the most successful companies to grow up since the Second World War. It is a true multinational, with plants producing high-quality cars around the world. Honda's Accord is the best-selling car model in North America. And its Acura division has been very successful as the first up-market entry from Japan. Honda is also the three-time Formula One champion, and has just parlayed that experience into the very hot NSX sports car. This is a company that is innovative in engineering and marketing. And it is also iconoclastic, forsaking even the direction of the powerful Ministry of International Trade and Industry, to pursue its own business strategy.

Despite this considerable success, its president, Nobuhiko Kawamoto, still drives his own, four-year-old sedan to work. There are no reserved spots in the Honda lot, so, like everyone else, the president tries to arrive early to get one close to the office. Once in the office, he puts on a Honda jacket, just like every other employee.[13]

This is humility in action. Such leadership sends the signal to the work force that everyone is of equal importance within Honda. Quality, innovation, and success are the results of the team, not the privileged leadership. Many argue that such Japanese business mannerisms can't be transported to North America, because of the cultural differences between our two societies. But this is naïve and simplistic.

As Sam Walton has shown, people everywhere respond to the power of symbols. The limousines, or reserved parking spots, or executive cafeterias, so prevalent in North American corporations, send signals to the employees that they are not as important as the executive elite. All the training programmes dedicated to making employees stakeholders, all the seminars on flattening the decision process, all the good intentions that accompany crusades for "sharing accountability," come to naught if the leadership remains removed, segregated by privilege, and un-humble.

The contrast in management style between North American and Japanese CEOs becomes downright ludicrous, when viewed in the context of overall business performance. Kevin Phillips has written a book about the foolish economic policies of the 1980s, and the dangerous redistribution of wealth that it caused. In *The Politics of Rich and Poor*, Phillips provides some startling data. While the U.S. share of the world's GNP will drop by twenty-five percent between 1983 and the turn of the century, Japan's will grow by a quarter. Despite that, American CEOs earn an average of twelve times the pay of the average hourly worker in their plants. Japanese CEOs earn one-third that level, or only four times what the average hourly worker takes home.[14]

As the globalization of the economy continues, there will inevitably be pressure to redress this imbalance in CEO compensation, just as there is pressure to improve blue-collar productivity to world-class levels. Until then, the imbalance serves to undermine many of the commitment-instilling programmes that North Americans are trying to implement, to improve their competitiveness.

The latest of these programmes, and one that is gaining wide acceptance throughout industry, is the newfangled gospel of *empowerment*. In the paradigm of empowerment, decision-making is in the hands of the people confronting the problem to be solved. This means that employees serving customers, and those in the plant manufacturing products, have the expanded authority and accountability for making decisions concerning quality, efficiency, cost and profitability.

This is an admirable and long-overdue restructuring of the decision-making process. Yet the full potential of empowerment can only be realized if the power is truly given away, and not rented or leased to employees. To genuinely place power in the hands of their customer-servers, company CEOs must develop the personal compassion and humility to release that power. Without compassion and humility, empowerment is but another drug that will, for a time, give relief to the symptoms, without curing the disease.

THE ENNOBLING POTENTIAL OF BUSINESS

With so many obstacles to overcome, with such blatant flaws and dangerous idiosyncrasies, the question to be asked is whether business, as an institution, is worth salvaging? The answer, unequivocally, is yes.

Business is among the most flexible, the most adaptable of human institutions. Its management techniques are constantly evolving, responding to the fleeting challenge of opportunity or the unrelenting pressure of competition. Business produces change, developing new technology, new products. And change drives business to overcome obsolete conventions, in order to remain current with the needs and attitudes of the marketplace.

Like any human institution, business can quickly become calcified and rigid. But the dynamics of competition are such that they force companies to respond to the initiatives of others. This cycle of competitive pressure has worked to keep business in closer alignment to the changing mores and concerns of our modern society than many of the classic political and religious institutions.

For example, although business has by no means recti-
fied its longstanding male bias, women have gone further,
faster in business than they have in either traditional religion
or politics. Business generally rewards intelligence, initiative
and contribution, and, again, while considerable progress is
still necessary, it has proven to be relatively easier to overcome longstanding prejudices in the conducting of business
than in religion or politics.

The Global Beacon

The hope that business affords humans is demonstrated by its
near-universal appeal. In April 1991, the Polish Stock Exchange
opened its doors in a former union hall of the Communist
Party. The pictures flashed through the media showed well-
groomed, eager young men, crowded around a purring computer terminal. Each wore bright red braces, providing both a
compliment and a parody to the sartorial trend that we so
strongly associate with Wall Street and Bay Street.

Throughout Eastern Europe, in Czechoslovakia, Hungary,
East Germany, the movement to a free market is proceeding at
an incredible pace. Obsolete, inefficient, government-
controlled plants are being closed. Private industry is sprouting.
The cost of moving from a controlled to a market economy,
in terms of human dislocation and sacrifice, is steep. Prices,
no longer set centrally, have doubled and tripled in only a few
months. Hundreds of thousands of people have lost their jobs,
as inefficient and hopelessly bloated state companies have
floundered, downsized or closed. Yet people generally accept
this sacrifice, because they believe that a market system based
on initiative, once established, will provide greater security
and opportunity for them.

Similar movements to free enterprise are evident in developing countries of the Far East, as well as in Central and
South America. Mexico's President Salinas is a Harvard MBA
graduate, who is working hard to run his country more like
a modern corporation than a state. He has undone generations of state involvement in business, and is fostering an
unprecedented degree of commercial linkage with the world beyond Mexico's borders. He is now on a one-man mission to
create a North American free trade zone.

For Mexico and Malaysia and Poland, the choice is clear. Capitalism is the only road for progress. Everywhere, the aspirations and the blueprint for development are the same. Industry is first attracted through low wages. Then, the benefits of that industrial base are plowed back into education and infrastructure-improvement, in order to graduate up the added-value ladder. As more added-value industries flourish, the balance of trade and the standard of living grow as a result. This, in highly simplified form, is the inherent promise of the initially Western, now global, commercial system.

With so much hope invested in business, for perhaps the first time in human history, those who have power and wealth and those who don't are both aligned behind one system. If we use our imaginations, we can see the historic potential in such alignment. The benefits, as well as the disadvantages of business transcend national, religious and ethnic differences. Evolving business to better deliver those benefits, and to correct those disadvantages, is in the interest of the whole human family.

Thomas J. Watson, the builder of IBM, saw the reciprocal benefits of world trade, several generations before globalization became the buzzword of business. Watson, perhaps because of his own very humble roots, believed business represented the great equalizer. Through it, systems and structures, people, communities and countries could all share in the benefits of initiative and smart business management.

Watson spun out a separate unit of his company, which he called, with some bravado, IBM World Trade. Unlike most multinationals of the era, Watson hired a majority of managers, including the most senior ones, from the domestic market in which IBM operated. Today, companies like Sony are applauded for such international management practices, and for the international representation on their board. Watson and IBM actually led the way, operating with such enlightened internationalism over fifty years ago.[1]

The Watson depicted in the book by his son, *Father, Son & Co.: My Life At IBM*, was, first and foremost, dedicated to his company's success. IBM's altruism, its international sensitivities, even its progressive use of architecture, all sprang from a very pragmatic, very focused desire to build the strongest, most competitive company possible. Yet Watson also believed that business afforded the greatest hope for humankind. The stronger the network of international trade, the more interdependent nations become, the less likely countries are to splinter away and entangle themselves in the conflagrations that have twice consumed our world, in this century.

Idealistic though this seems, trade, and the business that generates it, represent our best hope for collective security and prosperity. Business is not perfect. In fact, many of the divisive imperfections that have hampered our other human institutions are evident in business. It can be unfair, tyrannical, insensitive and exploitive. Yet, unlike religion, which is often only accountable to an anthropomorphized deity, and unlike politics, which is accountable only to those constituents who bestow power, business is accountable to the competition within the marketplace. Every day it must earn its custom. In every exchange, it must provide value. This competitive reality, this inexorable pressure, keeps business honest, or at least more honest, than other human structures and codes that we've developed during our history.

Business responds to opportunity. This is the progressive dynamic within business. Sometimes these opportunities are frivolous, like tailfins on cars. Increasingly, these opportunities are substantial, like the rush to provide air-bags and improve overall automobile safety. This process of finding competitive leverage creates an ever widening cycle of improvement, innovation, added value and added service. Society benefits. Individuals benefit. Companies prosper.

As the values of society change, they are intrinsically incorporated within this cycle. Concern for the environment, among communities, is already yielding considerable improvements in the environmental practices of business. Concern for racism and sexism within society is resulting in companies that are generally attempting to be more equal in their hiring practices and promotion criteria.

This is not to say that business is, by itself, a progressive influence within society. Business still has a long way to go, and it generally only goes as far as the pressure of the marketplace forces it to.

Like any other human structure, business has a proclivity to protect the status quo. Power, once accrued, is only reluctantly released and shared. Yet, even though it has sometimes taken the pressure of legislation or boycott to force business to accept its responsibilities, to redistribute or share its power, its accountability to the constituents of the marketplace has made it more malleable than any of our other dominant social institutions. Because competitive pressure is so dynamic and constant, business has shown itself to be responsive to a degree that, if we are diligent and thoughtful, can afford us considerable hope.

The Emerging Idea Economy

The modern world economy is coming to value ideas more than things. The Japanese have mastered the manufacture of things, including complex electronics and miniaturization. However, the VCRs and compact disc players and computers represent only one dimension of economic value. The movies and music and programmes, the software to run in those products, represent a huge, less tangible, but equally critical value.

The Japanese education system has, by the admission of their own government officials, produced a generation of smart managers and builders and manufacturers, with few idea people. Sony and Matsushita, while dominating the technology, have had to look to the U.S. for their ideas, purchasing Columbia and MCA respectively, to provide the "software" that ultimately gives value to the products that run it.

Naohiro Amaya, a retired senior official at MITI, suggests that Japan is "producing workers rather than full citizens." In his view, it is a great deal easier "to produce a good car than it is to produce a good human being," and he has been lobbying hard to expand the liberal-arts dimension of Japanese education.[2]

This transition in Japan underscores the growing importance of the individual in the evolving international economy. Ideas cannot be designed nor manufactured. They spring only from the minds of people. As George Gilder suggests in his book, *Microcosm*, economic value is no longer based on the hard resources of the past, not on minerals, mines and manufactured goods, but on knowledge.

As the world comes to acknowledge that it is exhausting the ability to create wealth out of things, it is finally recognizing the true value of ideas. "Gone is the view of a thermodynamic world economy, dominated by 'natural resources' being turned to entropy and waste by human extraction and use. Once seen as a physical system tending toward exhaustion and decline, the world economy has clearly emerged as an intellectual system driven by knowledge. The key fact of knowledge is that it is anti-entropic: it accumulates and compounds as it is used."[3]

With knowledge displacing hard resources as the raw material of business, the importance and value of the individual, creative mind increases. As human capital supersedes financial, people finally assume their paramount position within the priorities of the companies that rely on them for ideas and success.

While corporations have grown and succeeded by exploiting traditional resources of nature and labour, to develop the products and services of the modern economy, the attitudes and structures of exploitation must give way to those that liberate the human potential for creativity, new thinking and new ideas. In this context, companies must nurture human potential, not as an altruistic afterthought, but as a necessity of competition and future viability.

The ascension of ideas as the ultimate corporate resource will turn upside-down the traditional relationship between company and employee. Shoshana Zuboff, in her book, *In the Age of the Smart Machine*, examines the changes in the "nature of work and power" resulting from the expanding use of advanced computer technology in the workplace. She writes, "As the new technology integrates information across time and space, managers and workers each overcome their narrow functional perspectives and create new roles that are better suited to enhancing value-adding activities in a data-rich environment."

Zuboff is a professor at the Harvard Business School. She studied numerous companies in various industries that underwent rapid technological change. Even for manufacturing companies that were using computer technology to improve productivity, important changes in the roles and relationships between management and employees occurred. Zuboff notes that "authority comes to depend more upon an appropriate fit between knowledge and responsibility than upon the ranking rules of the traditional organizational pyramid."[4]

The redistribution of authority, to those with knowledge, from those with control bestowed by the hierarchy, is momentous, affecting the very foundations of how we work, how we create value, and the meaning derived from what we do. As Zuboff states, "Authority is the spiritual dimension of power because it depends upon faith in a system of meaning that decrees the necessity of the hierarchical order and so provides for the unity of imperative control. Authority requires collective participation in a system of meaning that extends beyond the immediate context, beyond those who command or obey, and reaches into the realm of transcendent values."[5]

Defining and giving impetus to these "transcendent values" will happen despite the will of companies, because they are not a fashion, a trend, but rather a tangible, inevitable result of the new nature of work. The idea is becoming the new economic unit, and the challenge for management is to evolve those systems and capacities that are most conducive to idea-generation.

While management, in the past, has sought to impose an order on the process of business, with ideas the process will impose a new style of management. Zuboff's studies show that one important consequence of more information-capability in the workplace is that it increases greatly the capacity to question. "Questions, in a fundamental way, are inimical to authority...yet the question is essential if information is to yield its full value."[6] So the very process of deriving full meaning from information—questioning—ultimately erodes the authority base of traditional, control-oriented business structures.

With ideas, power in an organization passes from the manager to the thinker. This means that the role of companies is no longer to harness the workers, but rather to support and inspire them. Zuboff notes that "as the work people do becomes more abstract, the need for positive motivation increases and internal commitment becomes all the more crucial." Most managers are still in the old headspace of serving the needs of shareholders, and we've not yet realized that we can only fulfil our obligations to them by according respect and support to the "ideaholders," who create real corporate value.

The challenges of developing and serving "ideaholders," of creating the progressive management structures to mine the cranium, are exciting, and portend great possibilities for business. Many business leaders, including those in communications industries, such as advertising, understand the unique management skills required to liberate ideas and unleash human potential. However, the conflicting demands of traditional finance have limited the ability of even the most visionary of managers to adopt more flexible, idea-conducive systems and approaches. Conventional accounting is simply inadequate to measure and provide guidance for managing idea companies.

My own industry is an example. Advertising is an industry of ideas, yet value is established by measures of cash flow, revenue and earnings that are really more appropriate for manufacturing concerns from another epoch. While these measures are important, there is, as yet, no way to assign value to the ideas created, nor to the people who create them. The failure of accounting to include such measurements has been tolerated, because industries like advertising have been peripheral to the larger economy.

Now, as ideas grow in importance within the overall economy, new accounting standards must be evolved to more accurately represent the value generated by creative companies. The global pressure for creativity, the demand for constant, unrelenting value-added, will force business to break from its traditional measurements of value, and finally factor the value of ideas into its equations of success.

Thinkers use different skills than doers. The equipment and capital support they require are inconsistent, if not incompatible. Yet, while a machine that produces a product can be evaluated by traditional financial formulas, its payout pegged to a certain level of productivity, the capital investment to support the creation of ideas is much harder to justify. The conventional concept of return on investment must be replaced by a broader, supra-financial notion of "return on ideas."

Towards A New ROI: *Return On Idea*

The current emphasis on conventional ROI is part of the reason North American companies have lost the lead to so many

European and Asian companies. Attention to financial results, particularly the quarterly measurement of performance, has handcuffed many North American companies. The longer-term perspective of our international competitors has given them the flexibility to invest in the new ideas that take time to gain momentum. The Airbus consortium has gained one third of the global marketshare for new jet planes. While we in North America criticize the government financing of Airbus, they have, nevertheless, developed an important technological base, which has a wide, cascading benefit to the whole economy.

Not only do European and Asian managers have the luxury of investing in ideas for their longer-term potential, but they've also developed the management skills to identify those ideas, nurture them through their organizations, and modify them in response to customers in the marketplace. Too many North American CEOs have learned skills of financial manipulation to meet the shareholder demands for quarterly performance. Ideas, particularly those that require time and funds to incubate, are often alien to the managers, who are evaluated for what they did that influenced results for the last three months.

Acknowledging the notion of "return on ideas" is the first step in breaking this cycle. Return on ideas will demand new measurement tools, and new measurement horizons. Financial payout will be but one consideration in a spectrum of measurements. These will include quality of people, people development and loyalty, the proclivity to create, frequency of innovation, patent registrations, strategic alliances for new products, new services and new ideas.

The financial alchemy, so prized for the last generation in North American management, will finally be understood as the short-sighted and simplistic skill it really is. Producing quarterly results is a lot easier than managing a company for the long term: fostering ideas, judging those with merit, investing and supporting their development, based on a vision of what the future opportunity will be, and then creating the execution of the idea.

One of the skill by-products of the North American orientation to numbers and regular profit delivery is that we've created a class of caretaker managers. These are the masters of finance, and they've spent a good part of the last generation creating returns for shareholders by buying, selling, stream-lining or dismembering companies. This managerial know-ledge base will not be enough, as the world economy shapes itself around the exchange of information and ideas.

With return on ideas as a measurement, managers will have the opportunity to open themselves to a whole new set of skills, which are not only more productive for the company and the economy, but also more fulfilling for the individuals in-volved. Linear skills of rationalization, downsizing and cost-control will continue to be important, but will represent only a small cluster of the needed managerial moxie. Imagination, creativity and inspiration will be the broader, more important skills of business managers entrusted with return-on-ideas re-sponsibility within the new economy.

The Equalizing Potential Of Ideas

As the currency of ideas takes its rightful place beside that of conventional finance, companies will be more likely to advance women, minorities, and the other segments of society, such as the physically disabled, who are currently under-represented in the positions of power within business. While manufactur-ing favoured the strong, and management favoured the con-formist, an economy based on ideas will favour those who can think, create, imagine and dream.

Business is a human invention, and incorporates human duality. As promising as it is in its potential, it has also shown an ugly capacity to exploit and exclude. During the last several decades, heightened social consciousness within society has resulted in greater equality in the workplace. Yet, while there has been progress, business has not fully embraced its social re-sponsibilities. Equal pay is, in some regions, the law, in many companies a stated policy, but in reality, it remains largely a myth.

In *Beyond Power*, Marilyn French reviews the chimer-ical progress women have made within the economy, during the 60s and 70s, after the first two waves of the feminist move-ment. The U.S. census data from those decades show that "the gap between male and female earnings has increased." White women earned only fifty-nine cents for every dollar earned by white males. For Black and Hispanic women, the ratio was fifty-four cents and forty-nine cents, respectively.[7]

Data for the 1980s are still being tabulated, but again the evidence is of a deteriorating, rather than improving, situation. Benjamin Friedman, the economics professor at Harvard, documents that many of the new jobs created during the boom of the 1980s were, in fact, in less attractive, less enriching and less rewarding industries. "Of all the new year-round jobs created since 1979, thirty-six percent have provided workers with *less than half* of what the average worker made in 1973." Many of these jobs fell to women.[8]

The inequality is not limited to women at the lower end of the wage scale. In management, business and government leaders acknowledge the presence of a "glass ceiling," which has continued to stymie the promotion of deserving women to senior management and CEO positions. The biases that prevent the most deserving from assuming their rightful roles within an enterprise obviously hurt the individual. Importantly, they also hurt the company, because they deny the organization the particular talents and vision of that most qualified individual.

As North American business leaders look into the mirror and study the reflection of their often-failing systems and beliefs, the need to equalize and promote the best people with the best ideas will become acute. Beyond the moral reasons for correcting the inequality is, ultimately, the pragmatic one of the new economy. To be competitive, business must be hungry for new ideas. And no source for that creativity can be overlooked or taken for granted.

The quest for ideas cannot be limited to executives in office towers. Japanese auto executives ascribe much of their product-quality achievement to the hundreds of thousands of suggestions and ideas that come from the plant people actually labouring to make the cars. To stimulate such ideas, to encourage such participation, North American management has no choice but to bring down traditional barriers and embrace the potential of all workers.

This is hard work, requiring that we overcome many of the biases and limitations that are currently interwoven into our management systems. At this time, whether the change is adopted from the top is academic. History has shown that ideas liberate, and an economy based on ideas will create its own liberating momentum and its own structures of equality and full participation. Managers can either accept and involve themselves in this process, or be overtaken by events which, in any case, they no longer can control.

Business managers aren't stupid and, although initially reluctant, I expect them to promote the notions that derive value from ideas. Business has shown itself to be very adaptable, moulding itself around the biggest opportunity to make money. As the realities of an idea-based economy continue to impose themselves, it's only logical that business will come to embrace them, and, in fact, probably accelerate their adoption to maximize competitive gain.

As the human potential of people becomes indispensable to the economic success of our companies, our companies will need to become ever better at providing meaning, satisfaction and creative fulfilment to the people producing the value. This is the compelling rationale for basing the new business model on reciprocity.

In his book, *The Industrialization of Intelligence*, Noah Kennedy concludes, "The best prospect for society is that the technological and scientific rationalization in the future will respond to the rational and freely expressed self-interest of a broadly defined community of humanity...This is another way of saying that humanity's future, as it has always been, is hostage to our desires and beliefs, and ultimately to our values. Our values guide our rationalizations, and values arise from the meaning we sense in our existence."[9]

The values of an economy driven by ideas are necessarily more human-centred, since only people have the capacity to imagine, create and think. This value-shift is essentially what is driving the code of business to be more reciprocal, more respectful of human priorities, while achieving profits. While reciprocity may be based on economic considerations, its net effect will be to support all humans who are involved with business to reach and quest for greater realization of their full potential.

If we are to secure North America's place in the economy of ideas, we obviously need to develop the capacity for ideas within our people and organizations. Once again, the interdependence between corporations and the society that supports them comes into play. Business, and the national and regional governments that support it, will be responsible for developing the mind-skills that such an economy requires.

Business has contributed to many of the problems that afflict our society, but it also holds within itself the capacity to help solve them. As we begin to focus the energy of business against those problems, as we define new opportunities for profit and corporate development, we will find business to be a progressive, productive force for change.

The creativity and inclination to innovation that business has shown will be indispensable to our society, as we grapple with the difficult issues of environmental clean-up, raw-material management and waste minimization. The flexibility of business, to achieve maximum benefit from its opportunities, also means that it will be receptive to evolving systems and structures that are more supportive of human aspirations and equality.

Most of the people in business are considerate, committed to their communities and to the progress and well-being of the next generation. Harnessing this inherent goodwill, and the vast resources that business commands, afford a unique opportunity for effecting progressive, productive, mutually rewarding change. Evolving business to enrich in human dimensions, as well as financial ones, can help solve some of the debilitating problems that we collectively face, while also providing corporate leaders, managers and employees a heightened sense of spiritual satisfaction for their achievements.

Business is not perfect, but it represents one of the few bright lights available to people around the world. We should challenge business to be better, while supporting it in its efforts. We should also make it more accountable, while unleashing its immense reserves of initiative and creativity to help people, and help society, realize dreams.

ADVERTISING AND THE RELEVANCE OF BUSINESS

Advertising is a mirror for business. Business is pervasive. Advertising is pervasive. Business is aggressive. Advertising is aggressive. Just as business sometimes captures dreams, causing the imagination to soar, advertising sometimes connects with its audience to evoke those dreams and stimulate imagination. And, just as business often disenfranchises people, because it exploits and pollutes, advertising often disengages its audience, because it clutters and repeats itself.

Advertising is not frivolous. On its most noble plane, advertising is a vehicle of free speech, a dynamic of our democracy, spreading information, communicating choice, and contributing to the competitive tradition of the free market. But, like capitalism itself, advertising can also be abusive, too intrusive and caught up in its own objectives to provide any relevance to society at large.

The values and ethics that guide business are most visible in the advertising that companies run for their products and services. How companies view themselves, what they believe about business, and how they regard their customers are, to one degree or another, evident in the selling communication that they design for themselves. In expressing how companies value their own products and their own customers, advertising tells us a lot about the general relationship between people and the advertisers talking to them.

Any evolution in the values of business requires a corresponding evolution in the values of advertising. Business needs advertising to communicate, to establish and develop the relationships through which its can conduct a commercial exchange with its customers. With the growing demand for more socially responsible business practices, companies will need to revitalize their advertising to reflect these changing values, and to build relationships with customers across a spectrum of human dimensions, beyond that of simply selling to them.

Advertising has proven its power in performing this role, with its very successful campaigns on socially important issues like drinking and driving and drug abuse. Advertising can move people, not only to buy hamburgers on $.99 discount, but also to reflect and react to complicated issues. This is important, not because all commercial advertising should become cause-oriented, but because such cause-advertising proves that advertising can engage people in more complete, more human terms than it traditionally has.

Disposable Advertising Is Going The Way Of Disposable Products

For a long time, and particularly during the last forty years, the industry of advertising has promoted itself as the communication specialists. Even today, most ad people would position themselves as consumer experts, able to distil people's needs and define strategies for communicating the selling proposition with the most impact. Like the business values that are only geared to profit, much of this expertise in advertising is now out of date, and out of sync with the goals and concerns of the public. Just as business is developing a new model for operating in a socially responsible way, so, too, are we in advertising struggling to come up with the new paradigm for genuinely reaching and moving people in our modern society.

Advertising effectiveness in North America is waning. Some of the reduced effectiveness is understandable. Many of the product and service categories that advertising supports are mature. In these instances, most advertising spending is defensive, attempting to hold people's awareness and protect market-share. Without the inducement of new growth, business and its advertising both settle into a fairly static maintenance pattern.

Another very important reason for the drop-off in advertising effectiveness is the growing callousness of the North American audience. This society, and particularly the generations after the Second World War, has been marketed to on a scale that is incomprehensible. The tools and devices of advertising have become second nature to them. And with this over-exposure, people have naturally built up defensive systems and screens of cynicism, through which they choose the very few messages that have meaning for them, while discarding the vast majority.

Marketers have, for a long time, used the metaphor of war to discipline their communications activities. They develop "strategies" for "aiming" their selling messages at selected "target groups," to realize specific "objectives." By implication, such a metaphor sets the prospect up as an "enemy," to be "hit" with advertising and "won over" with a sale. This language inescapably defines the relationship between customer and company as an adversarial one. Rather than cajoling and convincing, this premise for business is based on overwhelming. Not surprisingly, people have learned to fend for themselves, when it comes to advertising. As in any war, the "enemy" eventually absorbs the strategy of the opponent, and tries to build a defense against it.

So marketing-smart are many people that they've adopted some of the vernacular of the business as their own. The marketing wars between beer companies and cola companies, between fast-food chains and car marques, have familiarized the general public with business concepts such as "targeting" and "line extension." And they've heard the claim for "new and improved" so many times that smart companies have actually stopped using this phraseology, because its credibility has been so diluted. This, then, is a case in which the success of advertising, its very pervasiveness, has caused people to tune most of it out.

There are also very important, but often over-looked, cultural reasons for this decline in advertising effectiveness. We know, because we're so well-informed, that we are living in the information age. More accurately, our society and the whole human family is in the midst of a major revolution, the major catalyst for which is the information-supporting technologies of the computer, mass media, and communications. Because we are living through the volatile transition, most of us have lost our perspective and are unable to accurately gauge the degree and significance of the change our society is absorbing.

Although our world is profoundly shaped by this information revolution, many of the communications industries that have contributed to, and accelerated, that revolution are now themselves being overtaken by the rapid change. The TV networks, which linked the country, our North American continent, and then the whole world, are now overlapped by so many competitors that their very viability is in question. Advertising, too, has lost some of its viability and effectiveness, because of the very clutter it helped to create.

Within an overcommunicated society, people absorb information and formulate understanding in a different way. With less information to distract them, people in the past could extend more interest to the messages being directed at them. As those messages have proliferated, people have less time and less inclination to extend any interest, except to those few messages that are of significant relevance to them.

Most communications models that the advertising industry uses today were formulated well before the information revolution began. Advertisements had evolved to the point where they tried to meet the customer half-way, melding the selling message of the advertising company with the benefits and imagery that were of interest to the audience. However, in an overcommunicated environment, going half-way is no longer enough. Today, the needs of the product must be subjugated to the needs of the customer. The same lessons that companies are learning about customization of their products apply to advertising. Selling-communication must get closer and closer to the beliefs and biases of the audience, even if it means making the audience more important than the source of the message.

Rather than waging war against their prospects, marketers must learn to seduce them through superior service. Despite the obviousness of this need, most advertising strategies continue to be constructed around company-centred principles that were defined more than two generations ago. The creative strategies used by most clients and their advertising agencies continue to set out "objectives," "benefits," "tactics" and "target group" definitions, as if the war with consumers was still raging. The war is over, but the loser persists in adhering to an obsolete strategy.

The Great Distraction

Although there is a desperate need to experiment and develop new models for selling-communication, the advertising industry has been slow to respond. In large part, that's because we who work in advertising have been so distracted. The empires that defined the advertising industry for the last decade are unravelling, threatening to send it through a second paroxysm of change. First, as they assembled their worldwide networks of acquisitions and reverse take-overs, and now, during their prolonged restructuring and threatened dismantling, companies like Saatchi & Saatchi, and WPP (Wire & Plastic Products) have radically altered the advertising industry. This upheaval, while very traumatic, has not advanced the industry's understanding of communications by even one iota.

Rather than evolve new understanding for the changing, highly volatile marketplace, the management of many advertising agencies spent the 1980s distracted, caught up in the vortex of financial scheming and buy-outs that preoccupied so many businesses in the merger-mania decade. Instead of refining our expertise in the theory of communication and the art of persuasion, many of us got practice in managing the legal labyrinth of purchase agreements and the alchemy of accounting earn-outs.

In our own company, many hundreds of hours of senior management time were devoted to "future" planning—to the debate and negotiation of possible "deals." The energy expended in plotting possible purchase or selling scenarios was energy drained from the active management of our company and the progressive service of our clients. The expertise I personally acquired, the countless hours with legal and financial consultants, the contract negotiations, was largely empty, having little meaning or application in advancing the understanding or effectiveness of advertising.

It took us almost two years, after completing an alliance with a British partner, to recover a sense of purpose and equilibrium. It took that long for our people to settle in, after the dislocating rumours about a possible sale. It took that long to re-earn the trust and support of current clients, and to leverage their good will to successfully go after more new business. And it took that long for our company to achieve the improvements in our product that got us back to the standard we had originally set for ourselves.

Our company was not alone. The face of our industry was dramatically re-drawn during the 1980s. Of the seven Canadian companies that dominated the advertising scene before 1980, only two have survived as independents, and even one of those has been through a prolonged, distracting ownership struggle. Many smaller agencies followed the pattern set by the bigger agencies, having negotiated their own sell-outs and mergers. The net effect was thousands of hours spent, by among the best minds in the advertising industry, on the largely peripheral issue of ownership, and not on the substantive one of advertising effectiveness.

It is ironic that, while many of my colleagues and I were preoccupied with the intricacies of merger and finance, the very basis of our industry's validity shifted. Much of the body of advertising knowledge and communications experience that we were busy leveraging lost value and relevance. The consumers and customers from whom we derived our real equity were slipping away.

The timing of this distraction has been unfortunate. In effect, it drained the industry's dedication to the fundamentals of advertising, just as society was outgrowing many of the methods and tactics upon which the industry had based its validity. In poll after poll, the public demonstrates itself to be increasingly unmoved, sometimes even immune to the long-held strategies and creative approaches used by advertising.

Perhaps the most disturbing reminder of advertising's waning influence is the fact that the most of North American society dislikes the bulk of the advertising aimed at it. People actively express their displeasure by zapping commercials with their remote controls, or fast-forwarding them on their VCRs, or hissing at them when ads appear on movie screens. Passively, they simply ignore them.

For some marketers and advertisers, being liked is secondary in importance to being heard. This is flawed thinking, which not only disenfranchises people towards the disliked ad, but also dilutes the effectiveness and equity of advertising as an institution. Bad ads, and those that are disliked by people, serve to bring down the quality of the whole body of selling-communication.

For example, the sexist advertising, for products such as beer, has been justified on the narrow grounds that it works, appealing to the largely male "target group." However, by persisting in such sexist tactics, despite the growing sensitivity in society to issues of equality and sexual responsibility, beer companies have now alienated large segments of society. As a consequence, not only beer companies but all advertisers face the prospect of increased pressure from concerned special-interest groups, and more governmental regulation. The irresponsible actions of a few result in constraints on the majority.

Likeability is but one dimension of the impact and persuasiveness of an advertisement. The broader issue is that the average quality of advertising in the last decade has not advanced. With the changes in society—the heightened level of information overload, and the greater cynicism of the public—the failure to advance has meant that advertising has actually declined in effectiveness. Like the North American car companies, which lost touch with their customers, most advertising continues to speak in a language no longer used by the people it is trying to communicate with.

I am not overstating my case. Car makers have spent nearly a decade using the bribery of rebates, to win back customers whose quality expectations they failed to meet. Similarly, a great portion of advertising has degenerated into the promotional babble of give-aways and special-offer inducements, attempting to move customers whose hearts and minds have become deaf to its traditional messages and techniques.

The Leaders Have Become Laggard

Not only has advertising not kept pace with the psychological and values changes that have affected our over-communicated society, but increasingly, the very tools for reaching them have been transformed dramatically, as well.

Network television, the locomotive of marketing in the 1960s, suffered the same splintering, as a medium, that characterizes our whole society. Cable TV and Pay TV greatly expanded the options for viewing, so much so that the once-universal big three American networks, ABC, CBS and NBC, at times only reach *half* of the households viewing television. VCRs and video games further eroded conventional TV viewing. This is an incredible change. Yet, despite the massive restructuring of television, and the other dislocations caused by the explosion of information, the principles and measurement devices used in the advertising profession are largely left over from the Ed Sullivan era.

Currently, advertising in North America is based on a model of reach and frequency. In the simplistic mathematics of this approach, as many prospects as possible are reached as often as possible within the allocated budget. Exposures of advertising messages are measured in the millions. This theory holds that one message becomes more effective the more it is sent to, and received by, the intended prospect.

This theory of repetition in advertising is not unlike the theory of mass manufacturing, in whose service it was originally developed. Make more. Repeat more. Sell more. This is the cycle upon which most advertising campaigns have been based. As the theory of manufacturing has changed, to address the needs of the marketplace for customization and responsibility, it's logical that the theory of selling-communication must undergo a similar transformation.

Yet, a new paradigm for advertising has yet to evolve. Agencies and their clients are still measuring reach and frequency, and are still emphasizing repetition of message. This strategy fails to align to the new sensibilities of the very public it is trying to persuade. Consumers are increasingly rejecting disposable products, and increasingly recoiling from disposable advertising. Frequency, which once served to "pound home the message," may have been acceptable in a climate of few information alternatives, but it is illogical when consumers can so quickly turn their already-short attention spans to something that interests them more.

One of the still to be absorbed lessons of the age we're living in is that all of us have become voracious consumers of information. Unlike products that provide a specific utility, and are purchased again and again to perform that function, information, once consumed, must be recreated in order to engage attention and capture interest. Information is the most perishable product in the information age, yet we continue to advertise as if the message had the same currency after one hundred exposures as it did after its first.

With so many messages vying for our attention, it is only natural for any human being to respond positively to variety and new ideas, and to turn away from the repetitive and boring. If we are wondering where the current advertising model falls short, we need not look beyond the commonsensical notion that "variety is the spice of life." While a degree of frequency is obviously necessary, just to be heard in the marketplace, the unrefreshed, unrelenting repetition used by the majority of marketers leaves most people numb, immune to the objectives of advertising and disconnected from any relevance that it may provide to them.

Infusing New Substance Into Old Sizzle

Just as the trauma of market-share loss triggered a new appreciation for the customer among car companies, I'm confident that the shock of having its equity so depleted will refocus advertising executives on rebuilding the currency of their industry. This is important, because, to effect an overall renewal of business within our society, we need to have a healthy and relevant advertising industry.

Advertising seems to be too frivolous to warrant such importance. One British advertising maven has called advertising "the rock and roll" of business, and most people perceive advertising to be relatively insubstantial. Advertising seems to be neither a profession nor an art. Yet, for all the apparent frivolity of its messages, for all the idiosyncrasies of its practitioners, advertising plays a critically important role in the interchange between companies and the people who buy their products.

Traditionally, advertising has sold aggressively, formulating its communication mostly from the point of view of the product being advertised. This product-centred view of advertising reflected the product-centred view of the advertiser. Some of this advertising has been very loud. Some of it, offensive. Much of it, imitative. But, as long as it worked, by the traditional measure of generating sales results, advertisers and their agencies persisted in adhering to its sometimes-abrasive precepts and devices.

Now, as society becomes more discerning in its consumption patterns, and as it demands more responsibility of its business institutions, product-centred marketing and advertising are much less relevant. Many companies have acknowledged this transition by adopting more customer-oriented strategies. These have yet to yield an improvement because, for the most part, marketers and advertisers refuse to accept that they are no longer in control of the marketing and advertising process.

Their outdated perceptions are even evident in their titles and job descriptions. People who work in marketing are often called Product Managers. And the marketers who work in advertising are called Account Executives. These designations reinforce the old hierarchy. The *product* and the *account* are no longer the first priority, but are secondary in importance to the customer, who must be reached, served and satisfied. However, it is easier to accept the notion of change than the reality of a loss of power. And most people in marketing and advertising have yet to face the reality that this power has passed irrevocably from the company to the customer.

Rather than making the investment to search for new models, many marketers and advertising people are content to accept the erosion of the current one. Studies among clients show that they perceive advertising effectiveness to have dropped during the last five years. These same studies indicate that clients believe that the professionalism and expertise of the people planning and creating the advertising have also dropped.

Among the consequences of these seriously held perceptions is that advertising is decreasingly viewed as an investment in opportunity, and more and more as a defensive expense, a cost of doing business. The advertising budgets in many companies are under constant pressure, exactly because clients now see it as discretionary, and not intrinsic to marketing.

The climb back to credibility and relevance is important, not only for the vitality of the advertising industry, but for the broader health of business. While it is often confused with its tactics and devices, advertising is more than a message, more than an attempt at memorability and persuasion. Advertising is, quintessentially, a means of building and nurturing a relationship. The credibility and relevance of business rests, in large part, on the credibility and relevance of its selling-communications.

Making Human Connections

Relationship-building between a company and its customers and public will be one of the most important priorities of socially responsible business enterprises. Through its process of communication, of engaging its audience and delivering a message, advertising closes the distance between a company, its products, and the people who buy and use them. Advertising creates familiarity. Really good advertising also creates empathy and emotional connection. Out of these grow the bonds between customer and company, between buyer and seller, between user and brand.

We know from our personal lives that relationships are often complex and fragile. Miscommunication and misunderstanding are not only possible but prevalent in even the closest of friendships, and the most intimate of relationships. Instead of exploring this complexity, most advertising has avoided it, resorting to simple, simplistic, rational selling messages to promote rational purchase decisions. This approach goes against one of the most basic mysteries of human nature—our endless capacity to defy logic, to use reason only occasionally, and almost never when making big decisions.

For Canada to go to war in the Persian Gulf, for our country to run up a deficit so huge that future generations will be taxed heavily to fulfil its obligations, for Canadians to pit their armed forces against the Native people, for us to accept the possible disintegration of Canada itself, are some examples of how illogical and emotional even the most important of our decisions are. Buying detergent or a new automobile involves points of rational assessment, but most of these are obscured in a domineering cloud of emotion, tradition and imagery.

While a considerable amount of advertising claims to be working on an emotional plane, most tries to sandwich a rational point of "hard-sell" within an interesting or clever "soft-sell." For the most part, the communications-sandwiches defeat themselves. What is viewed as "hard-sell" is often what is important to the marketer. What is seen as the "soft-sell" is often what is important to the prospect. In reality, most advertising has only a naïve understanding of the psychology and value system of the people it is trying to sell to. More important than either "hard-sell" or "soft-sell" is relevance.

Building relevance is what will revitalize the advertising industry, and restore the value of its product to marketers. As we move into an era in which it will be important for business to connect on a much wider, much deeper band with society, advertising, with its capacities for connecting people and ideas, has the potential to affect not only sales, but the quality of the new relationship between business and society. By building new bridges between companies and their customers, between business and its broader community, advertising can help revitalize North American business, to meet both its commercial goals and interlinked social challenges.

The work of advertising will always be primarily to get sales results. But increasingly, the achievement of those results will require that business meet obligations that are far broader than the simple delivery of the promised product benefit. Advertising will logically need to engage prospects on this band of wider, deeper obligation.

Already, the reciprocity that society is demanding of business is having an impact on advertising. Companies that have adopted green marketing initiatives are using advertising to express their environmental sensibilities to consumers. In addition to planting ideas to sell products, such advertising helps align the values and sensibilities of the advertised product with those that are deeply held by the people buying those products. This fosters a relationship of greater depth and dimension.

As the competitive cycle of product improvements heats up, and as consumers become more educated about the environmental impact of their purchases, a circle of reciprocity is created. The environment benefits from products that are less damaging. The consumer benefits from products that fulfil psychological, as well as functional, needs. And the marketer benefits from the greater loyalty that its socially responsible business practices engender. Importantly, advertising interconnects the interdependencies, to make this circle work.

In time, as business gives more back to the society that sustains it, it is very likely that advertising itself will be expected to do more than simply promote. Advertising, like business, will be expected to make a contribution, as well as make a sale. Some of this pressure, already apparent, may come in the form of regulation. But probably the more significant and lasting pressure will come from the dissonance of current advertising techniques, and society's demand for ever more sensible and responsible business and selling practices.

One important consequence is that a typical advertising campaign will require a significantly greater variety of messages. This again represents a paradigm-shift for most marketers and advertising people. In the industry's current thinking, the creation and production of these messages are viewed as being of secondary importance to the expenditure required to expose the message. In the gospel according to "reach and frequency," the spending in media is actually referred to as "working" dollars, while the spending for the production of the commercial message is called "non-working."

These designations, and the underlying operating strategy to limit spending on the actual message, contribute to the very clutter they try so hard to break through. With its focus on repetition, the current model of "working" and "non-working" is working no longer. If we were to take the perspective of the customer, the prospect at whom the advertising is being directed, we would see that this logic is, in fact, reversed. Repetition benefits the advertiser, because it provides greater efficiency. But it fundamentally ignores the need of the prospect to be engaged in a new, fresh, interesting, active and interactive manner.

In advertising, as in life, a relationship is renewed and kept vital through constant interaction and interchange. Since most people being sold to are passive participants in this relationship, the onus is on the advertiser to provide the stimulus to keep the relationship current and growing. We don't tell our friends the same story over and over again. We don't expect them to pay attention, to respond, unless we are saying something that is of interest to them, that challenges their imaginations, that evokes their emotions, that enriches their lives.

As the complexity of the relationship between business and its customers grows, it is only natural that the advertising that feeds that relationship become more complex, more multidimensional. More variety, more intrigue, more empathy, and not greater frequency, will win customers for companies, and support the more diverse relationship that today's more competitive business environment warrants.

A communications model based on the premise of developing deeper, more fully human relationships between companies and people is very challenging. The creative talent of the advertising industry will finally be accorded the importance in the communications process that their ability to create meaningful messages deserves. With this respect, however, there also come attendant responsibilities, which advertising people must acknowledge and accept accountability for.

First among these responsibilities is a much more comprehensive understanding of the psychology and beliefs-structure of the people the advertising is trying to engage. Many advertising people, by reason of their creativity, talent and intelligence, view themselves as superior to the people they are trying to reach and touch. This arrogance is cancerous, and it explains why so much advertising, even some that is highly innovative, ends up talking to itself.

Agencies and the people who actually create the advertising are to blame. The understanding of the prospect, the customer, is often clinical and indirect. Creative people generally read briefs prepared by their marketing counterparts. Their exposure to customers is usually through research. Often these are no more than numbers on a page. Even when creative people sit through focus groups, to gauge the priorities and responses of customers, the contact with the consumer is filtered through the world-distorting glass of a one-way mirror.

Separated from real people, from a profound understanding of their real values and instincts, it's no wonder that most advertising has had only a superficial impact on those it is trying to persuade. In the future, creative people, those who actually conceive the selling ideas, write the words and art-direct the visuals, must take greater responsibility for delving deeper into the psychology of consumers. They, and not the Gestapo-like account service group, must look face-to-face into the eyes of the people they are trying to engage.

This new responsibility will require that creative people step out from behind the aura of artistic idiosyncrasy. To earn their expanded role within the marketing process, they must accept their professional responsibilities, and with the humility that all of us must learn in business, they must put their talent at the service of the hearts and minds of the people being advertised to.

The second important responsibility is to revise the strategic formulae for advertising, to reflect the ascendancy of the consumer and the subservience of the product. Most creative strategies are written as if the war with the customer is still being waged. "Objectives" are defined from the point of view of the company. Prospective customers are singled out as "targets." A "benefit" to be derived from the product is identified and substantiated. The alienating effect of this approach warrants a cease-fire.

New words, new concepts that reflect the changing priorities of the customer must be developed. Creative strategies, in the future, will strive to direct advertising to build relationships. The human and psychological insights that contribute to that relationship—that engage interest, that elicit involvement and participation—will be the key components of that strategy. Its language will be more human, replacing the false precision of business-speak, with words that respect the individuality of the person whose custom advertisers are trying to earn. Importantly, these documents will seek to define the terms of reciprocity; what the product and company will give to both the consumer and society, in exchange for a purchase.

Reciprocity means giving something back. In advertising, it will not be enough to simply communicate what the client or product is giving back. The advertising itself must express and evoke reciprocity. Each advertisement must, therefore, contain its own "benefit." Only if the advertising itself rewards the viewer, be it through entertainment value, humour, or news value, can we expect the promise and reward of the advertised product to come through. Only by demonstrating its own reciprocity, by being relevant, can we expect advertising to be effective in planting the selling benefits and expressing the reciprocity of the advertised product.

The ethics of advertising, like the ethics of business, must be above reproach. Interacting with people, on terms that embrace their full humanity, increases the responsibility for advertising to be honest and respectful of its audience. Upon this base of credibility, it will be possible to revitalize advertising to be relevant and highly creative, selling products, reinforcing the broader values of the company, and using the full spectrum of artistic expression to gain the attention and interaction of people. Overcoming concerns about advertising's credibility must be as important a priority to business as overcoming its clutter, in our over-communicated but less-than-understanding world.

Advertising, in its heyday, was called the locomotive of business. The changes in the marketplace have relegated this industry to caboose status. It now seems to follow, more than lead. And, from its trailing position, it seems always to be under threat of being cut back by clients. This metaphor dates the conceptual innovations of advertising, since most of them were made by people like David Ogilvy and Roser Reeves, in the era of rail travel.

It's time to update the currency of this important tool of business. It's time to start the experimentation and academic learning that will advance the concepts of advertising, revitalizing them to be as vital and valid, at the end of the information revolution, as they were in the beginning.

EXPANDING THE HUMAN AND PROFIT POTENTIAL OF BUSINESS THROUGH ART

Many managers are genuinely searching for new ideas with which to revitalize their operations, stimulate their employees, and enhance company performance, in terms of both customer satisfaction and profit achievement. The process is dynamic. New problems befuddle even the most well-managed companies. Competitor initiatives, industry evolutions, customer defections, and employee listlessness keep company leaders on their toes.

With so many variables to manage, it has become common practice in the last decade for companies to import ideas. Consultants transplant their views and notions, to solve specific problems. Books and seminars offer transfusions of still other concepts, which have proven themselves in other circumstances with other companies. After almost ten years of dissecting excellence as preached by Peters and Waterman, and absorbing quality as promulgated by Demming, and aspiring to the leadership as taught by Kotter, and designing competitiveness as strategized by Porter, most companies have only gotten marginally better, without getting the desired breakthrough advantage.

The reason for the widespread mediocrity that afflicts North American companies is that many of these ideas, while valid unto themselves, are not inspired by, and integrated within, the core culture of companies. My own company's experience, and that of many of our clients, is that, although our minds understand the benefits of these concepts, our hearts lack the conviction to implement them thoroughly, to derive the full benefit of the concept we are importing.

D. Quinn Mills, an economist and professor at the Harvard Business School, has found this gap between intent and achievement in many of the companies he's consulted with. In his book, *Rebirth of the Corporation*, Mills finds many managers who have been through various attempts at revitalization and say, "We talk the talk, but do we walk the walk?"

Emergencies and crises often propel dramatic change in a company. In these survival-threatening circumstances, new beliefs are more readily encoded in the corporate psyche. But the change that gnaws at our companies every day is generally far less traumatic, and the responses we contrive or import often lack the urgency to impel deep and genuine conviction.

The issue we face, as leaders of companies, as managers, and as employees participating in the venture, is to develop within companies a near-genetic capacity for change. To encode change is an almost contradictory notion, because the response must be as dynamic as the change that stimulates it.

There are devices and tactics for prompting change, and for encouraging people to break one pattern of behaviour and accept another. Some companies, like IBM, use frequent restructurings to infuse new ideas and new challenges into their massive bureaucracies. Counterintuitively, IBM "fixes things that aren't broke," believing that change is best made when things are going well and the company is in a position of strength.

Many of the companies going through the heightened disruption of a merger have learned that even in these most traumatic of circumstances, change is very difficult to execute, and it is nearly impossible to impose productively. Consultants suggest different strategies for weaving together two disparate enterprises. Teams comprising managers and workers from both companies are given the responsibility to shed inappropriate or obsolete equipment, systems and traditions, retain those that enhance competitiveness, and develop new practices that align with the strategy of the merged new entity.

Usually, this well-intentioned planning works much better in theory than in reality. People resist change. It understandably threatens the comfortable rhythm of expectation and habit that people have developed. Even with the most obvious and rational impetus to change, like the health risks that support stopping smoking, it is very difficult for people to let go of the comfortable.

While we all know that the rate of change is accelerating, our society and business institutions have provided very little training, very little guidance, in how to manage the emotional upheaval of an ever-shifting reality. The energy of most institutions is, in any case, usually directed to achieving stability, to preserving and protecting that which has been institutionalized. Implanting within a company's culture a heightened capacity for change is something that business managers acknowledge to be important, but which, because of its fluidity, ultimately threatens the very structure that spawns it.

Opening To Art: Opening To Change

To become a society that embraces change, and to create companies that thrive on constant change, requires a more fundamental redesign of our institutions. Among the under-valued, under-appreciated factors that can help us manage change and participate in its manifestation is art. Artistic experience, for the artists and for those who respond to it, is transformative, thereby contributing to our own human capacity to experiment, to try the new, to risk, and to change.

In our current North American culture, art is very much on the periphery of of our social consciousness. After the necessities of life and commerce are attended to, art is accorded some marginal attention at the fringe of our interests. We've consigned art to the far corners of our museums and galleries, to occasional programming on PBS. Throughout our culture, we approach art as if it were a discretionary commodity, something to dabble in, to support occasionally and, in few moments of reflection, to be inspired by.

Art is far more fundamental to the human experience. Throughout human history, art has reflected people's aspirations and fears, their sacred and secular preoccupations and concerns. Art has been very important in providing a source of meaning, helping to translate the ebb and flow of life into patterns of nobility, dignity and worth. Art has expressed vision, capturing in its colours, movements and forms the self-image of nations, generations and entire eras. Most fundamentally, art has stretched the imagination, giving warning, offering hope, defining the futility and the ascendant that push and pull at every human life.

Materialism blinds us to the true source and meaning of art. The interchanges between a person and the archetypes, moods and meanings of art are not discretionary, but rather, if we are to genuinely accept our continuity as human beings, are essential concerns and preoccupations. By neglecting our human inclination to art, our society has deprived itself of a wonderful source of renewal, refreshment and regeneration. And, by limiting art to just an occasional corporate investment, business has deprived itself of a powerful tool for enhancing the development, productivity, and quality of life of its people.

Change has been a fairly constant dimension of human experience. However, there are several periods throughout history, including ours, where the spurt of change is of unprecedented proportions. The widespread dislocation of our society, wrought by the explosion of information into our lives, is very similar to the transformation that European society underwent during the Renaissance. Science and primitive industrialization were beginning to transform the predominantly agrarian culture of Europe. The superstitions of the Dark Ages were giving way to the enlightenment of thoughtful, methodical, scientific exploration.

It is hard for us to imagine the shock to the system that the discoveries of Copernicus and Galileo represented in their time. Seemingly immutable beliefs were shredded. Deep cultural convictions, many of them based on centuries-old religious dogma, were uprooted. The fundamental self-image of society changed from one of fear, darkness and dependency to one of self-confidence, enlightenment, and self-sufficiency.

As the society grappled with the mind- and soul-boggling changes of the Renaissance, it exploded with artistic achievement. The historical reasons for this are many. The expanding merchant class provided a wider base of patronage for the arts. New techniques and technology pushed out the boundaries of art. And the more extensive trade patterns allowed for a more frequent, dynamic exchange of ideas and concepts between cities, countries and continents.

While this explains why the Renaissance was so fertile a period of artistic achievement, it does not adequately convey the role that art itself played in helping European society come to terms with its revolutionary rate of change. As science began the highly distressing process of displacing religion as the source of life-meaning and understanding, society turned to its art to provide an expression of the emerging vision of itself.

Art provided new symbols for a society in transition. It evoked images of awe, and also of comprehension, as art mirrored how humans saw themselves, within a universe that science was unfolding in ever greater detail for them. Art became a guidepost, helping people come to terms with the society they were creating. It expressed new values. And art helped to exorcise those demons of inadequacy that haunted the psyche of society.

Although there were many economic and political factors that conspired to end the repressive feudal traditions of the Middle Ages, much of the meaning and process of liberation, initiated during the Renaissance, was advanced by art. Poetry, painting, music and sculpture gave expression to the dreams of society. Art demonstrated the ascendant qualities of human nature, providing emotional and spiritual reinforcement for the notions of equality and egalitarianism that were promoted by moral philosophers and political scientists.

Today, we are again in the midst of a great social transformation. Information is changing what we know, what we do and how we do it. Importantly, information is also changing how we see our lives and our society. Another great liberation is taking place. Access to information liberates people and opens them to new possibilities. The democracy movements in Eastern Europe, the demands for greater personal freedom in Korea, the aborted, but still fermenting, democracy movement in China, were all inspired and, in large measure, fueled by information and the electronic media that convey it.

Information is also liberating the workplace. First in offices, and now in factories, information is shifting power within commercial organizations, from those who manage to those who do the work. The feudal working system, based on standardization and control, is being replaced by one that liberates the individual to contribute on a much more expansive dimension of thinking and creating.

As with other great movements of change, the economic transition we are undergoing is very distressing. Many people, both in blue- and white-collar jobs, are ill-prepared to cope with the constant shifting and churning characteristic of an era on the way to becoming something else. Security has evaporated, and with it, the beliefs and concepts that have underpinned people's relationships with the communities they live in and the companies they work for. And we are so busy trying to cope with change that there is little time for reflection.

During the war in the Persian Gulf, the world was inundated with information, but still lacks fundamental understanding of what was achieved, and at what human cost to the vanquished. We know too much, but understand too little. We have access to an abundance of information, yet we seem to be suffering from a dearth of meaning.

While art became a source for this understanding during the Renaissance, we've so segregated it from the day-to-day process of our social interchange that we've lost the capacity to mine it for meaning. Art is so outside of our social experience that it has been reduced to a largely irrelevant novelty. Rediscovering the power of art will help us come to terms with the society we are becoming. Integrating the experience of art into our lives, and into the commercial structures that we work within, may actually help us increase our capacity for change, as well as our resilience and flexibility in accommodating it.

Companies already use art. Thomas Watson Jr. commissioned some of the greatest architects available, to design not only IBM's offices but also its manufacturing plants and warehouses. The style that IBM developed reinforced its modernity, and provided employees with an environmental expression of their goal—to be dynamic participants in creating the future with their products and services.

Many other companies have such architectural traditions. Frank Lloyd Wright designed the headquarters building for Johnson's Wax, providing a structure of great grace and imagination, which still evokes awe and delight among people who work within the space, and those fortunate enough to visit it.

Companies also frequently buy art, as an investment, as an expression of support for the broader arts community, and as decorative punctuation for the corporate character expressed in the working environment. Company collections sometimes become very large, very valuable, but they also often remain in the hallowed halls frequented only by the corporate elite. The exclusivity of such corporate art makes it a badge, a fringe benefit for those executives who already have a company car. Like the princes of the Middle Ages, such corporate benefactors use art to express both their self-importance and power.

Most large corporations and many smaller companies contribute to the arts through sponsorships. Texaco has sponsored broadcasts of the Metropolitan Opera for over fifty years. General Motors sponsored Ken Burns's brilliant TV documentary, *The Civil War*. American Express and Pepsi are sponsoring the production of the art-spectacle, *The Phantom of the Opera*, across Canada. The list goes on and on.

Sponsorships genuinely enrich the community. Art is presented to a wider public than it would otherwise have been exposed to, because of the support provided by the corporate contributor. Just as many companies have charity funds, many also have arts funds, so that they can provide some support, and reap the attendant goodwill and visibility that their contributions warrant.

While important, and to be applauded, the involvement of companies with the arts is, at best, only superficial. Art generally sits outside the corporate interest. It is not a vital, fundamental concern of commercial institutions. When connected to the company, art is most often a source for business entertainment. Openings and box seats and expositions are used to reward employees, or treat special customers to a non-business, but still commercially motivated, event. So, because it sits at the periphery of corporate interest, art is often misused or under-utilized by companies.

As we strive to create business enterprises that provide more meaning and fulfilment to our employees, art can be an important conduit for people, through which they connect their thoughts, emotions and spiritual longings to what they do for a living. Art is essentially an exploration of meaning, and bringing the questioning and perspective of art to the workplace can help to formulate the deeper satisfaction that people hope to derive from what they do.

Questioning In Art Stimulates Thinking In Business

Art in the workplace does more than provide an environmental boost for employees. Art, in its creation and with the responses it elicits, stimulates the quality of thinking and reflection that most companies need to be competitive today. The artistic mind looks beyond convention, stretching the expected to explore what can be. This mental questing is exactly what we need for our North American companies to grow and remain vital in the global economy of ideas.

Often, art is seen as a qualitative experience that is inconsistent with the quantitative world of business. The two, like other aspects of our humanity, are, in fact, interwoven and complimentary. The Russian artist and philosopher Ernst Neizvestny sees a symbiotic relationship between art and science. "In the human spiritual sphere, the creative activity of the artist and the scientist is necessarily interdependent. The artist broadens the circle of associations and feelings, including the scientist. The scientist broadens humanity's concept of the world and reveals new possibilities for the artist's creative work."[1]

This interplay between the creativity of art and the quantification of science provides business with a mechanism for creating a culture of pragmatic innovation. Neizvestny writes, "The scientist and the artist both increase knowledge of the world to an equal degree, although the external form of their contribution differs. Image and intuition, concept and symbol enter into the creative work of an artist and scientist in different stages and in different proportions. But the nature of art contains presentiments of scientific truth." The relationship between art and business holds the same potential.

In learning about art, in learning to unleash their own artistic sensibilities and talents, people within business are developing skills that can enhance their productivity, as well as their self-worth. In working with information, the only way to achieve productivity gains is by increasing the capacity for understanding. The artistic mind, in its questioning and experimentation, is open to the new interconnections of thoughts and the new combination of ideas that provide understanding. As people become more comfortable with involving themselves in the unique spatial dimensions of art, their aptitude for somersaulting new ideas in business increases.

Art is a medium, facilitating the communication of thoughts, concepts, emotions and vision. As more and more workplaces are inundated with information, art can provide new models for its transmission and dissemination. We know how limited memos and business plans are, in their ability to inform and inspire, and the tools of art may provide the means for extending comprehension to the intuitive level that is more and more important to us in business.

Art expresses the silence between spoken words. It explains the message concealed in the white space between written words. Art provokes and evokes, giving form to the emotional and spiritual notions that go beyond our rational range. As business attempts to overcome the stultification of the rational, and attunes itself to the broader potential of the human beings who work within its structures, it is only natural that artistic expression will be used to stretch that potential and realize its full promise.

As more people seek greater meaning from what they do for a living, as they look to include more spiritual and fewer secular values in their lives, art affords business a medium for relating to these deeply held needs. Neizvestny calls art "an objective form of meditation." To immerse oneself in art is to immerse oneself in reflection. The heightened capacity to reflect fulfils the individual. Inevitably, it also spills over, and improves the focus and thinking power that the individual can apply to his or her job.

The benefits of infusing greater artistry and artfulness into the cultures of our companies are not abstract, nor need they be classified as long-term in their payback. Art can be exposed to people, and its appreciation nurtured, within the conventional training programmes that many companies are using to help develop the skills of employees.

Professional Development Through Art

So much of what we do in business involves expression—writing reports, making presentations, sharing data to win support or endorsement or concurrence. All of these communications skills can be directly and dramatically improved by greater artfulness and artistry. Training programmes that focus on writing and presentation skills can be broadened to explore the arts-side of literary and visual expression.

Business generally believes that precision is the hallmark of good business writing. While precision is important, the written word in business today must also convey a broader, intuitive and emotional understanding. Commitment of people to a cause is best achieved not only through understanding, but also through inspiration, and those documents and presentations in business that have this capacity to inspire are evoking an art-like response.

Exploring poetry as part of a business-writing programme may seem far-fetched, but in fact, it helps people come to terms with the meaning of words. The more they understand the power and fragility of words, the better communicators they become. In fostering an appreciation for the beauty of communication, companies are also bestowing greater dignity on the everyday tasks of communications managers. This helps people derive even greater psychic rewards from their jobs, so that meaning is achieved on two levels.

This is not to suggest that reports should be written in iambic pentameter. Nor should people be spending an inordinate amount of time trying to make a memo work as a sonnet. The goal is to make people better communicators, and helping them to explore the most evocative, most expressive of communications forms, simply adds to their skills base.

Presentation skills are even harder to develop among people than those of business writing. Many people feel very awkward about public speaking. Most have not had the training or reinforcement for it. Again, the arts may provide a vehicle for developing a new level of communications-competency. Borrowing from the theatre or from the visual arts can provide participants in corporate training programmes with the tools, devices and traditions for enhancing their presentation ability.

Presentations, although we don't regard them as such, are, in fact, theatre. Their purpose is to engage people, to involve them in the material being reviewed, to impress them, and finally, to move them to action. The skills of the theatre are ideally suited to helping make the presentation more meaningful and inspiring to the audience it is intended to move. Designing presentations to intrigue their audiences, to provide compelling lessons, to make meaningful and lasting impressions, makes them not only more interesting to perform and to behold, but also more productive.

Such theatrics often break out spontaneously at company Christmas parties or golf tournaments. After a lampooning skit or serious presentation, people inevitably remark that they didn't know that this person was so "good on her feet," and that another person "had so much talent." Opening the corridors of companies to such artful exchange every day is a way of tapping the immense creative energy that most people suppress, and can't find expression for in their current work environments. By supporting such creativity, by making work itself more of an artistic endeavour, companies are availing themselves of the fuller human potential of their employees.

Art is not a distraction. Nor is it easy and facile. Art takes very hard work. It requires developing a mastery over fundamental details, and involves a great amount of input before it is capable of generating output. Van Cliburn, the highly accomplished concert pianist, recently came out of retirement to perform at the one-hundredth anniversary of Carnegie Hall, in New York City. He advocates that classical music be taught as a basic in elementary school, because it provides students with the invaluable discipline of focus. Whether they apply their learning to music or not, students will be enriched by the capacity to concentrate.

Art in business can work the same way. Art demands the concentration that so many of us in business are distracted from providing to the issues and topics that affect our companies' long-term health. So, as we become better artists, come to better appreciate the value and meaning of art, we become better managers and business people.

Enrichment

Infusing art into a company's culture can take many forms, and, of great importance, the very process of bringing the art in can help bond, challenge and inspire people. One idea is to appoint a company Poet Laureate. Supported by the company, this person would have the financial freedom to pursue his or her art. This person would also be the artistic shaman for the company. The company poet would be called upon to write poems that celebrate the accomplishments of a company, or mourn its losses or failures. Poetry would be available to salute indivi-duals or teams for their various contributions. It would also express changes in strategic direction, recording lessons from the past and setting forth the vision for the future.

A company poet enriches the company and the community, creating another "circle of reciprocity." Employees have access to a deeper form of communication, both to provide meaning to events, and to possibly enhance their own communications and artistic capacity. The company benefits from greater employee cohesion, plus the creativity to push up productivity. And the community benefits, with more poets to translate the disturbing and exhilarating vortex of change into something that is meaningful and important to our society.

The pragmatic and important benefits of art to business have been among the surprising things that I've learned about, through the process of writing this book. I am an account person by training. While I've worked in advertising for over fifteen years, and have worked with some of the best creative people in our business, my skills have, for the most part, been directed to devising marketing strategies and serving clients. Throughout my career, I've remained rather ignorant of the process and pressures of creativity.

Writing this book has forced me to confront the process of art on a new level. As a student of creativity, I've been intrigued by its mystery and awed by the ideas, imagery and evocations it produces. As a practitioner, I've found that creativity is a far less enigmatic process than I imagined. It is highly rewarding, but also very tedious and demanding, and filled with alternating experiences of euphoria and self-doubt.

Whatever creativity I've expressed in this material required a lot of work. Input had to be managed. Output had to be regulated. Far from being a haphazard interconnection, achieving creativity requires the discipline and perseverance that we usually associate with research scientists. There is a part of me that played, and a part of me that worked. There is a part of me that soared, and a part of me that slogged through the mud.

In my case, the discipline involved reading and research. These intermingled with my own experience, to connect the observations and ideas that are the basis for this book. Surprisingly to me, although this has been a labour of love, the joy of true inspiration has been rare and fleeting. Most of the work has been in the doing; choosing the words, building the sentences, constructing the meaning, to give expression to those infrequent (although I must admit, highly satisfying) moments of inspiration.

This process has demanded that opposites be reconciled. The spirit of reflection, which takes time, has fluidity, and resists containment, has been constantly challenged by the pragmatic pressure of a deadline. This tension between thinking and doing, between inspiration and execution, is, I found, very difficult to manage. It is very much like trying to synthesize the strengths of an entrepreneurial company and a huge corporation. Both activities are valid, but reflection without execution is limp, and execution without inspiration is deadly.

In growing as an artist, I've grown as a business person. My capacity to reflect, to envision, has been practised and stretched. The frenetic character of my usual work will be enriched by the contemplation of writing. And, in forming and communicating these ideas, I've come to understand them better, so that I can refine their execution in my own life, within our company, and among our clients.

While writing a book is not a tool for everyone, the process of immersing oneself in an artistic endeavour is a means of enriching life. By stretching ourselves, by releasing the inner dreams and fears and visions that seek expression in art, we are expanding our human potential to see, to think, to feel. Companies that encourage this expression, that support the inherent artistry in people, will be enriched by employees who are more satisfied, and who contribute on a broader spectrum than the work traditionally expects of them.

Art is a means of channelling change. Importantly, its transformative effects will not be limited to the company itself. A company with art engraved in its culture will be open to the currents around it. It will derive inspiration from the world beyond its walls, and naturally seek to share its artistic accomplishments with that world. In this way, art can help us integrate our commercial enterprises more fully into the rhythms of human society. The value of art, once fully appreciated, can help us construct companies that deliver more than just profit. Operating with a love and respect for art means that companies will necessarily operate with greater love and respect for the people who create it, and the natural world that sustains it. Without art, companies can never have souls.

WORKING TOWARDS A TRUE BALANCE SHEET

The themes in the essays of this book have consistently reflected the perspective that our business institutions must evolve to embrace the broader needs and potentials of human beings, and that they must do so in a way that is harmonious with the planet and natural system that sustains us. Thinking, sensible people will generally agree with these goals, but we remain befuddled by the actual process and details of the evolution. How do we move business, with its ingrained traditions, with its enormous power, and with its self-interest-based resistance to change, to become more environmentally benign and more humane in its practices?

History and human experience teach us that nothing can change until the need for change is acknowledged.

Last fall, I had the opportunity to participate in a panel, sponsored by CBC Newsworld and Queen's University, which dealt with the broad, disturbing topic of violence towards women in our society. For a very long day, the forty-five members of this panel discussed, dissected and debated this issue from various standpoints; violence towards women in the media, in the workplace, in the home. While the dimensions of the problem are enormous, and we only began to scratch the surface of possible solutions, we felt that we were at least building momentum for change, by "naming the problem."

Just as an alcoholic cannot begin the process of healing until that person acknowledges alcohol as a problem, so, too, our companies and corporations cannot begin the process of healing themselves and reconciling themselves to the society and planet they are damaging until we and they "name the problem." I hope that this book has begun that "naming" process.

Of course, in "naming" the problems, in acknowledging accountability, we also start the momentum towards finding solutions and resolutions. To point fingers is not enough. Business is too important to our well-being in North America, and too important to our international security, to be allowed to burn itself out. We must reform it, evolve it, and have business come to terms with its shortcomings, in order to help it realize its fullest potential.

What We Audit Is What We Value

All of the changes I've suggested involve developing new values and new measurements for business. Perhaps the most fitting place to begin this evolution is the balance sheet. This financial document details a company's assets and liabilities, and it helps investors, tax auditors and managers to assess the value of the company, at a specific time. The assets and liabilities detailed on the balance sheet are exclusively financial; cash on hand, retained earnings, value of inventory, accounts payable and receivable, long-term and short-term debt, the value of plant and capital equipment.

The current balance sheet reflects the primary and somewhat distorted preoccupation that our companies have with dollars. The worth of companies, if they are to be relevant and viable to our society in the future, must go beyond the financial and include the less tangible, but equally important, values of human development and natural support. These are not incidental values but, in fact, reflect the real worth of a company, and the management sophistication and contribution that the leaders of our companies are making.

A balance sheet details off-setting strengths and weaknesses. Given our declining reserves of fossil fuels, and the increasing degradation of life that their use entails, it makes sense that the use of energy should be regarded with the same scrutiny and discipline as the use of cash. How much energy is used, to achieve how much production, should be a mandatory measure of efficiency included on all corporate balance sheets.

As all companies within industries present information about energy use, relative to production, we can evaluate which are, in fact, providing greatest value, not only in financial return, but also in return on energy deployed. Such measures would force managers to look beyond the quarterly results, and make the investments that will yield high-energy productivity, as well as profitability.

Economists and industry associations can establish common measures, such as units of energy consumed per unit of production. While perhaps initially very crude, these ratios will at least offer a relative base of comparison. Using the mathematical formulas similar to those that do the number-crunching for financial spreadsheets, it will then be possible to rate and track a company's energy performance, relative to competitors and to previous years. Shareholders, environmental agencies, and government taxation auditors can use these energy indices and ratios to determine whether sufficient investment in energy efficiency is being attained, and whether profitability is being achieved at the expense of long-term viability.

Balance sheets measure the inflow and outflow of money. This in-and-out measurement can also be applied to other environmental and human factors. How much raw material was used? How much direct waste was created from the process of manufacturing? How much secondary waste was created by packaging and the final usage of the product made by the company?

In the case of diaper manufacturers, such as Procter & Gamble and Kimberly-Clark, the balance sheet would detail the number of trees used to manufacture their products. The energy costs of production and distribution would be disclosed. And the volume of waste produced by these products could finally be quantified.

Since the intent of a balance sheet is to balance, we can then view whether the reforestation policies of these companies are, in fact, on the scale of the logging practices. We can also assess whether the true costs of making and using these products, in terms of the energy they consume and the amount of waste they create, is justified, relative to price charged and profits generated. Re-working the balance sheet, to include these more accurate measurements, is not intended to stultify innovations such as disposable diapers. Rather, it ensures that the true price for the convenience is fully assigned, and that the damage to the environment is balanced with investments that restore nature to approximately the same degree that it is mined, logged, depleted, or dirtied.

These environmental considerations should not be regarded as non-financial. In fact, they reflect the reality that there is a cost for everything. The cost of waste disposal, for instance, is very real and growing for the municipalities and communities that are scrambling to absorb more garbage in already-saturated landfill sites. Taxpayers are, therefore, already paying for the waste inefficiencies of products, such as disposable diapers, that are used by a minority of people. An environmental balance sheet will help us do the difficult job of re-assigning those costs that are now in the public sector to those companies that are making, and those consumers who are using, inefficient, expensive products.

Responsible Business Is Smarter Business

While such progressive balance sheets may be regarded as socially responsible, they actually more accurately reflect the costs and values of the free market. Much of our production is subsidized by government. Federal and provincial lands are logged, providing an artificially low cost of raw materials to the milling operations. Farmers are paid to produce massive amounts of crops, so much so that the resulting world-wide gluts in dairy and grain prices are keeping prices so low that no one prospers.

An environmentally comprehensive balance sheet would capture and pass on the true cost of these subsidized operations. This would allow us to charge the price of products directly to the consumer at the cash register, rather than through the greying, indirect, inefficient process of taxation. It would also encourage a better debate, among policy makers and their constituents, about where to invest public—our—money.

Many will argue that consumers and voters will rebel, if they—we—have to pay real prices for products, at supermarkets and department stores. The sad reality is that we are already paying, through one of the highest tax rates in the world. Not only that but, despite our subsidies, and maybe even because of them, many of our protected industries are uncompetitive and inefficient, in comparison to their global counterparts.

Canadians, while we complain about energy and gas costs, relative to the United States, are still paying far below world prices for our energy. Despite this advantage, much of it subsidized, Canadians have yet to realize a significant competitive advantage from this lower-cost energy. In terms of future competitiveness, this easier access and lower cost of energy could well become a handicap. Unlike the Europeans and Japanese, who pay much higher prices for their energy, North Americans have yet to make the investment in more efficient plants and technology.

One of the reasons why oil prices dropped and stabilized, during the volatile period of the Persian Gulf War, was that oil-dependent countries like Japan have greatly increased their economic efficiency, relative to energy use. Since the original oil shock in the mid-1970s, Japan has halved its consumption of oil, while nearly doubling its industrial production. Such energy efficiency provides a real and substantial long-term competitive advantage. Weaned on the false assumption of cheap oil, North American managers have yet to face the discipline of producing more with less. The technical and managerial know-how is still to be learned, while our international competitors are already in the second and third generation of applying this very valuable expertise.

It is ironic that, while we are prescribing the medicine of market pricing to the newly capitalistic nations of Eastern Europe, we in North America are ignorant of the degree of centralized control of our own economy. By failing to heed our own advice, by not taking the medicine, we as a society are contributing to our decline in competitiveness.

The interdependence of public policy and private enterprise is one of the themes of this book, and a fully accountable balance sheet is one of the tools for us to measure, not only how well our companies are doing, but also how well our government leaders are performing.

California, in the midst of a severe water shortage, finds that eighty percent of its precious water is going to agriculture, which generates less that ten percent of the state's GNP. Subsidized water has profited a few, to the disadvantage of many. Part of the problem is that most water, agriculture, logging, mining, and energy policies are left over from another era. These industries are mature, and should be fending for themselves against world competitors. Whatever subsidies we invest should be not to support the industries of the past, but to nurture those of the future.

In Japan, prices for rice and beef are ridiculously high by our standards, but reflect the small portion of arable land available for agriculture. Despite its high prices, the productivity of the Japanese worker in the most modern and cutting edge of industries have helped Japan realize the highest standard of living in the world. Japan's investment in the education of its children and in the progressive training of its workers is an example of how smartly applied subsidies can realize a significant return in the future.

This, again, is not to suggest that we model our society after the Japanese, but rather that we learn some of the lessons of their enhanced competitiveness. By leading the world in adopting expansive balance sheets, North Americans can more accurately diagnose those aspects of our performance that are world-leading, world-class, or in drastic need of renewal. And, as we've led the world in the implementation of environmental standards for pollutants from car emissions, so too we can use the still-formidable economic clout of North America to pressure those countries that trade with us to pursue better environmental practices.

Phil Thurston, one of the OPM programme professors at Harvard, suggested to my classmates and me that we conduct regular, non-financial audits of our companies. His logic was that financial audits are but one indicator of a company's health and vitality. The non-financial audit is open-ended and flexible, accommodating the goals, pressures and needs that are unique to each operation. Quality-of-life issues, human-resource development and management, personal growth and fulfilment, community service, research and development needs, are but a few of the potential components of the non-financial audit.

Given the importance of business in our modern society, as well as in our personal lives, it is appropriate that we begin to formalize such qualitative audits, as part of the expanded balance sheet that business will be measured against. The impact of a business, beyond its bottom line, on its customers, on the people who work within its structures, on the community, and on the natural environment, needs to be assessed. The calipers for measuring this qualitative impact are not yet available to us, but again, can be agreed upon by leaders in specific industries, in collaboration with ecologists and public representatives.

Companies are already responding to the need for such enhanced performance measures. Quality-recognition programmes, such as the Malcolm Baldridge Award in the U.S., are attempting to acknowledge, encourage and reward superior performance. Modelled on the Demming Prize, which the Japanese award to the company that most advances the art and science of quality, such programmes have considerable, if hard to quantify, value.

Firstly, the recognition builds confidence and pride within an organization. This enhances both morale and motivation, encouraging people to go even farther in pursuing the goals of the company. Secondly, the public endorsement of such an award provides unique and meaningful opportunities for marketing, tangibly demonstrating to existing and prospective customers that the company is delivering superior value. As the prestige of the award grows, so too does its internal and external value to a company.

In Japan, award programmes have gone beyond quality. A recent cover story in *Fortune* magazine explored the development of interdisciplinary teams in the workplace. Such teams are helping companies like Rubbermaid develop new products faster, more tailored to the needs of customers, and with greater quality built in. The article refers to a nationwide competition among manufacturers' teams in Japan. "Sponsored by the Union of Japanese Scientists and Engineers, the competition pits teams selected by their companies against one another. Once a year, the teams travel to Tokyo to make presentations before judges, who decide which performs best at everything from solving quality problems to continuously improving a manufacturing process. The winners get showered with prizes and media attention."

Highly visible, highly publicized public recognition programmes are a tool for rewarding those companies that perform well in those progressive areas that may still be beyond the measurement of traditional accounting. The more involved the public becomes in these award programmes, the more significant and valuable they become to the companies competing for the honours. This is important, both to reinforce and reward performance that generally benefits our society, and to embarrass those companies that are laggard in facing their greater social responsibilities.

The interdependence I'm advocating works two ways. Not only are companies more accountable for their actions, but the public must also assume greater responsibility for its relationship with business. Creating a new balance sheet, one that measures companies on their social responsibility as well as fiscal delivery, will help demystify current annual reports, making them more accessible and understandable to the public at large.

I've repeatedly asserted that we are all intimately affected by business, even by companies that we don't work for and don't buy from. Because society shares in both the expansion and contraction of business, because we are directly affected by its competitiveness and environmental policies, all of us are emotionally, if not actually, shareholders in North American companies. The more involved we are in their operations, the more knowledge we have about their financial and non-financial performances, the better able we are to judge which companies deserve our custom and policy support. Expansive balance sheets can open companies to this healthier, more insightful public scrutiny.

Recognizing The Duality: Striving For Balance

Once business accepts the premise of a supra-financial balance sheet, then it will be possible to list and reconcile more opposites than just assets and liabilities. In a recent issue of *Canadian Business* magazine, Professor Henry Mintzberg reiterates his belief that North American management suffers from over-analysis and over-reliance on its rational faculties. The article explains that his concepts for more intuitive management were inspired by "the psychological research into the differing functions of the left and right side of the brain. In his seminal text, *The Psychology of Consciousness*, California-based research psychologist Robert Ornstein argues that the left side of the brain regulates our quantitative and rational functions while the right regulates the emotional and creative."

Mintzberg preaches that the most effective executives manage "by balancing images and feelings with words and numbers."[1] The left-brain, right-brain model has provided a psychological support for his view of management. It also provides yet another set of variables for inclusion in the new balance sheet.

The measures for creativity will require considerable creativity unto themselves, to establish and define. While the left-brain dimensions of a company are largely already on display in the numerical matrices of conventional balance sheets, the right-brain ones are more elusive. For innovative companies, such as 3M, Sony and Rubbermaid, a straightforward index of sales from new products provides one measure.

For those less-tangible creative dimensions that may not directly relate to revenue contribution, measures can be expressed, relative to previous years and to industry standards. For instance, training and development time per employee can be tabulated and compared to trends the company achieved historically, and to averages in the industry, or among international competitors. This would indicate whether companies are making the investment to keep their people current with developments in industry, and developing, within that work force, the ability to adopt competitive new technology or practices.

In the most enlightened companies, the right-brain column of the balance sheet will include measures of commitment for enriching the lives of employees and the community, with art. Productivity per employee on the left-brain side of the balance sheet will be compared to indices of artistic achievement, indices of play, indices of fun, on the right-brain side. Left-brain charts that track sales and profitability trajectories will be matched with right-brain charts that track contribution to the quality of life and the quality of the environment.

Such a holistic balance sheet cannot be a fantasy. The collective wisdom of the human race strongly supports the concept that health and fulfilment are only achieved when we balance the inner and outer, the emotional and the rational, and all the other dualities that make up our human nature. Business, as an institution of humans, can only realize its fullest potential if it, too, strives for balance. The misalignment of values is too threatening, too damaging, to our species and to our home, to perpetuate "business as usual."

Every generation faces a transition point, at which time it must confront the issue of its legacy to its children. We, who inherited so much, and who grew up in a North American culture that supported us in the expectation of even more, face the sobering reality that what we will leave behind is considerably less than what we started with.

The planet and its fragile environment are imposing their own reckoning. Only recently, U.S. health officials announced that the depletion of the ozone layer is happening at twice the rate previously estimated. This will effect an increase in the incidence of skin cancer, claiming an additional 200,000 victims in America alone. On what balance sheet do we add up this cost in lives? What accounting offsets can we balance against this destruction of the life-supporting ecosystem that took billions of years to evolve? What are the commercial assets that justify such tragic, enduring liabilities?

While we can't give up on business, neither do we have to accept the status quo. The challenges are daunting. These macro-pressures must be addressed, while we also sharpen our basic business skills to meet the relentless competition from Europe and the Far East. Making such large-scale social change, at the same time as we need to enhance competitiveness, seems like a staggering conundrum. In fact, the solutions for one may well hold the solutions for both.

North American business can best meet its considerable challenges by interacting with, and involving, the deep and full potential of the human beings who work in its offices, who manufacture in its plants, and who live in its communities. By tapping into the basic human need for meaning, business can channel the considerable energy and ingenuity of our people to tackle the formidable problems we face. People will give more if they get more. This simple formula is the key for our companies to use, to unlock the enormous latent potential of our human resources.

In the final analysis, the only balance sheet that can endure, that can sustain our companies and maintain life, will be based on reciprocity. The business that gives, deserves to receive. As we struggle to work through the many obstacles that are preventing the implementation of this basis for business, we will, one hopes, come to learn yet another lesson—one that is waiting to be discovered in the depths of the human heart. Giving has its own value. And the meaning that giving provides transcends any balance sheet.

BIBLIOGRAPHIC NOTES

Why Meditations?

1. Drucker, Peter F., *The Frontiers of Management*, (New York: Harper & Row, 1986), p. 33.
2. See above, p. 233.
3. Drucker, Peter F., *The New Realities*, (New York: Harper & Row, 1989), p. 181.
4. Depree, Max, *Leadership Is an Art*, (New York: Doubleday, 1989), p. 26.
5. *Fortune*, December 31, 1990, p. 72.
6. Tracey, Diane, *The Power Pyramid*, (New York: William Morrow and Company Inc., 1990), p. 12.
7. See above, p. 48.
8. Levitt, Theodore, *Thinking About Management*, (New York: The Free Press, 1991), p. 21.
9. *BusinessWeek*, October 15, 1990, p. 20.
10. Peters, Tom and Austin, Nancy, *A Passion for Excellence* (New York: Warner Books, 1985), p. 262.
11. Heider, John, *The Tao of Leadership*, (New York: Bantam Books Inc., 1985), p. 1.
12. Convey, Stephen R., *The 7 Habits of Highly Effective People*, (New York: Simon & Schuster Inc., 1989), p. 292.

Business and the Quest for Meaning

1. Brown, Lester R., *State of the World 1988*, (New York: W.W. Norton & Company, 1988), p. 11.
2. Brown, Lester R., *State of the World 1987*, (New York: W.W. Norton & Company, 1987), p. 6.
3. Campbell, Joseph, *The Power of Myth*, (New York: Doubleday, 1988), p. 207.
4. Mintzberg, Henry, *Mintzberg On Management*, (New York: The Free Press, 1989), p. 318.

5. See above, Brown, 1988, p. 13.
6. Schumacher, E.F., *Small is Beautiful*, (London: Abacus, 1974), p. 37.
7. *Financial Post*, February 5, 1991.
8. See above, Mintzberg, p. 351.
9. *The Globe & Mail Report on Business*, August 16, 1990.
10. Maccoby, Michael, *Why Work?* (New York: Touchstone Books, 1988), p. 28.
11. Frankl, Victor, *The Will to Meaning*, (New York: Meridian Books, 1969), p. 55.
12. See above, p. 75.
13. La Bier, Douglas, *The Emotional Fallout of Success*, (Reading: Addison-Wesley, 1986), p. 71.
14. See above, Depree, p. 44.
15. Howard, Robert, *Harvard Business Review*, *"Values Make the Company"* September/October 1990, p. 136.

Business and the Sin Against the Planet

1. *Harpers*, March, 1991.
2. Sale, Kirkpatrick, *The Conquest of Paradise*, (New York: Alfred A. Knopf, 1990), p. 81.
3. Galbraith, John, K., *Economics in Perspective*, (Boston: Houghton Mifflin, 1987), p. 64.
4. Berry, Thomas, *The Dream of the Earth*, (San Franscisco: Sierra Club Books, 1988), p. 119.
6. See above, p. 17.
7. See above, p. 10.
8. World Commission on Environment and Decelopment, *Our Common Future*, (Oxford University Press, 1987), pp. 39, 111.
9. See above, p. 211-212.
10. See above, Berry, p. 33.
11. *MacLean's*, November 5, 1990.
12. *The New York Times*, April 28, 1991.
13. *The Economist*, June 16, 1990.
14. *MacLean's*, March 11, 1991.
15. Ohmae, Kenichi, *The Borderless World*, (New York: Harper, 1990), p. 175.
16. *Newsweek*, January 21, 1991.

The Growing Irrelevance of Business

1. See above, Drucker, *The Frontiers of Management*, p. 283.
2. Gilder, George, *Microcosm*, (New York: Simon & Schuster, 1989), p. 17.

3. Schlosstein, Stephen, *The End of the American Century*, (New York: Congdon & Weed Inc., 1989), p. 21.
4. See above, p. 36.
5. *Fortune*, November 19, 1990.
6. See above, Mintzberg, p. 346.
7. *Fortune*, January 21, 1990.

The Dehumanizing Vocabulary of Business

1. Lesham, L. and Margenau, H., *Einstein's Space & Van Gogh's Sky*, (New York: Collier, 1982), p. 26.
2. Halberstam, David, *The Next Century*, (New York: William Morrow & Company, 1991), p. 89.
3. Carlzon, Jan, *Moments of Truth*, (Cambridge, Mass: Ballinger Publishing, 1987) pp. 64, 89.
4. *Sony Management Newsletter*, January, 1991.
5. See above, Drucker, *Frontiers of Management*, p. 224.
6. *Fortune*, January 29, 1990.
7. *Fortune*, May 6, 1991.
8. See above, Drucker, *Frontiers of Management*, p. 223.

The Crumbling Mythology of Business

1. Jung, Carl, *Man and His Symbols*, (New York: Dell, 1964), p. 76.
2. See above, Mintzberg, p. 140.
3. Capra, Fritjof, *Uncommon Wisdom*, (New York: Simon & Schuster, 1988), p. 237.
4. *BusinessWeek*, November 24, 1990.
5. Ginzberg, E. and Vojta, G., *Beyond Human Scale*, (New York: Basic Books, 1985), p. 130.
6. *Fortune*, March 11, 1991.
7. See above, Ginzberg and Vojta, p. 188.
8. See above, Mintzberg, p. 365.
9. *The New York Times*, April 28, 1991.
10. See above, Schumacher, p. 46.
11. *Canadian Business*, May 1991.
12. Mills, D. Quinn, *Rebirth of the Corporation*, (New York: John Wiley & Sons, 1991), p. 113.

Searching for the New Heroes of Business

1. French, Marilyn, *Beyond Power*, (New York: Balantine Books, 1985), p. 428.
2. See above, Sclosstein, p. 34.

3. Rose, Frank, *West of Eden*, (New York: Viking, 1989), p. 166.
5. Friedman, Benjamin M., *Day of Reckoning*, (New York: Vintage Books, 1989), p. 7.
6. *The Economist*, February 16, 1991.
7. See above, Schumacher, p. 81.
8. Campbell, Joseph, *The Hero With A Thousand Faces*, (Princeton, N.J.: Princeton University Press, 1949), p. 11.

The Feminine and Masculine in Disequilibrium

1. See above, Levitt, p. 109.
2. See above, Drucker, *Frontiers of Management*, p. 35.
3. Kidder, Tracey *The Soul of a New Machine*, (New York: Avon Books, 1981).
4. *BusinessWeek*, June 11, 1990.
5. *Canadian Business*, May 1991.
6. See above, Levitt, p. 57.
7. Koestler, Arthur, *The Act of Creation*, (London: Arkana, 1964), p. 211.
8. See above, Berry, p. 161.
9. Fox, Matthew, *A Spirituality Named Compassion*, San Franscico: Harper & Row, 1990), p. 202.

Business Is Serious but Its Practice Doesn't Have to Be

1. See above, Levitt, p. 6.
2. *U.S. News & World Report*, March 14, 1991.
3. *Fortune*, March 12, 1990.
4. See above, Koestler, p. 45.
5. *The Globe & Mail Report on Business*, July 27, 1990.

Using History to Plan the Future

1. See above, Depree, p. 16.
2. See above, Levitt, p. 6.
3. Neustadt, Richard and May, Ernest, *Thinking in Time*, (London: The Free Press, 1986), p. 14.
5. Boorstin, Daniel J., *Hidden History*, (New York: Vintage, 1989), p xi.

Leadership Through Following

1. Kottier, John, *The Leadership Factor*, (New York: The Free Press, 1988), p. 123.

2. Waterman, Robert H. Jr., *The Renewal Factor*, (Toronto: Bantam Books, 1987), p. 311.
3. Kidder, Rushworth, *An Agenda for the 21st Century*, (Cambridge: The MIT Press, 1989), p. 85.
4. *BusinessWeek*, March 18, 1991.
5. Boyett, Joseph and Conn, Henry, *Workplace 2000*, (New York: Dutton. 1991), p. 292.
6. *Fortune*, March 20, 1989.
7. See above, Depree, p. 10.
8. See above, Waterman, p. 196.
9. Zemke, Ron and Schaaf, Dick, *The Service Edge*, (Toronto: Penguin Books, 1989), p. 24.
10. See above, Depree, p. 9.
11. See above, Zemke and Schaaf, p 360.
12. Love, John F., *McDonald's: Behind the Golden Arches*, (New York: Bantam, 1986).
13. *BusinessWeek*, July 9, 1990.
14. Phillips, Kevin P., *The Politics of Rich and Poor*, (Random House, 1990).

The Ennobling Potential of Business

1. Watson, Thomas J., *Father, Son & Co.*, (New York: Bantam, 1990), p. 176.
2. See above, Halberstam, p. 116.
3. See above, Gilder, p. 378.
4. Zuboff, Shoshana, *In the Age of the Smart Machine*, (New York: Basic Books, 1988), p. 6.
5. See above, p. 222.
6. See above, p. 291.
7. See above, French, p.464.
8. See above, Friedman, p. 159.
9. Kennedy, Noah, *The Industrialization of Intelligence*, (London: Unwin Hyman, 1989), p. 196.

Expanding the Human and Profit Potential of Business Through Art

1. Neizvestony, Ernst, *Space Time and Synthesis in Art*, New York: Mosaic Press, 1990).

Working Towards a New Balance Sheet

1. *Canadian Business*, May 1991.